BRIDGING SCHOLARSHIP AND ACTIVISM

D1452151

BRIDGING SCHOLARSHIP AND ACTIVISM

REFLECTIONS FROM THE FRONTLINES OF COLLABORATIVE RESEARCH

Edited by BERND REITER and ULRICH OSLENDER

Michigan State University Press | East Lansing

♾ The paper used in this publication meets the minimum requirements
of ANSI/NISO Z39.48-1992 (R 1997) (Permanence of Paper).

Michigan State University Press
East Lansing, Michigan 48823-5245

Printed and bound in the United States of America.

21 20 19 18 17 16 15   1 2 3 4 5 6 7 8 9 10

LIBRARY OF CONGRESS CONTROL NUMBER: 2014941661
ISBN: 978-1-61186-147-1 (pbk.)
ISBN: 978-1-60917-434-7 (ebook: PDF)

Book design by Charlie Sharp, Sharp Des!gns, Lansing, MI
Cover design by Shaun Allshouse, www.shaunallshouse.com

Michigan State University Press is a member of the Green Press Initiative and is committed to
developing and encouraging ecologically responsible publishing practices. For more information
about the Green Press Initiative and the use of recycled paper in book publishing, please visit
www.greenpressinitiative.org.

Visit Michigan State University Press at www.msupress.org

Transformations in Higher Education: Scholarship of Engagement

The *Transformations in Higher Education: Scholarship of Engagement* book series is designed to provide a forum where scholars can address the diverse issues provoked by community-campus partnerships that are directed toward creating innovative solutions to societal problems. Numerous social critics and key national commissions have drawn attention to the pervasive and burgeoning problems of individuals, families, communities, economies, health services, and education in American society. Such issues as child and youth development, economic competitiveness, environmental quality, and health and health care require creative research and the design, deployment, and evaluation of innovative public policies and intervention programs. Similar problems and initiatives have been articulated in many other countries, apart from the devastating consequences of poverty that burdens economic and social change. As a consequence, there has been increasing societal pressure on universities to partner with communities to design and deliver knowledge applications that address these issues, and to co-create novel approaches to effect system changes that can lead to sustainable and evidence-based solutions. Knowledge generation and knowledge application are critical parts of the engagement process, but so too are knowledge dissemination and preservation. The *Transformations in Higher Education: Scholarship of Engagement* series was designed to meet one aspect of the dissemination/preservation dyad.

This series is sponsored by the National Collaborative for the Study of University Engagement (NCSUE) and is published in partnership with the Michigan State University Press. An external board of editors supports the NCSUE editorial staff in order to ensure that all volumes in the series are peer reviewed throughout the publication process. Manuscripts embracing campus-community partnerships are invited from authors regardless of discipline, geographic place, or type of transformational change accomplished. Similarly, the series embraces all methodological approaches from rigorous randomized trials to narrative and ethnographic studies. Analyses may span the qualitative to quantitative continuum, with particular emphasis on mixed-model approaches. However, all manuscripts must attend to detailing critical aspects of partnership development, community involvement, and evidence of program changes or impacts. Monographs and books provide ample space for authors to address all facets of engaged scholarship, thereby building a compendium of praxis that will facilitate replication and generalization, two of the cornerstones of evidence-based programs, practices, and policies. We invite you to submit your work for publication review and to fully participate in our effort to assist higher education to renew its covenant with society through engaged scholarship.

HIRAM E. FITZGERALD
BURTON BARGERSTOCK
LAURIE VAN EGEREN

Contents

Introduction, *Ulrich Oslender and Bernd Reiter* · ix

Part One. The Promises and Pitfalls of Collaborative Research

Of Academic Embeddedness: Communities of Choice and How to Make Sense
of Activism and Research Abroad, *Bernd Reiter* · 3

New Shapes of Revolution, *Gustavo Esteva* · 15

The Accidental Activist Scholar: A Memoir on Reactive Boundary and Identity Work
for Social Change within the Academy, *Rob Benford* · 31

Can Development Bridge the Gap between Activism and Academia? *Cristina Espinosa* · · · · · · · · 49

Leaving the Field: How to Write about Disappointment and Frustration
in Collaborative Research, *Ulrich Oslender* · 63

Invisible Heroes, *Eshe Lewis* · 75

Part Two. Negotiating Racialized and Gendered Positionalities

El Muntu en América, *Manuel Zapata Olivella* · 99

Activism as History Making: The Collective and the Personal in Collaborative Research
with the Process of Black Communities in Colombia, *Arturo Escobar* · 105

Out of Bounds: Negotiating Researcher Positionality in Brazil, *Elizabeth Hordge-Freeman* · · · · · 123

Between Soapboxes and Shadows: Activism, Theory, and the Politics of Life and Death
in Salvador, Bahia, Brazil, *Christen A. Smith* · 135

State Violence and the Ethnographic Encounter: Feminist Research
and Racial Embodiment, *Keisha-Khan Y. Perry* · 151

The Challenges Resulting from Combining Scientific Production and Social-Political
Activism in the Brazilian Academy, *Fernando Conceição* · 171

The Challenge of Doing Applied/Activist Anti-Racist Anthropology in Revolutionary
Cuba, *Gayle L. McGarrity* · 181

Conclusion, *Ulrich Oslender and Bernd Reiter* · 201

About the Authors · 205

Introduction

Ulrich Oslender and Bernd Reiter

One advantage of a bridge is that it allows walking in both directions.

—Gustavo Esteva, 2008

S hould you find yourself wandering one day around Highgate Cemetery in London, stop by at Karl Marx's tombstone, easily recognizable by a towering bust of the bearded man. One of the engraved epitaphs reads: "Philosophers have only interpreted the world differently; the point is to change it."[1] This dictum is the eleventh of Marx's *Theses on Feuerbach*, which he wrote in 1845, but which were only published as an appendix to Friedrich Engels's *Ludwig Feuerbach and the End of Classical German Philosophy* in 1886. The Eleventh Thesis is also one of the most cited expressions of Marx. In 1953 the government of the German Democratic Republic (GDR) had it engraved into the entryway of the Humboldt University in Berlin. There, in a now reunited Germany, it still proudly greets the visitor and the passing academics on their daily way to work—maybe as a reminder of their true purpose in life?

Marx critiqued Feuerbach's version of materialism as "conceived only in the form of the object or of contemplation, but not as sensuous human activity, practice, not subjectively" (Marx 1998, 570). He deplored the philosophical stance of the contemplative materialism of the young Hegelians, one that failed to comprehend practical activity and the changing of circumstances as revolutionary practice. It is starting from this critique that Marx developed his ideas into the revolutionary framework of historical materialism. Marxist or not, it would not be far-fetched to suggest that most, if not all scholarly-based activism today takes Marx's dictum to heart: *the point* of our work is not simply to interpret the world but to *change it.*[2]

The idea of "bridging scholarship and activism" is not an entirely new one. In fact, it has a long history, one that we do not intend to review exhaustively in this book. It has also gone through various phases or cycles of activity. The 1970s, for example, saw a plethora of methodological advances in the field, from Alain Touraine's proposition of an *intervention sociologique* (Touraine 1988), via

Paulo Freire's concept of *conscientização* developed in his *The Pedagogy of the Oppressed* (Freire 1971), to Participatory Action-Research (PAR), which was initially developed in Colombia by Orlando Fals Borda and others (see Oslender in this volume for a review of these approaches). Postmodern uncertainty in the 1980s and 1990s somewhat dampened these advances in academia, even though activism remained strong in the real world. The twenty-first century has seen a renewed emphasis on collaborative research and participatory methodologies. Research councils are increasingly interested in funding collaborative research proposals and are seemingly willing to listen to and learn from the experiences of subaltern groups. We can possibly talk of a "methodological turn" in some—if not all—of the social sciences. Methodological considerations are regarded as integral to most PhD theses and academic publications today.

This means that there is also a plethora of personal experiences that activist-researchers increasingly share through their publications with the wider world. Self-reflexivity has become a key concern for those who consider themselves as doing some of the bridging between academia and activism. Activist-researchers ask questions about their role in the research process. About how to relate to the people they do research with, or indeed for. Yet these activist-researchers, through their own practice, also challenge the established social sciences in a more profound way. They ask questions about the viability of conducting research that does not have the research subjects' interests at its center. Some go even as far as to question the very legitimacy of established social-science practice that ignores relations of power in the field and fails to address Marx's second part of his dictum: the imperative for change.

The "methodological turn" that we hint at in this book may also be seen as intersecting with broader epistemic shifts, such as proposed in the recent "decolonial turn." The latter has been influential in much of the current literature on collaboration and activism. In the words of one of its main proponents, the decolonial turn marks "an attempt to shift the geography, and the geo-politics of knowledge, of *critical theory* to a new terrain of *decoloniality* (Mignolo 2005, xx). At the heart of this approach lies the concept of "coloniality," the idea that colonial relations have extended past the colonial period itself and into every part of the modern global system. These ideas were initially developed by a group of Latin American scholars in a research project called modernity/coloniality/ decoloniality (MCD; see Escobar 2008, 163–176), although it should be acknowledged that parallel developments can also be observed in writings in African and African Diaspora scholarship, most notably perhaps in Ngũgĩ wa Thiong'o's *Decolonising the Mind* (1986), Faye Harrison's *Decolonizing Anthropology* (1991), or Carole Boyce Davies et al.'s *Decolonizing the Academy* (2003). The MCD project preoccupies itself with unearthing and articulating alternative ways of thinking from its dwellings in double consciousness, mestiza consciousness, border thinking, and subaltern epistemologies. Decolonial thinking is thus seen as an option from which to be critical of existing master/universal narratives that pervade society and academia. The parallels to our call for a methodological turn are many. While not all authors in this volume relate directly to decolonial thinking, a call for "epistemic decolonization" underlies most of their contributions.[3]

This book is the partial result of an ongoing dialogue among a group of social-science scholars and activists from different countries who first met in 2010 and then continued to exchange ideas and proposals for social change. While the involved scholars are seeking for ways to meaningfully share their findings with those who were the subjects of the research, the activists are looking for partners in their efforts to improve the lives of poor and marginalized communities in the Western Hemisphere. For the involved scholars, this exercise necessarily entails a good portion of self-reflection, as their efforts often run against established research paradigms of mainstream social-science practice and its quest for objectivity. The questions, critiques, and suggestions presented in this volume thus are first and foremost questions that engaged researchers are asking themselves. While some of these questions might seem unduly harsh, the motivation that brings us all together is to ask the hard questions in the hope that critical self-awareness can indicate the path that we must take if we want our work and efforts to have more resonance and impact beyond the academic world.

Asking the Hard Questions: Social Science and the World

Is a medical science without patients still a valuable endeavor? Hardly. How about social science without people? If we follow some social scientists, the social component of the social sciences becomes less and less obvious. Not only because the work produced in this field is not read by a broader public—which is in part due to the way it is written. But also because some social scientists seem not to care much for their relationship to "the social." Instead, in the words of Clarke and Primo (2012), some economists, political scientists, and sociologists suffer from "physics envy" and seek to imitate the hard sciences with ever more abstract models and formulas. They want to be *scientists* first and foremost. While this trend is not new and is understandable to some extent, given the need to produce the kind of knowledge that is "hard," confirmable, reliable, and hence beyond personal doubt and opinion, it seems to raise a series of rather intricate problems. First, what if the realm of the social is not capturable with hard instruments, because social life is at least to some extent willful and not lawful? In other words: What if the social world escapes any attempt to describe and explain it along rigid guidelines? What if there are no predictions to be made? If that were the case, all attempts to approach the social world—that is, the world in part constituted by meaningful human interaction—with a rigid analytical framework would then be ill begotten and in vain. What could a social science under such circumstances look like? This is one of the challenges that the authors assembled in this book seek to address.

The other challenge bringing together the authors who decided to gather their work under the title *Bridging Scholarship and Activism* is the one that results from having found a niche for oneself in either academia or social-justice activism—and then seeking ways to bridge the gap that so often divides those two realms. Can there be meaningful social activism if it ignores the latest, or maybe even the most basic findings of the social sciences? How long can we afford, as activists, to ignore what some social scientists have to say about local activism? To be sure, the constant pressure to develop and execute projects and to raise external funds for their execution leaves almost no time to read up on and follow the latest academic discussions on such essential topics as social movements. However, some social scientists do produce analyses about the effectiveness of social intervention and change, as well as research on social justice, equality, civil society, NGOs, social movements, peasants, landless movements, and the like—but most of it does not reach those who could actually benefit from these findings. Several factors stand in the way of a more fruitful sharing of information. Oftentimes, no real effort is made to share the findings reached by researchers with those communities that served as objects during the execution of the research project. In many cases, the findings of research projects conducted with local communities in Latin America, Asia, or Africa, for example, are published in American academic journals and in English—thus making a reception among local activists difficult, if not impossible. The incentive to publish in English-language journals comes from the pressure of earning tenure at an American university, and it evidences the different systematic logics involved: social change on one side, and an academic career on the other. While much of the blame for not sharing relevant information with those who could apply it locally certainly lies with the researchers, local activists must also ask themselves if they do enough to reach out and integrate academia into their daily work and strategies. A social activism that ignores academic research about the effectiveness of different mobilizing strategies, for example, may lose out on important insights for its own benefits. It risks becoming self-centered, self-serving, and less effective.

At the same time, social scientists cannot afford to ignore the social world. Questions about the reception, circulation, and influence on social-justice activism, politics, and policymaking processes cannot and should not be avoided. If sociology, political science, anthropology, geography, and, yes, the social science of economics do not or cannot produce any knowledge about the social world that is also *for* the social world—then these disciplines face a legitimation crisis. What can a social science contribute to a broad audience if it is not received by such a broad audience?

Any realistic social scientist should ask herself what purpose her latest paper serves—other than her own career and travel ambitions. This seems particularly pressing for those social scientists producing the kind of knowledge that could potentially be of great relevance and influence for social activists—such as the work of Jürgen Habermas, Michael Hardt and Antonio Negri, Alberto Mellucci, and many others. Most of this work is, however, written in such a cryptic way that a broader reception among nonacademics is made impossible. If research *on* social movements is not at least in part also written *for* social movements—whose interest does it serve?

The authors assembled here are all post-naive in this sense—i.e., they are facing this dilemma in one way or another. Successful or not, it seems clear at this moment in time that avoiding this question is not a legitimate strategy. It is opportunism at best, and cowardice at worst. The courage to ask hard questions not just about others but about oneself and one's job or activity thus unites the authors gathered here—and we have assembled them to help raise some of the questions we all should be asking ourselves more often. There are, however, no clear and one-size-fits-all answers. What we do hope to achieve by this exercise of critical self-reflection is to create an impulse that hopefully reaches other members of the discipline and other social-justice activists. Clearly, if our ambitions reach beyond our own identities (in the case of activists) and beyond our own careers and bank accounts (in the case of academics), then we cannot afford not to critically engage with each other, seek ways to cooperate, share our knowledge, and make our knowledge and experience available to others—particularly nonspecialists. This requires a critical reflection about our language and outreach strategies, but it also demands a rethinking of such established practices as tenure and tenure-related demands, such as peer-reviewed publishing. Questions of (participatory) methodology have to be asked, and a philosophy of science has to be found that allows for the professional production of knowledge that is still receivable by a nonprofessional audience.

The contributions assembled here are the result of several efforts. First, there was a conference, convened by Bernd Reiter at the University of South Florida (Tampa), in April 2010, under the title "Afrodescendants Still at the Bottom?" This conference sought to break the monotony of discipline-based self-promotion by having local activists and funding-agency representatives share panels with scholars. Out of this first effort came a first book, entitled *Afrodescendants, Identity, and the Struggle for Development in the Americas* (Reiter & Simmons 2012). A panel under the title "Bridging Scholarship and Activism?" followed at the Latin American Studies Association Annual Meeting in 2012. Some of the contributions assembled here come directly from that panel. Others are part of another, related effort, to bring scholarly work about local black communities of the Americas to those same communities. This initiative, also coordinated by Bernd Reiter, seeks to create the Frantz Fanon Summer Training Institute for Afrodescendant Community Leaders of the Americas. The preparation of this Institute has taken many rounds and led to many encounters, seminars, conferences, and planning meetings, most of which were held either in Tampa, Florida, or in Panama, and some in virtual space. Some of the contributions assembled here come out of this concrete effort to give meaning to scholarly work by bringing scholarly knowledge production to those who can actually benefit from it—even more so if this knowledge production is about them.

The first, necessary—while not sufficient—step in that direction is a critical self-awareness of one's own positionality, with all its gendered, racialized, national, and class-based dimensions. Only when one knows not only one's reach and limitations, but also how one is perceived by those others with, about, or even for whom one wants to work—only then can one, be it as a researcher or an activist, contribute in an honest and meaningful way. To maintain lies about oneself must lead to dishonest interactions and can only undermine the fabric of trust upon which any social research or social-activist intervention must rely. The authors assembled here face this difficulty of first seeing themselves before they can really see others with admirable courage. None of the contributors have become cynical about their work. All point to possible ways to make sense out of one's work and praxis. All detect and describe difficulties in order to join in a collective effort to overcome them—in the true spirit of both social-justice activism and social-science research.

Chapter Overview

Part 1 of this collection, The Promises and Pitfalls of Collaborative Research, addresses general themes and problems encountered by engaged researchers in the field.

In "Of Academic Embeddedness," Bernd Reiter ponders the consequences of increased mobility for scholars and their work. Drawing on ideas from a confluence of social theory on postmodernity, globalization, and the role of intellectuals in order to address the social alignments and solidarities that activist scholars negotiate in the course of their lives and careers, he argues that if scholars lose their embeddedness in local communities, then not just their work, but their legitimacy as social scientists suffer. Reiter argues that "global thinking" is impossible and undesirable. Concretely, he argues that increased mobility, sometimes voluntary and sometimes not, has potentially severe consequences for the involved scholars, for the communities they leave behind, and for the communities they choose to visit and conduct research in and on. To still maintain a meaningful and constructive practice, Reiter puts a strong emphasis on "sharing" and "giving back."

In "New Shapes of Revolution," the much respected and loved Mexican intellectual-activist-scholar Gustavo Esteva recounts his own experiences when seeking to bring the lifeworlds of historically excluded groups into the academic realm. As a self-confessed deprofessionalized intellectual, Esteva has built close relationships with the Mayan communities of Oaxaca, Mexico, with whom he has worked on the construction of an entirely new university, the Earth University (Universidad de la Tierra). His voice is one of a true organic intellectual, deeply embedded in subaltern communities. In this chapter, Esteva narrates his experience as a participant in a visit to a Zapatista self-governing pedagogical experiment of the *escuelita* (literally meaning "little school"). He was one of almost 2,000 people from thirty countries and all parts of Mexico who had been invited to attend a course the Zapatistas had titled "Freedom According to the Zapatistas." It was a lesson in self-governing at the community level and a pedagogical experiment that left Esteva deeply impressed.

"The Accidental Activist Scholar: A Memoir on Reactive Boundary and Identity Work for Social Change within the Academy," by Rob Benford, recounts, in auto-ethnographic style, the struggles that the author had to face throughout his academic career—and how he was able if not to overcome, at least to address the difficulties that being considered an activist created for him. His story highlights the dangers of confinement of academic discipline all the way from the hiring process—he almost was not hired, being considered an activist and hence "not a serious scholar"—to getting tenure, promotion, and respect from peers and university administrations. While Rob Benford's journey highlights the difficulties and problems he faced at different academic institutions, his life and career also offer inspiration on how to navigate such slippery terrain successfully and how to make sense of it all.

In "Can Development Bridge the Gap between Activism and Academia?" Cristina Espinosa relates her experience as an activist for social justice in Peru, which she would later channel into her career as a scholar and professor. For Espinosa, "activism" means professional, 100 percent dedication to the struggle of indigenous people in Peru. She is less sanguine than others about the possibilities for actually bridging scholarship and activism. From her vantage point, both demand all our time and energy. Thinking otherwise is, according to Espinosa, an illusion at best and a self-lie at worst—that is, a guilt-driven effort to still relate to "the struggle" while no longer in it. It is, in other words, driven more by the need to forge, maintain, and maybe sell a certain identity than by real possibilities.

"Leaving the Field: How to Write about Disappointment and Frustration in Collaborative Research" is written by the geographer Ulrich Oslender. He takes a less pessimistic view on the same issue. Instead of denying the possibility of bridging scholarship and activism, he rather asks, What happens once you leave the fieldwork site? What are the responsibilities that field research among poor, historically excluded, and racialized others imposes on the researcher? How does one protect their vulnerabilities and avoid exploiting and exposing them, for example, in one's own writing? What if one becomes the bearer of "special knowledge" that is not meant for outsiders? This chapter raises important questions about the ethics of research, particularly when it is conducted among and on vulnerable groups. Oslender draws here on methodological considerations advanced in Participatory Action-Research, or PAR, particularly as developed by the Colombian sociologist Orlando Fals Borda. He also ponders the important question of the legitimacy of a researcher to talk about and on behalf of the communities she/he researches. Can outside researchers legitimately represent them? Should they? In what ways? Oslender provides some answers to these questions drawn from his research with Afro-Colombian communities in the Pacific Coast region of Colombia.

"Invisible Heroes," the last in this section, is a collection of interviews conducted during a workshop held in 2013 in Panama with a group of Afro-descendant community leaders and organizers from different Latin American countries. Eshe Lewis interviewed these national Black Power leaders to document their life stories. To better situate these stories, she also provides some background information on each individual, their country, and the organizations they lead. All interviews were first conducted in Spanish, then reviewed by the interviewees, and after their final approval, translated into English by Eshe Lewis. As the title indicates, the six individuals whose lives are presented here are all "invisible," in the sense that Ralph Ellison gave the term; i.e., they are Afro-descendants in countries that have only very recently, and at times reluctantly, admitted that they even had populations of African descent as part of their national bodies. For some five hundred years, these bodies had been imagined, crafted, cut and bruised, bent, and forcefully mixed to be as white and as European as possible. *Blanqueamiento*—or whitening—was the order of the day. The Afro-descendant leaders presented here and the communities for which they advocate have been rendered invisible by those "whitened" state elites. As they now speak up and slowly gain national and international recognition, visibility, and a voice, their stories offer much insight into the lifeworlds of historically excluded and racialized groups. Their inspiring activism offers hope and guidance to all those seeking to add their voice to theirs.

The essays assembled under part 2, Negotiating Racialized and Gendered Positionalities, zero in on some of the core issues and problems raised in part 1. A critical self-awareness among social scientists engaged in empirical research projects in countries of the "global south" and in vulnerable communities whose members have long suffered from exclusion, discrimination, marginalization, invisibilization, stigmatization, and misrecognition will necessarily raise questions of identity. Race, class, gender, and nationalism all play an important role in how a researcher is able to enter a community, how he or she is perceived by this community, and what expectations are raised by different community members about the researcher. Within this force field of perceptions and expectations, the identity of the researcher is questioned and their role is scrutinized—not just by the community members, but first and foremost by herself. How to reconcile one's own identity with the performance of identities that spring out of the need to relate and cater to those one has learned to care about? What happens if one's own identity has in effect changed in the course of conducting long-term research—something that is very likely to occur when true learning and engagement are involved? What happens when one returns from the field, having to translate and explain one's life "over there" to those who stayed at home—be it family members, colleagues, or tenure and evaluation committees?

We start these reflections with a poem by the Afro-Colombian ethnographer, writer, and public intellectual Manuel Zapata Olivella (1920–2004). His poem "El Muntu en América"—translated here by Jonathan Tittler as "Our People in America"—provides a poetic introduction to the terrain of identity construction, identification, and of becoming one with a people, maybe even with a continent. A haunting piece, the Muntu stands for the collective experience of people of the African Diaspora—their original uprootedness, but also their many strategies of appropriating new spaces in this world. Zapata Olivella masterfully narrated this complex story of the Muntu in his epic Afrocentric masterpiece *Changó, el Gran Putas*, available in English under the title "Changó, the Biggest Badass" (also translated by Jonathan Tittler; see Zapata Olivella 2010). Throughout his life, Zapata Olivella stressed the implication of the "encounter" of the three main ethnicities in the Americas, which produced a continent of "trietnicidad," according to him. As the individual chapters in this second section deal with the experiences of African-descendant populations in Latin America, we thought it fitting to introduce the section with this poem of one of the most important voices of the African Diaspora in Latin America.

The Colombian anthropologist Arturo Escobar explores in "Activism as History Making: The Collective and the Personal in Collaborative Research with the Process of Black Communities in Colombia" his own experiences of conducting research with people of African descent in the southern Pacific Coast region of Colombia. Escobar's work over the last twenty years has become synonymous with the Process of Black Communities (PCN), one of the most dynamic sectors of the social movement of black communities in Colombia. In his narrative, Escobar shows how his own encounter with movement leaders changed the ways in which he perceived his research. In fact, he all but abandoned his initial interrogations and began, together with movement leaders, to draw up a common research agenda. It quickly became obvious to him that beyond the more material struggle over land rights lay a complex process of identity construction within structures of alterity that the movement intended to mobilize, and which he describes in detail in this chapter. More than an observer, Escobar became a friend to the movement. Not only has his work benefited from such a close, even organic, relationship with the movement—in his latest book, *Territories of Difference* (2008), he acknowledges the intellectual input of PCN leaders into the series of nested frameworks that he presents there—but he is also one of the most vocal defenders of the movement's claims of autonomy. Mobilizing his own position as a full professor within the U.S. academy, Escobar has invited movement leaders on awareness-raising campaigns to the United States, providing them with an important platform for transnational mobilization and solidarity. Together with one of the book's coeditors (Ulrich Oslender), Escobar is also a founding member of GAIDEPAC, a loosely organized alliance of academics and intellectuals that has organized in defense of the Colombian Pacific Coast. His commitment to the struggle of PCN has also earned him accusations of a lack of objectivity in his analysis, a reminder of the constant struggle activist-scholars lead to be both academically relevant and socially engaged.

"Out of Bounds: Negotiating Researcher Positionality in Brazil," by the sociologist Elizabeth Hordge-Freeman, offers an insightful approach to positionality and "activism." The latter is seen as a form and an ethic of practice that are grounded in everyday forms of consciousness-raising and service. Activism in the author's analysis ranges from hair braiding and her cooperative efforts to get someone out of jail to collaborating in community-based research. The author mostly examines everyday activism, which typically remains unnamed and underrecognized vis-à-vis activisms connected to named organizations or movements. Hordge-Freeman allows the reader a glimpse into the very fabric of identity construction, performance, and perception that gets interwoven, and often entangled, when conducting in-depth, long-term research in a place such as Bahia, Brazil. In order to gain access, Hordge-Freeman had to find a position and role for herself that could be understood and fit into the sense-making efforts of the people she sought to understand, namely, African-descendant families living in the city of Salvador. Given her very sensitive research topic, how racism affects families, Hordge-Freeman needed to find a place and a role for herself that gave her a chance to build relationships of trust strong enough to talk about such uncomfortable issues as racism in one's own family. Attempting to do so forced Hordge-Freeman to revisit her own identity—the image she had about herself and the image that different others formed about her. Her own blackness in itself, as she had to learn, was no guarantee for access, and the perceptions of African Americans from Brazil do not necessarily overlap with the perceptions of African Americans from the United States. While Hordge-Freeman's way to construct trust and gain access highlights again the importance of honesty, transparency, giving back, and sharing as a way to build trust (she started braiding hair in the local neighborhood, for example), this strategy also produced unintended consequences and raised problems of ethics, as she was used as a cultural asset by one of the local community members. In sum, Hordge-Freeman's chapter highlights some of the inherent tradeoffs and limitations of "going native." It also puts the positionality of shared racial backgrounds across different countries of the Americas into perspective.

"Between Soapboxes and Shadows: Activism, Theory, and the Politics of Life and Death in Salvador, Bahia, Brazil," by cultural anthropologist Christen A. Smith, draws on recent theoretical and philosophical discourses on anti-blackness, social and physical death, lethal policing and paramilitarism, and the racialization of urban space. Smith takes the reader to the very limits of the experiences one can have as a researcher abroad. Also focusing on the city of Salvador, Brazil, she recounts her brushes with violence, death, killings, and torture of poor black community members. The violence these communities are exposed to comes in part from the state—that is, a police force that is widely known to perpetuate gross human-rights violations by targeting urban black communities, particularly black youth. As she witnesses different efforts and actions by the affected communities—in most cases, family members of killed youth—Smith realizes that the violence to which poor black communities in such places as Bahia are routinely exposed has a symbolic and spiritual function that has a long history in the effort of controlling enslaved Africans and their descendants. By committing brutal acts of violence and then displaying it openly, black communities are to be scared, warned, and contained. Becoming aware of this function, Smith concludes by stating that "In order for me as an activist-researcher to even approach the question of practice/theory/discourse/power, I must get comfortable with the complexities, contradictions, and unromantic realities of what it means to live as a black person within the context of violence that is the subject of my research, and this means confronting the realities of spiritual terror, and acknowledging the stakes of speaking up and speaking out."

"State Violence and the Ethnographic Encounter: Feminist Research and Racial Embodiment," by fellow cultural anthropologist Keisha-Khan Perry, further explores the encounter of black female researchers from the United States with violence and death in peripheral poor neighborhoods of Salvador, Brazil. Offering a black feminist analysis, Perry, like Smith, recounts her experiences with police violence in Salvador. When the police invade the neighborhood of Gamboa de Baixo, where Perry conducted her ethnographic research living among local families, she finds herself exposed to the same risk as all the other residents. From this experience, Perry is able to draw several learnings and reflections. How to handle one's own fear of death? How to present it to the people of the community—and how to one's mostly unsuspecting family back home? How far can solidarity go—and how far must it go? The most affected groups of such police raids on poor neighborhoods that are perceived as suspicious and dangerous by middle- and upper-class Soteropolitans (i.e., inhabitants of Salvador, Bahia) are women, as they are the ones who are physically present in the homes when the raids occur. They are readily targeted by male police violence. As a black female U.S.

researcher in the middle of such a raid, Perry is faced with strong and very consequential choices. By choosing to stay, to witness, to testify, and to add her voice to those of the local women, Perry is able to add a very meaningful component to her academic work—without letting go of being a researcher. She concludes by stating, "The building of ethnographic relationships and the production of knowledge based on those relationships becomes a way for me as a diaspora black woman researcher to understand how to belong politically to a social movement in Bahia; to be in place as an anthropologist, rather than *out of place*; to break down that wall; and to stay alive." As such, Perry's experience not only highlights the possibilities of conducting ethnographic research—it also leaves no doubt about its risks and potential costs.

"The Challenges Resulting from Combining Scientific Production and Social-Political Activism in the Brazilian Academy," by the Bahian professor of journalism Fernando Conceição, provides a final perspective on conducting research in Salvador, Brazil—a city often labeled as Brazil's "Black Mecca." As a Black Power activist who was involved in such path-breaking and historically important actions as the foundation of the Black Consciousness Nucleus of the University of Sao Paulo, Brazil's number-one research university, and the lawsuit for reparations against the Brazilian state, Conceição can dwell on a vast personal experience as a black activist, advocating strongly for black rights and empowerment. In this chapter, Conceição tells the story of how his personal background and his activism affected his path towards becoming a professor at a federal university and, once there, of advancing in his career. His life thus becomes a parable for the general state of racial justice in Salvador, Brazil, and beyond, as his life also takes him to São Paulo and confronts him with federal state apparatuses. His trajectory makes it very clear that being black in Brazil—and at the same time studying racial issues in that country—exposes him to the same critique that Perry references in the previous chapter: his "scientific objectivity" becomes challenged, and because of this, his legitimacy as a social scientist is undermined. This, of course, is not something that routinely happens to white scholars, foreign or not, when they study "race" from a purely "neutral" standpoint. Brazilian hegemonic common sense, similar to that prevailing in the United States, thus elevates whites out of an ethnic position and bestows on white researchers the symbolic capital of observing from a neutral place—from nowhere—thus performing the much-quoted God-trick of being simultaneously nowhere specific and everywhere. Under such conditions—and they dominate not only in Brazil, but elsewhere as well—being a racialized subject becomes a major hurdle when seeking to achieve an academic career. This condition, as Conceição shows, gets even worse when a racialized subject defines him- or herself as an activist who is invested in the cause of improving the lives of his or her own people.

The book closes with "The Challenge of Doing Applied/Activist Anti-Racist Anthropology in Revolutionary Cuba," in which the applied anthropologist and activist Gayle McGarrity retells her own experiences in revolutionary Cuba. As a black women, educated in Jamaica, the UK, and the United States, and also keenly aware of the lives of African-descendant people in places such as Brazil, McGarrity critically scrutinizes the Cuban revolutionary reality, where, according to official doctrine, racism was a thing of the (pre-revolutionary) past that effectively ended in 1959. As an applied anthropologist and activist with a focus on health, especially the well-being of African-descendants, McGarrity questions Cuba's official rhetoric of racial harmony. While she is aware of the improvements made under the Castro regime to ban overt racial discrimination and hate crime, she still finds dominant opinions and outlooks imbued with racialized notions of white merit and black backwardness. To address these issues in a society that so sternly clings to its progressive and anticapitalist—that is, anti-exploitation—image became extremely difficult, as she recounts. Openly accusing Revolutionary Cuba of such a thing as racism, McGarrity had to learn, brings one quickly into conflict with otherwise like-minded "radicals" on the political left—particularly among academics. Publishing her findings in critical academic journals became an uphill task. While earning the wrath of most paper radicals, McGarrity instead found herself in company that she did not seek: radical right-wingers, who welcome any chance to discredit Castro's Cuba. As the account provided by McGarrity shows, in such a highly politicized environment, serious scholarship and meaningful social-justice activism are rendered highly complex and outright difficult, if not impossible.

The conclusion, jointly written by the editors, ventures into some of the consequences of the insights and learnings the contributions to this volume suggest.

NOTES

1. Original German: "Die Philosophen haben die Welt nur verschieden interpretiert; es kommt darauf an, sie zu verändern."

2. See, for example, a recent publication by critical geographers who borrow Marx's injunction as their title (Castree et al. 2010).

3. For a presentation of the decolonial perspective and a set of references, see Escobar (2008, ch. 4). The main names associated with it are Enrique Dussel, Aníbal Quijano, and Walter Mignolo. See also the edited collections by Moraña, Dussel & Jáuregui (2008) and Mignolo & Escobar (2010).

REFERENCES

Boyce Davies, C., Gadsby, M., Peterson, C., & Williams, H. (Eds.). (2003). *Decolonizing the academy: African diaspora studies*. Trenton, NJ: Africa World Press.

Castree, N., Chatterton, P., Heynen, N., Larner, W., & Wright, M. (Eds.). (2010). *The point is to change it: Geographies of hope and survival in an age of crisis*. Oxford: Wiley-Blackwell.

Clarke, K. A., & Primo, D. M. (2012). Overcoming "physics envy." *New York Times Sunday Review*, April 1, SR9.

Escobar, A. (2008). *Territories of difference: Place, movements, life, redes*. Durham, NC: Duke University Press.

Freire, P. (1971). *Pedagogy of the oppressed*. New York: Herder and Herder.

Harrison, F. (Ed.). (1991). *Decolonizing anthropology: Moving further toward an anthropology for liberation*. Washington, DC: American Anthropological Association.

Marx, K. (1998). *The German ideology*. Amherst: Prometheus Books.

Mignolo, W. (2005). *The idea of Latin America*. Oxford: Blackwell.

Mignolo, W., & Escobar, A. (Eds.). (2010). *Globalization and the decolonial option*. New York: Routledge.

Moraña, M., Dussel, E., & Jáuregui, C. (Eds.). (2008). *Coloniality at large: Latin America and the postcolonial debate*. London: Duke University Press.

Reiter, B., & Simmons, K. E. (Eds.). (2012). *Afrodescendants, identity, and the struggle for development in the Americas*. East Lansing: Michigan State University Press.

Thiong'o, N. (1986). *Decolonising the mind: The politics of language in African literature*. London: J. Currey.

Touraine, A. (1988). *The return of the actor*. Minneapolis: University of Minnesota Press.

Zapata Olivella, M. (2010). *Changó, the biggest badass*. Translated by J. Tittler. Lubbock: Texas Tech University Press.

The Promises and Pitfalls of Collaborative Research

Of Academic Embeddedness: Communities of Choice and How to Make Sense of Activism and Research Abroad

Bernd Reiter

Das Äußerste liegt der Leidenschaft zu allernächst
—Goethe, *Wahlverwandtschaften*

Postmodernism has caught up with all of us in one way or another. We are all decentered to some degree. Advances in education and increased exposure to a globalized media have corroded traditions everywhere and challenged monistic worldviews and belief systems in the remotest corners of the globe. While we are becoming more and more aware of Others everywhere, we can rely less and less on those traditional values and guiding systems passed on to us from the past. The postmodern condition, as Jean-Francois Lyotard (1979) has argued, is one of uncertainty and of disconnection, as traditional bonds, both vertical and horizontal, are losing their strength. The physical, or bodily, component of this loss of traditional value systems and ways to make sense of the world is one of increased mobility. Some of us can now be everywhere, but when doing so risk being nowhere at all. Others remain stuck in their localities while being increasingly aware of their being stuck—not at least due to the international visitors they now receive. Zygmunt Bauman has described this phenomenon better than I could. He writes: "Some can now move out of the locality—any locality—at will. Others watch helplessly the sole locality they inhabit moving away from under their feet" (Bauman 1998, 15). Bauman further explains that "Being local in a globalized world is a sign of social deprivation and degradation. The discomforts of localized existence are compounded by the fact that with public spaces removed beyond the reaches of localized life, localities are losing their meaning-generating and meaning-negotiating capacity and are increasingly dependent on sense-giving and interpreting actions which they do not control—so much for the communitarianist dreams/consolations of the globalized intellectuals" (3).

The postmodern, globalized world is a polarized world, with elites routinely jetting through the skies as preferred gold and platinum clients of major airlines, while the majority of the population witnesses helplessly the erosion of the systems that give meaning to life. The driving force, according to Bauman and others, is the ability to communicate instantaneously across great distance, thus erasing the differences between inner-community and inter-community communication. We can all talk to everybody, no matter how far away they are. As a result, physical proximity has lost its value. Or, in Bauman's words: "The present-day fragility and short life-span of communities appears primarily to be the result of that gap shrinking or altogether disappearing: inner-community communication has no advantage over inter-communal exchange, if both are instantaneous" (Bauman 1998, 15).

This ability to communicate instantly with everyone is met by the increased ability of some to leave. Some of us are now in a position to simply up and go, leaving behind oppressive families, controlling small towns, restrictive economic situations, and any other unpleasantness and restrictions imposed on us, thus giving some of us unprecedented opportunities to "fulfill ourselves" and satisfy our egotistic dreams, while leaving others, who are less able to move, behind. Of course, as with anything else in market systems, the amount of assets an individual or firm is holding determines the ability to take advantage of these opportunities, leading to the widely recognized polarization of the world where the rich get richer and the poor get not just poorer, but more exposed, helpless, and frustrated, as now they have much better tools to understand how screwed they really are and who screws them on a daily basis.

This essay is a very personal reflection about my own trajectory as a former social-justice activist and social worker turned scholar and researcher. Maybe more than most of my colleagues I have been thrown into the quick waters of the academic market, which has taken me to new places several times and eroded my connection to the places I have left behind. With every change of place I made—from Germany to Colombia, to Brazil, to New York, to Lisbon, Portugal, to Tampa, Florida, to France, Spain, and back to Germany—my ability to make sense out of my academic work seemed more threatened, as my attempts to connect it to local communities seemed to grow more and more tenuous. Having moved through such a great number of "new homes" probably makes my case an extreme one—but I hope to be able to offer, by way of introspection, at least some insight that also applies to others. My case might not be so extreme, after all.

Framed more generally, this essay proposes to analyze some of the consequences of the mutually reinforcing powers of postmodernism and globalization on academics and their connection to local communities. I will show that the postmodern, globalized condition we face has eroded the embeddedness of scholars in their lifeworlds and exposed them to look for new, artificial communities that allow for some sort of second-degree sense-making out of academic activity. Most scholars leave "their" communities and connect to new communities of choice at least once during their careers—particularly if their careers are taking off. Doing so, however, is problematic on three levels—namely, for the scholar herself, as the bonds to these communities of choice tend to remain tenuous and require active investment for their maintenance; for the communities left behind, because while people, or firms, leave, the problems they created tend to stay; and third, for the receiving communities of choice, who are increasingly exposed to agents of a kind of change that is not gradual, but born thousands of miles away. I will go through the three levels one by one.

The Globalized Scholar: At Home Everywhere and Nowhere

Many contemporary scholars face a double dilemma: on one hand, scholars employed in some Northern and Western universities enjoy some of the advantages of the economic elites Bauman has in mind, namely, access to information and global mobility. In terms of their access to information (I am reluctant to say "knowledge"), they are elites. On the other hand, their work and status have been severely devalued and exposed to the narrow utilitarian framework of the economic market, which does not ask, "Who are you?"—but "How much are you worth?" Particularly for social scientists and humanists, the answer is more often than not: "not much." Most academics are thus tenuous elites, characterized more by their gatekeeping and performance anxiety–driven behavior than by their relaxed elite habitus. In academia, vanity and egotism tend to be displayed in a crazed game of exalted egos trading in "who knows best" (Latour & Woolgar 1986).

This, it seems, is caused by the fact that most academics are not truly "elites," while at the same time they enjoy some of the elite-only advantages of global mobility. Like artists, they have to believe that they are important so they can muster the drive to sit down and write to the world—while at the same time fearing that "the world" is not listening and the only ones reading their work might be their own students, who have no choice in the matter. Academic books rarely sell over one thousand copies, and the readership of most academic journals is even smaller—and reduced to those who are obliged to read them: graduate students and a handful of colleagues.

Pierre Bourdieu has thus called academics "dominated dominants, that is, the dominated among the dominant" (1991, 655). As dominated dominants, professional scholars, while enjoying some relative privileges vis-à-vis the other dominated, are nevertheless exposed to the dynamics of globalized academic markets, which most of them face without much financial or symbolic capital and with very limited agency. The average recent PhD has little choice and almost no power of agency when facing an extremely competitive market for jobs, grants, postdocs, and fellowships.

To many scholars, being a professor thus means having left one's traditional community behind after having exposed oneself to the global maelstrom of PhD admissions and job searches. My own trajectory might serve to illustrate this point: While growing up in Germany and living in Colombia and Brazil, I went to graduate school in New York, did a postdoc in Portugal, and finally found a tenure-track position in Tampa, Florida—a place I had never even heard of before. Since then, I have also spent several months living and working on time-limited research projects in France, Spain, Colombia, and Germany.

The academic market dominates and dictates most of the choices academics like myself make, and it exposes us to high levels of nonvoluntary mobility and undesired flexibility. On today's academic postdoc and job market, finding a job where one lives is almost impossible. For married academic couples, finding tenure-track positions at the same universities is almost a miracle. The last job search my own department conducted produced some two hundred viable candidates— none of whom already lived in Tampa.

My own case, then, seems less extreme and more typical: Every time I leave, I remove myself more and more from those communities to which I had a genuine connection and a bond. Every time I arrive, I am forced to find ways to insert myself into the already existing local communities

I encounter. The older I grow in this process, the less "natural" or "organic" these relations tend to be—so that the postmodern condition becomes a self-fulfilling prophecy and I can no longer differentiate between traditional and modern, original and simulacrum. You can only call so many places your "home." Any reference to a rhyzomatic network of horizontally dispersed relationships seems but a cheap language trick and a bitter euphemism unable to compensate for the sense of loss arising from being disconnected.

The ability to forge meaning out of chaos (or sense out of complexity) relies on having strong and meaningful connections. It is a relational effort and as such requires having robust relations to begin with. When living in a world where one cannot distinguish between original and simulacrum lifeworlds, we run the risk of moving entirely into a simulacrum world without even recognizing the difference—*a plastic world*, in the words of Ruben Blades.[1] After over twenty years away from "home," my hometown feels probably the most foreign of them all—and the one that makes me the most aware of the price I have to pay for my high level of mobility.

As scholars, why do we need communities, someone might ask? Why not embrace the fate of the solitary thinker? The problem, however—particularly for social scientists—is: in the absence of community embeddedness, where to get inspiration from? What questions to ask? What to write about and for whom? After having lived and worked in Brazil for some seven or eight years, trying to add my work and voice to those seeking to improve the lives of the excluded and marginalized—I moved to New York. For the first few years I still had plenty of empirical material to reflect upon. But how long can one maintain a meaningful connection to a community left behind? How long can one legitimately speak about, let alone for, this community? At what point is it more truthful and honest to say: "Better ask a Brazilian, or at least someone who still lives there"?

The academic market, like all capitalist markets, relies on branding, which demands: once a Brazilianist—always a Brazilianist. Removed from the communities they once lived in and studied, many Northern and Western scholars are driven into a niche of specialization that is less and less grounded in genuine participation and local knowledge. As a result, the work of many scholars has long been a reflection of their condition: they write only for themselves and their academic community—a group of experts without any connection to other experts, let alone lay people and the local communities that they have studied.

To make matters worse, forced to "publish or perish" by the logic of a narrowly defined academic system, most of us write only to advance our own interests—that is, to get tenure, promotion, and more money. Tenure review boards simply do not care about how many of the research subjects involved in a study were actually able to benefit from their participation—be it only through a sharing of findings in local outlets, published in the local language. What matters to most tenure review boards instead are impact factors, where "impact" ironically excludes those local communities that might benefit from the produced research. This, again, might be an extreme case of highly unreflexive political-science departments, and I know that some other departments do a better job—but the logic of how to define, let alone assess, academic impact and success among social scientists in general certainly deserves some critical review. The criteria for assessing the merits of "tenure" seem to work, to the best of my knowledge, directly against any attempt to share one's findings with local nonspecialists. As a result, on top of being anxious quasi-elites, some of us risk becoming hysterical egomaniacs without any consequence.

Worse, and any metaphors of "rhizomatics" notwithstanding, the disconnected individualism that springs from uprootedness makes it increasingly impossible for many of us to even grasp the problems that plague local communities—let alone do anything to help local activists to make a difference. This uprootedness condemns us to become "global citizens" and pushes us into the trap of commitment-free scholarship about "global forces." However, there is no such thing as "global thinking," and in most cases, global activism is but a cheap excuse for not being willing to commit to the causes of local people and groups (Esteva & Prakash 1998). While "the strength of weak ties" (Granovetter 1973) lies in being able to take personal advantage of loose connections to many people and communities, understanding, commitment, responsibility, solidarity, and reciprocity all demand strong ties.

As Gustavo Esteva and Madhy Suri Prakash (1998) so convincingly argue, "global thinking" is mostly a meaningless stand-in, born out of the necessity to offer a positive framework for thinking without consequence and commitment. In their view, as well as in my own, only multiple local efforts and collaborations between them have the power to change the world—a view also shared by Ernesto Laclau and Chantal Mouffe (1985). Committed academics can assist these efforts by adding their work and voice to those of local people, communities, and activists. "Global scholars" who engage in "global thinking" and deal in "global problems" at best can give advice to those few hyper-elites that actually have the power to influence global politics. But how many of us can really become advisors to the U.S. Department of State, Tony Blair, Kofi Annan, or even lower-level foreign policymakers? The great majority of "global thinkers" run the risk of undermining the limited local actions of local activists by belittling their efforts and importance. Most "global thinkers" do not even seem to care about social and political change to begin with, so that their choice of a research domain is a truthful reflection of their snobbish elitism. They want to be global brokers, diplomats, and players in a game of no other consequence but the effect such engagement has on their own careers. True and lasting change, on the other hand, must come from below, i.e., from local communities. In the words of Esteva and Prakash, "Since none of us can ever really know more than a miniscule part of the earth, 'global thinking' is at best an illusion, and at its worst the grounds for the kinds of destructive and dangerous actions perpetuated by global 'think tanks' like the World Bank, or their more benign counterparts—the watchdogs in the global environmental and human rights movements" (Esteva & Prakash 1998, 22). Even from a narrower, scientific viewpoint, objective knowledge cannot be universal. Only partial and situated knowledge promises to advance our collective effort to better understand our different worlds. If "changing it for the better" is our objective, universalist platitudes draped in "global thinking" certainly represent the least promising strategies (Harding 1991; Haraway 1988).

The almost unavoidable outcome of "global thinking" more often than not is a sort of irrelevant arrogance. It is the kind of arrogance that claims to have solutions for others without ever bothering to know those others, let alone provide them with a voice. This arrogance is also the one that asks, *what ideas can I offer to others or the world?*—as if the problems of the world were caused by a lack of smart people and ideas. To think so is not only arrogant, but naive (Easterly 2007). Thinking that one knows better what is good for others is also the kind of attitude that more and more local activists, influenced—and sometimes led—by native or first people, struggle against (Escobar, this volume). Grassroots activists are not the only ones, however, rendering such scholarship irrelevant.

With but a few exceptions, the productions of most global thinkers go unheard. Who really reads the books and articles of even the most prominent academic global thinkers, most of whom work for international-relations departments and publish in highly specialized academic journals? The "big debates" routinely waged in this field among "realists," "liberals," and "constructivists" have not had any reception, to the best of my knowledge, outside of the circle of the same specialists that have formulated them in the first place. The work of such prominent global scholars as Robert Keohane, the 2012 recipient of the Harvard Centennial Medal and the main proponent of "neoliberal institutionalism," must necessarily be a reflection of their own positionality and situatedness. What else but "high politics" could elite scholars such as Keohane write about? It seems hardly coincidental that international relations is an American discipline. After all, U.S. hegemony *is* the standpoint of most authors writing in this field—even if most of them might not realize it (Tickner 2013).

Instead of offering ill-received prescriptions to those waging global power over "the world," I contend that the important question to ask instead is *With whom do I want to stand?* and *For whom do I want to work; that is, to whom do I make my work accessible and for what purpose?* In my own experience, the answer to these questions will necessarily influence not only what one writes about and where it is published and distributed, but also what kind of language code one uses. While such global scholars as Jürgen Habermas, Gilles Deleuze, Felix Guattari, Jean Francois Lyotard, Michael Hart, and Antonio Negri might have valuable insights to offer to those suffering from poverty, exclusion, and discrimination, they have certainly made sure, by choosing cryptic and convoluted language codes, that most of the affected groups will never be able to read, let alone use, their books and articles.

To sum up: One cannot stand with anybody if one is constantly on the move. Against the fashionable trope of the rhizome (Deleuze & Guattari 1987), standpoint theory demands that one has a point on which to stand to begin with. I am not sure how many different viewpoints a scholar can adopt, but it seems that our range is limited, if not by time and resources, then by our own positionality, which enables some views but forecloses others (Haraway 1988).

The Ones Left Behind: Communities Thinner than Air

In the agglomerate, if more and more people constantly and frequently move, local community bonds become thinner and thinner, and eventually local communities become mere agglomerations of self-interested individuals who enter new communities with strategic interests in mind, making them instrumental and a tool for profit-seeking of some sort. When this happens—and it has of course happened for a long time, particularly in the communities of the advanced capitalist world—leaving becomes easier and easier, as local communities offer less and less genuine embeddedness and less and less guidance for action and thought. They impose restrictions and exercise control without offering comfort and meaning.

Those who leave—once they have been duly treated by the different disciplining machines that transform them into utterly disconnected and self-interested strategic actors—tend to spread meaninglessness by introducing it like a virus into those communities that they find so attractive: communities that still offer meaning and guidance to their members. Those communities are typically found in those regions of the world yet not thoroughly structured by instrumental rationality, and not yet inhabited by the rational, profit-maximizing zombies unleashed from those communities already further into the maelstrom of globalizing capitalism (Comaroff & Comaroff 1999).

Hence the moral dilemma of any astute and self-aware researcher or transnational scholar: we know that we make our career by exploring the lifeworlds of those stuck in their locality, and in doing so we risk becoming active agents in the very destruction of the locality we seek to defend, and whose destruction by the unbound forces of globalized capitalism we so eloquently deplore. Worse: we also know that nobody really cares about the loathing of academics so that our radical critique goes mostly unheard, our messages not impacting the world. We are unable to remedy the structures we criticize, while our transnational actions and our mere presence in local communities never fails to introduce globalization into the lifeworlds of the people stuck there—making those even more aware of how stuck they actually are.

Given local scarcity of academic jobs and the global opportunities advertised in such outlets as the *Chronicle of Higher Education*, where academic job offerings from Turkey, China, Singapore, etc., are routinely advertised, those seeking academic careers have no other choice but to apply worldwide for training opportunities, fellowships, postdocs, and tenure-track positions. Not every local community, after all, has its own university offering graduate training. As only a few recent PhDs get a well-paid, tenure-earning job immediately after completing their degree, chances are that they will spend some time "community hopping" before they finally land a good, permanent job. They are, however, not the only ones engaged in this sort of community destabilization. They are merely the vanguard. Particularly in the United States, where market forces are the most unbridled, personal lives have long adapted to the forces of impersonal markets. On average, Americans move some twelve times during their lives; they have children once they have enough income, and they try out different life partners according to more or less standardized tests that take into consideration such criteria as income, health, housing situation, etc. (called "dating"). When they can, when they must, or when better opportunities await elsewhere, those endowed with enough assets move, following the same rational logic as firms. Their lifeworlds have been thoroughly colonized by the logic of capitalist markets (Habermas 1985). According to Bauman, "The company is free to move; but the consequences of the move are bound to stay. Whoever is free to run away from the locality, is free to run away from the consequences. These are the most important spoils of victorious space war" (Bauman 1998, 8f).

In the case of humans, Albert Hirschmann's (1970) assessment is probably still the most telling: the easier it is for someone to just move, the lower are the incentives to actively engage with local problems. Under conditions of increased mobility, exit trumps voice and loyalty. While companies move and leave problems behind, people move and leave problems unresolved, or for others to solve. Furthermore, if many people move, as is the case in the United States, the bonds that hold communities together get thinner and thinner, to the point where local communities become mere residual places of people unable to move away. In Germany, where I grew up, this phenomenon has led to entire villages emptied of young and active people, but also to an exodus of local shops catering to them. A few years back, the last bakery of my home village closed, and the majority of elderly people living there are now stuck and unable to get to the supermarket in the next urban center. What once was a vibrant local village community has become the residence of those unable to move. For them, there are no small shops, no deliveries, no spontaneous gatherings in front of houses and alleys. The benches in front of the old houses, once built so that the older generation could sit down in the evening and watch the younger generation promenade, now go unused. Nor could they be used, as all one can see pass by today are cars. The milkman does not come anymore, nor does—this is Germany—the beer truck. Almost all of my former high school classmates have left. Some have moved to bigger cities, and some, like myself, to foreign countries. The only difference from the social poverty of suburban America is that the buildings and the urban structure remind everybody how much social life these streets must have hosted only a few decades back. The stone benches stand as silent totems, like gravestones to a community life that has vanished and died. Very much like the average American suburbanites and the village dwellers in those other parts of the world that have undergone economic development, those that were unable to leave are stuck. More often than not, they are also lonely. This loneliness seems only in part explained by a physical lack of company; it rather seems to reflect a weakness of community bonds—even if others are present, and sometimes precisely because they are.

Some of the new communities I joined along the way did not feel like communities at all, but rather like a bunch of people thrown together against their own will and sharing nothing but a common wish to take advantage of each other. Most prevalent in those was not a sense of community, but an angst that one might get taken advantage of by another member, acting quicker than oneself.

Communities of Choice: Where to Dump Next?

The solution to this devastating emptiness of anemic communities for many scholars lies in actively engaging in other communities—communities of choice. If my own community feels empty and thin, then why not spend more time in Guatemala, Brazil, India, or elsewhere, where communities are still genuine, people are welcoming and hospitable and do not calculate every move for the sake of personal gain. To many social scientists, spending time away and partaking in genuine community life abroad is the first time they ever experience what community can mean, or how important culture can be to sustain community life. Engaging in the community life of others, particularly if those others are poor, excluded, mistreated, and in general on the defensive, allows for the achievement of several goals at once: Most poor and exploited people, because they are at the nadir of power, make for easy research subjects. They appear willing and open, even when they are not. They tend to be welcoming to the foreigner and outsider. They often cooperate willingly, without raising uncomfortable questions about intellectual ownership and rights. They pose no risk of pursuing the researcher if anything goes wrong, as their access to legal systems is precarious at best. On top of that, they allow the researcher to engage in work that appears meaningful to him or her. After all, his or her work helps the wretched of the earth and allows one to feel cozy and warm in the middle of so much sense and meaning. These are, of course, only the spoils of successful academic work, if successful it is. The core benefit for the researcher abroad is that a whole career can be constructed upon such work. Books, articles, and conference papers are the most immediate outcomes of research, abroad or not—and these products can carry tremendous symbolic value and lead to other jobs, promotions, and repeated research grants. They represent a major investment in the credibility currency in which scholars trade (Latour & Woolgar 1986).

This might sound hyperbolic, but my own experience, again, might provide an example—whether extreme or typical is up for grabs. Conducting research on school reform in Bahia, Brazil, I encountered local community schools where the local activists told me that they "had enough of white, middle-class researchers coming to their school, taking their time, but never bothering to come back and share any of their findings" (Reiter 2009).

The problem is, again in the words of Zygmunt Bauman:

> If the new exterritoriality of the elite feels like intoxicating freedom, the territoriality of the rest feels less like home ground, and ever more like prison—all the more humiliating for the obtrusive sight of others' freedom to move. It is not just that the condition of "staying put," being unable to move at one's heart's desire and being barred access to greener pastures, exudes the acrid odor of defeat, signals incomplete humanity and implies being cheated in the division of splendors life has to offer. Deprivation reaches deeper. The "locality" in the new world of high speed is not what the locality used to be at a time when information moved only together with the bodies of its carriers; neither the locality, nor the localized population has much in common with the "local community" . . . Far from being hotbeds of communities, local populations are more like loose bunches of untied ends." (Bauman 1998, 23f)

As visiting researchers inevitably leave local communities after their research is concluded, locals stay behind, hoping that some of their time and effort spent assisting the researcher somehow returns to benefit them, even if only in the form of learning what all their work and effort led to, "over there." However, most researchers do not return and locals never learn what became of their contributions and efforts. While an academic might make a career out of the work done in a locality, that same locality might never learn about it. Having participated and supported foreign researchers thus puts local participants into the position of Vladimir and Estragon in *Waiting for Godot*, or the Brazilian villagers who participated in Orson Welles's unfinished documentary *It's All True*—still hoping decades later that they would hear from Mr. Welles and maybe become famous. Most researchers I have encountered, however—particularly those not spending much time in a locality—do not even leave copies of the photos they take of locals, and very few actually go back after their work is completed to share the results and findings of their research with their research subjects. Many simply take—and very few give back. A local Casa da Mina priestess in the city of São Luis told me once that the famous researcher and specialist of Afro-Brazilian religion, the Frenchman Pierre Verger, had taken an old photo that showed some of the now diseased dignitaries of this cult and had never bothered to give it back. The priestess, similar to the local school activists in Salvador, had developed a deep distrust of white, foreign researchers—and rightly so.

Of course, while being "soiled" by a previous researcher and rendered uncooperative for future researchers, such communities might use the experience of academic exploitation as the beginning of their own empowerment, conquering agency and making deliberate decisions about whom they want to collaborate with and under what conditions. The traveling scholar will most likely meet such attitudes and regulations with discontent, as they question the privileged positionality of Northern researchers and their right to impose an unconstrained gaze upon those they want to examine. However, taking active control, by local communities, of the conditions and terms of researching them can help them to secure much-needed knowledge, avoid abuse where Human Subjects Approvals fail to grip, and it can lead to more respectful and mutually beneficial relationships among visiting researchers and local communities. Such steps are thus potentially important and necessary to take, particularly in such "hip" communities as, for example, the Mexican Zapatistas, who have become every Latin Americanist graduate student's research nirvana.

What Is to Be Done?

The picture painted so far is of course overly gloomy. I painted it that way to provoke some hard thinking and hopefully some action among those who often unwillingly become agents of destruction, or at least agents contributing to the eroding of local sense-making efforts—namely, professional scholars. The risks I have depicted are all pitfalls I have encountered myself, as a white, European-descendant male conducting research among mostly poor black communities in Latin America, Africa, and in Europe. Instead of accusing, I hope to have shared some of my own worries and fears, as some of the problems described above are difficult to avoid. A "going back" and sharing is not always financially feasible once a research project is concluded. Tenure pressure is an imposing reality and its dictates are difficult to ignore. The constant search for jobs and academic opportunities that triggers the kind of "community hopping" deplored here has structural components that are difficult, maybe impossible, to avoid.

However, some of the same literature that points out all of the pitfalls and dangers of globalization and postmodernism also offers some guidance on how to navigate the slippery domain of academic work under globalizing and postmodern conditions. The decentering of the individual and the loss of hegemonic scripts that guide our morals pose problems, but they also provide opportunities. As the "good old days" are fading, more of us are becoming aware that the good old days were not that good after all. Analytical frameworks more aware of the gendered and racialized dimensions of exclusion and privilege are slowly conquering more space and starting to command more visibility and authority. Decoloniality frameworks of reading and understanding the world have gained more prominence even among the academic mainstream—at least in some disciplines. These new frameworks offer new ways to make sense of the world without relying on the old dogmas of hegemonic white male dominance, dressed up as universalism. This king, at least, has been denuded quite a bit, and more and more people are able to see his nudity. Social scientists can and must play a central role in this process of destruction of the old and biased mantras that still provide the legitimation for exclusion, exploitation, and unjustified qua unexamined privilege. A decentering of individuals has invited Others in, not only into individual consciousnesses, but also into dominant discourses of knowledge production and distribution. The role of critical social scientists and humanists in this process has certainly been significant—even if much more needs to be done. Pierre Bourdieu has highlighted this role by stressing the importance of critical reflexivity. To him, "Critical reflexivity, in other words, is the absolute prerequisite of any political action by intellectuals. Intellectuals must engage in a permanent critique of all abuses of power or authority that are committed in the name of intellectual authority; or, if you prefer, they must submit themselves to the relentless critique of the use of intellectual authority as a political weapon within the intellectual field and elsewhere" (Bourdieu 2000, 41).

Some of us, particularly in such fields as international relations and economics, clearly need to be much more courageous when analyzing ourselves and the roles we play in the different games we engage in—academic as well as political, economic, and social.

Scholars who are actively engaged and involved in communities of choice abroad can, due to their practical experience, become true agents of change, not just in the communities they visit and work with, but also back "home," because their practical experience should allow them to better evaluate the priorities of academic life (e.g., how important is it really to publish in this or that "highly regarded" journal when the readership is miniscule). My own practical experience with courageous activism in the face of poverty, exclusion, and precariousness abroad has certainly put some of the academic activities deemed important back home in perspective. Witnessing courageous local activism has also allowed me to detect and recognize the very prevalent "paper revolutionism" and "campus radicalism" (Bourdieu 2000, 41) of so many Northern scholars who often denigrate the concrete but small victories local activists tend to achieve. It is easy to be radical when one is a tenured professor with a cozy office, a guaranteed job, and a retirement plan, and it is cheap to seek academic recognition by offering the most radical assessments while not risking anything—least of all to put one's words into practice.

I have also learned that the disconnected professors tend to be the ones who complain the most about their own "precarious" situations while not even considering the situations of some of the staff who support their daily activities—some of whom receive indecent wages, without access to pension, health, and social security provisions (I work in Florida, mind you). Hence, having lived and worked under truly precarious conditions in the global South puts perspective onto the "plights" of Northern academics and allows for a reassessment of one's role and position in producing social change. It helps avoid "mistak[ing] verbal sparring at academic conferences for interventions in the affairs of a city" (Bourdieu 2000, 41). Paper radicalism is, I suspect, one of the results of community disembeddedness that can be remedied by a genuine involvement with local communities and their struggles.

Communities of choice can become "genuine" (for lack of a better word) communities to the visiting researcher, as researchers can truly embrace the lifeworlds and problems of the local communities they study and become active supporters of local efforts towards change and improvement. Visiting scholars are of course not bound to unwillingly introduce the virus of a corrosive capitalist mentality into these communities, because any human interaction is at least in part willful and offers choice. By becoming "outside members," researchers can and have helped local communities in their struggles, giving them visibility and legitimacy through the research they conduct there. Research, instead of objectifying subjects, can also empower them—if done in knowledge-respecting, and knowledge-sharing way. The burden to make sense of one's uprooted life lies, after all, not with the local community, but with the visiting researcher.

Knowledge shared with the local communities makes all the difference. So does sharing in general—be it a sharing of food, books, or photos. Once a researcher comes back and shares, she also puts an end to the vicious cycle of leaving waste behind while making a career and money out of whatever was extracted locally. If you dump your baggage somewhere else, then at least go back and help clean it up. And when you do that, share your research findings, leave some books behind, share your photos. Don't steal from or lie to locals—be it only information you steal and lies you tell about your own life, pretending to be equal. Care. I have learned that if you do, a community of choice can also become a true community, even if you stay away for long periods of time.

NOTES

1. From the Salsa song "Plástico," by Ruben Blades.

REFERENCES

Bauman, Z. (1998). *Globalization: The human consequences.* New York: Columbia University Press.

Bourdieu, P. (2000). For a scholarship with commitment. *Profession*: 40–45.

Bourdieu, P. (1991). Fourth lecture. Universal corporatism: The role of intellectuals in the world. *Poetics Today* 12 (4): 655–669.

Comaroff, J., & Comaroff, J. (1999). Alien-nation: Zombies, immigrants, and millennial capitalism. *Codesria Bulletin* 3 & 4: 17–26.

Deleuze, G., & Guattari, F. (1987). *A thousand plateaus.* Minneapolis: University of Minnesota Press.

Easterly, W. (2007). The ideology of development. *Foreign Policy* (July/August): 30–35.

Esteva, G., & Prakash, M. S. (1998). *Grassroots post-modernism.* London: Zed Books.

Granovetter, M. (1973). The strength of weak ties. *American Journal of Sociology* 78 (6): 1360–1380.

Habermas, J. (1985). *The theory of communicative action: Reason and the rationalization of society.* Vol. 1. Boston: Beacon Press.

Haraway, D. (1988). Situated knowledges: The science question in feminism and the privilege of partial perspective. *Feminist Studies* 14 (3): 575–599.

Harding, S. (1991). *Whose science? Whose knowledge?* Ithaca, NY: Cornell University Press.

Hirschman, A. (1970). *Exit, voice, and loyalty.* Cambridge, MA: Harvard University Press.

Laclau, E., & Mouffe, C. (1985). *Hegemony and socialist strategy.* New York: Verso.

Latour, B., & Woolgar, S. (1986). *Laboratory life: The construction of scientific facts.* Princeton, NJ: Princeton University Press.

Lyotard, J.-F. (1979). *The postmodern condition.* Manchester: University of Manchester Press.

Reiter, B. (2009). Inequality and school reform in Bahia, Brazil. *International Review of Education* 55 (4): 345–365.

Tickner, A. (2013). Core, periphery and (neo)imperialist international relations. *European Journal of International Relations* 19: 627.

New Shapes of Revolution

Gustavo Esteva

> Such revolution is an art. That is: it requires the courage not only of resistance but also of imagination.
>
> —Howard Zinn, *La Jornada* 30 (October 2010)

An Alternative to Education

In 1997, after a year-long reflection and debate, the indigenous people of Oaxaca offered a firm public declaration: "The school has been the main tool of the State to destroy the indigenous people." This was a historical truth. In Mexico, as in other countries, the educational system was born with the obsession of de-Indianizing the Indians; the elite preferred culturicide to genocide. After the declaration, some communities began to close schools and kick out teachers, scandalizing everyone. Two years later, tests showed that children not going to school were better prepared in everything than those going to school. Yet, the communities were still concerned: How could their young people continue their studies outside their communities, if they so wanted, without any formal diploma? Therefore, a new university was created with them and for them, in which no previous certification of studies is required.

Universidad de la Tierra en Oaxaca is a coalition of indigenous and nonindigenous organizations. It is an organization, a space, and a web for learning, studying, reflecting, and doing. An organization: those collaborating in Unitierra are organized to learn and act together. A space: Unitierra is an open space for other people and organizations. A web: Unitierra operates in interaction with a wide web of friends and acquaintances, with whom we learn and do.

In Unitierra there are no teachers, classrooms, curricula, campuses, or diplomas. We understand *learning* as an aspect of daily life that can be cultivated, and *studying* as the leisurely and autonomous activity of free people. We call our research activities, both theoretical and empirical, *reflection in action*. In all our activities we give special importance to the *intercultural dialogue* and to the *construction of autonomy*.

We are affiliated with the Sixth Declaration of the Selva Lacandona of the Zapatista Army for National Liberation (EZLN). We are convinced that no real solution to the current social and political predicaments can come from the top down, through social engineering. We are looking for the reconstruction of society from the bottom up, reclaiming and organizing a convivial way of life. As substitute for nouns like food, education, and health, creating dependency on the market or the state, we are reclaiming verbs like eating, learning, healing, settling—that is, our autonomous capacities to live in dignity.

We are deeply immersed in the processes of social transformation happening around us, of which we are an expression. We think that the world as we know it is coming to an end. We are seeing everywhere increasing authoritarianism and dispossession, imposed as a substitute for the current political and economic regime. We consider that some of the political initiatives in which we are involved, in Oaxaca and Chiapas, are a good illustration of the struggles to transform society that are happening everywhere.

The idea of Unitierra is becoming contagious. New, autonomous Unitierras currently exist in Chiapas and Puebla in Mexico, in California in the United States, and in Toronto in Canada.

The Lacandona Commune

Today, the main challenge in Mexico is to resist forces dispossessing and oppressing the people with a wave of violence that may precipitate vicious forms of civil war. At the same time, we need to connect the points of resistance, giving to them an organizational form adapted to their nature. What is needed is to construct a political force that can stop the ongoing disaster, prevent its continuation, and begin to reorganize the society from the bottom up.

There are clear symptoms that such a process has already started. Many initiatives are connecting desire to reality and thus giving to political action a joyful and effective sense. An increasing number of people are ceasing to dance to the tune of the powerful, in order to play their own music.

The main catalyzer, which may precipitate the social emulsion transforming society, is coming from the Lacandona Commune in Chiapas. For many analysts, both the Zapatistas and subcomandante Marcos are history: they lost their opportunity, their time, and are increasingly irrelevant. The media have "disappeared" them; they ignore them, except to disqualify them. Allies and sympathizers have begun to share such an impression. For prominent thinkers like Chomsky, González Casanova, or Wallerstein, however, *Zapatismo* is today the most radical and perhaps the most important political initiative in the world.

The Zapatistas were the first in challenging the intellectual and political mood, which until 1993 had surrendered to neoliberal globalization. Since the Zapatista uprising, all antisystemic movements have acknowledged that it was a wake-up call, creating the opening later expressed in the World Social Forum as "Another World Is Possible," whose more vigorous and creative sectors seem inspired by the Zapatistas.

But there is something more, at a deeper level. Teodor Shanin described it years ago in the following terms:

> We believe that there are no alternatives, and when you don't have alternatives you must create them. Socialism was a magnificent guide even for non socialists . . . There was an alternative. But we are no

longer there. Some still think that they can still find in capitalism an alternative. Very soon they will be disillusioned.

But perhaps that's not the question. We already see the end of state socialism (and there's no other socialism in the real world), but also the end of real capitalism in a very concrete sense: capital can no longer govern a country . . . The real societies, which are in the form of nation-states, can no longer be governed using capitalism. (Esteva & Shanin 2005, 14)

Such conviction dominated: There were no alternatives. There was the need to create them. That is what the Zapatistas did. A rumor currently circulating in Mexico is that their new initiatives can fulfill again that function. They are marking the contour lines of new social and political paths when the crisis has created new opportunities, and threats and many dead ends are proliferating everywhere.

For almost twenty years, the Zapatistas have been exposed to the attention of the public and the media. In fact, as surprising as it may seem to those who insist on forgetting them and who periodically bury them, no contemporary social or political movement has attracted public attention as much as Zapatismo has, in both quantitative and qualitative terms.[1] The Zapatista rebellion, Wallerstein (2005) wrote, "has been the most important social movement in the world, the barometer and alarm clock for other anti-systemic movements around the world." No one would dare to attribute to the Zapatistas the amazing expansion of transnational networks of solidarity and the mutual support that have emerged in the last twenty years. But only an intolerable blindness can negate the weight that they have had in their creation and continue to have as a cause of inspiration.

One of the reasons why so many seem to want to forget Zapatismo, to send it to the past or to reduce it to a few municipalities in Chiapas, is the depth of their radicalism. The Zapatistas challenge in words and deeds every aspect of contemporary society. In revealing the root cause of the current predicaments, they tear to tatters the framework of the economic society (capitalism), the nation-state, formal democracy, and all modern institutions. They also render obsolete conventional ways and practices of social and political movements and initiatives. In reconstructing the world from the bottom up, they reveal the illusory or counterproductive nature of changes conceived or implemented from the top down. Their path encourages everywhere resistance to globalization and neoliberalism, and inspires struggles for liberation. They also contribute to articulating those struggles.

Nothing about the Zapatistas is more important than their contribution to hope and imagination. When hope is destroyed, that sheet-anchor of every man—says the *Mahabarata*, the sacred book of India—great grief follows which forsooth is almost equal to death itself. For Ivan Illich, "The Promethean ethos has now eclipsed hope. Survival of the human race depends on its rediscovery as a social force" (Illich 1971, 105–106). That is exactly what the Zapatistas have done.

Pan-Dora, the All-Giver, closed the lid of her amphora before Hope could escape. It is time to reclaim it, in the era in which the Promethean ethos threatens to destroy the world, and the expectations it generated vanish one after the other. In liberating hope from its intellectual and political prison, the Zapatistas created the possibility of a renaissance, which is now emerging in the net of plural paths they discovered, or is daily invented by the imagination they awakened and made brighter. They are still a source of inspiration for those walking along those paths. But they do not pretend to administer or control such a net, which has its own impulses, strength, and orientation. We all are, or can be, Zapatistas.

Behind our black mask, behind our armed voice, behind our unnamable name, behind what you see of us, behind this, we are you. Behind this, we are the same simple and ordinary men and women who are repeated in all races, painted in all colors, speak in all languages, and live in all places. Behind this, we are the same forgotten men and women,

- the same excluded,
- the same intolerated,
- the same persecuted,
- the same as you. Behind this, we are you.[2]

In 250,000 hectares of Selva Lacandona, surrounded by thousands of troops, daily attacked by paramilitary groups, demonized by the government and the political classes, isolated and disqualified by the "institutional" Left, the Zapatistas persist in their amazing sociological and political construction. They refused to get funds from the government, not even for their schools and health centers. When civil society asked them to follow "the political way," they tested in a dignified way the government's capacity for dialogue. The Accords of San Andrés, agreed upon with the government, were ignored and violated by successive administrations. But the Zapatistas have demonstrated their sense and feasibility by applying them with autonomy in the area under their control.

A Provisional Evaluation

The record of the Zapatista impact until now is impressive.

- The Zapatistas were a decisive factor in the dismantling of the oldest authoritarian regime in the world, Mexico's *ancien régime*.
- They created a political option to the dead end of globalization.
- The situation in Chiapas changed dramatically; thousands of peasants, mostly indigenous, got the land they had been struggling for, and a new balance of political forces is redefining the social fabric in that state.
- In the territories occupied by the Zapatistas, in spite of military encirclement and continual paramilitary threats, they have been doing what they said from the very beginning that they wanted to do: after reclaiming their commons, they are regenerating their own forms of governance and their art of living and dying. They have been able to operate autonomously, improving their living conditions, without any kind of services or funds from the national or provincial government. They are in fact living beyond the logic of the market and the state, beyond the logic of capital, within a new social fabric. This does not imply, of course, that they have escaped from the capitalist social fabric defining Mexico and the world, the dismantling of which requires weaving another social and political fabric, as the Sixth Declaration of Selva Lacandona states.
- Thanks to the Zapatistas, autonomous municipalities flourishing in different parts of Mexico have now increased visibility and political space. Daily attitudes exhibiting Zapatista influence are proliferating. The convening power of the Zapatistas grew from a few thousand in the first

week of 1994, to 3–4 million for the national and international consultation of 1996, to the more than 40 million (40 percent of the Mexican population)[3] for the 2001 March.

• All over the world, there are gestures, changes, mobilizations, that seem to be inspired by the Zapatistas. The highly visible social movements against globalization, neoliberalism, or war quote the Zapatistas as a source of inspiration and support them. Thousands of committees, which call themselves "Zapatista committees," operate across the world. They were founded as an expression of solidarity with the Zapatista cause. They are still ready to offer such solidarity, and some of them are actively engaged in doing something with or for the Zapatistas. Most of them are rather involved in local or issue struggles: *for* their own dreams, projects, initiatives, or *against* a specific or general development or injustice: a dam, a road, a dumping ground, a McDonalds . . . or a war, a policy, a government.

• One must go back very far in history to find another political initiative with similar global repercussions. As the Zapatistas themselves already noted, what today looks like Zapatismo, walks like Zapatismo, speaks like Zapatismo, and thinks like Zapatismo, is no longer in the hands of the Zapatistas.

While the Zapatistas continue the long process of consolidation of their political option, the ever increasing and general breakdown of the political classes in Mexico has been deepening. The three constitutional powers as well as the political parties deteriorate continually. The spectacle is pathetic and painful, not so much because there are many things worth saving in everything that is being broken down, but because of the consequences of the mess. A few years ago, the Zapatistas called for attentive observation of what is going on.

> The relentless and frenzied dismantling of the nation-state, driven by a political class lacking professional capacities and decency (clearly accompanied in no few occasions by some of the media and all of the juridical system), will result in a chaotic nightmare that not even primetime shows of suspense and terror could equal. (Subcomandante Marcos 2004, August 20, 27)

Mexico is already in that chaos, that nightmare. It is not an encouraging perspective, nor the breeding ground of a revolution. It is not about a necessary and sensible transformation for the progressive substitution of broken or useless parts in an obsolete machine. It is a turbulent and tense process in which the fragments of what used to be the Mexican political system try clumsily and uselessly to express themselves anew, or fight among themselves, clumsily and endlessly, guided by an eagerness to get rid of their rivals on a path that only in the illusions of those involved is an upward path.

As disintegration is deepening, the Zapatistas continue advancing. Their Juntas de Buen Gobierno (Boards of Good Government) "are proof that Zapatismo doesn't pretend to hegemonize or homogenize the world in which we live in either its ideas or its methods." What they have been doing is proof that "in the Zapatista lands there is no aim to pulverize the Mexican nation. On the contrary, it is here that the possibility of its reconstruction is being born" (Subcomandante Marcos 2004, August 23, 28).

When all is said and done, it is all about not being afraid of continuing to create autonomy, because the indigenous villages should organize themselves and govern themselves, according to their own ways of thinking and understanding, according to their interests, taking into account their cultures and traditions. (JBG 2004, August 10)

In Zapatismo, say the Zapatistas, communities make their decisions at variance with the dominant regime.

Ours is neither a liberated territory nor a utopian commune. Neither is it the experimental laboratory of an absurdity or a paradise for an orphaned left. It's a rebellious territory in resistance. (Subcomandante Marcos 2004, October 2, 31)

The Lacandona Commune, observes Luis Hernández,

is not a regime, but a practice . . . a laboratory of new social relations . . . [that] recovers old aspirations of the movements for self-emancipation: liberation should be the work of those it benefits, there oughtn't be authorities over the people, the subjects of the social order must have full decision-making capacity over their destinies. Their existence isn't the expression of a moral nostalgia, but the living expression of a new politics. (Hernández 2004, 21)

In their own way, as usual, the Zapatistas continue to test the speed of dreams, with a liberating spirit, accompanied from time to time by those who come to learn and collaborate with them—who in recent years came from more than fifty countries and many regions of Mexico.

The radical promise of the Zapatistas is not a new ideological construction of possible futures. It is continually self-fulfilled in their deeds, in their daily behavior, as a redefinition of hope. Their position is not equivalent to expectation, as the conviction that something will turn out well. It expresses the conviction that something makes sense, regardless of how it turns out. "Hope is that rejection of conformity and defeat." Its name is also dignity:

Dignity is that nation without nationality, that rainbow that is also a bridge, that murmur of the heart no matter what blood lives in it, that rebel irreverence that mocks borders, customs, and wars. (Zapatistas 1998, 13)

They are fully aware that the expanding dignity of each man and each human relationship is challenging existing systems. Their localization is a feasible and effective alternative to both localism and globalization. Their autonomy marginalizes the economy and resists modern and capitalist individualization promoted by both internal and external colonizers.

Rooted in their dignity, the Zapatistas have been erecting some landmarks and signposts of what looks like a net of plural paths. Whoever walks these paths can see, with the diffuse and intense quality of a rainbow, a large range of political perspectives that herald a new social order, beyond the economic society (be it capitalist or socialist), beyond formal democracy and the nation-state. *Más allá* (beyond) the current conditions of the world and their intellectual, ideological, and institutional underpinnings.

The Zapatistas are one of a kind, and at the same time typical. They come from an ancient tradition, but are immersed in contemporary ideas, problems, and technologies. They are ordinary men and women with an extraordinary behavior. They are still mystery and paradox, as the grassroots epic now running around the world of which they are the best example (Esteva & Prakash 1998).

The Zapatistas are no longer the Zapatismo circulating in the world. At the Intercontinental Encounter against Neoliberalism in 1996, the Zapatistas told all the participants that they did not get together to change the world, something quite difficult if not impossible, but to create a whole new world. The phrase was received with fascination and enthusiasm . . . but also skepticism: it appeared unfeasible and romantic. Step by step, however, as soon as people started to escape from the dominant intellectual and ideological straitjackets, they discovered in themselves a dignity similar to that of the Zapatistas, and also discovered that the statement was in fact very pragmatic.

As the crisis is widening, with its trail of disasters and dramas, and the social breakdown also deepens, battalions of discontent are multiplying, ever more organized and lucid, but often with a peculiar uncertainty: the crisis of imagination. Many of the discontented do not know what to do.

Escuelita—The New Initiative

On December 21, 2012, some 40,000 Zapatistas marched in silence in a disciplined and peaceful way in the same towns they had occupied during their uprising on January 1, 1994. They left a brief communiqué: "Did you listen? It is the sound of your world falling apart. It is the sound of our world re-emerging. The day that was the day was night. And night will be the day that will be the day."

A little later, a flood of communiqués announced the course "Freedom according to the Zapatistas," to be held on August 11–16, 2013. The communiqués explained that the teachers of this course would not be certified professionals, and no expert pedagogue would be around. None of the formal requirements of a classroom or an academic space would be met. The idea would be to learn not about the world but from the world, and to learn from those constructing a new world. The teachers in the course would be those constructing a world without exploitation or social classes, without oppression or hierarchies, a world in which the patriarchal and sexist mentality has been profoundly broken, a space that is no longer utopian because it exists in the real world.

The most difficult aspect of the course would be its content: Freedom.

The word produces an immediate association with those who have lost it, and generates solidarity with those in jail. We must, of course, care for them; many of them, perhaps most of them, are innocent. We must express the profound injustice of having them in jail while those responsible for the horror around us walk with impunity in the streets.

But the course would not be about that kind of freedom. A few years ago the poet John Berger observed that if he were forced to use only one word to express the current condition of the world, he would use the word "prison." We are in it, even those of us who pretend we are free. The *escuelita*,[4] as the Zapatistas called the experience, would attempt to show what freedom is for them. In that way, we might perhaps learn to see the bars of our own prisons.

Almost 2,000 people, from thirty countries and all parts of Mexico, were invited to attend the course. I was one of them. What we saw, smelled, tasted, and experienced was a new world, with a new kind of human being: the Zapatista world, constructed in the course of the last thirty years.[5]

The people starting the movement in 1983 and organizing the uprising in 1994 had been totally dispossessed. In the 1970s and the 1980s they were dying like flies from hunger and curable diseases, oppressed by a very violent and barbaric structure of power. Many of them were working as semi-slaves on private ranches or as servants in the cities. "In the villages," subcomandante Marcos said once, "there were very few children; most of them were dying." Since 1994, they have been continually exposed to harassment, physical and psychological aggression, paramilitary assaults, and encircle-ment stricter than the Cuban embargo. They constructed their new world from scratch, against all odds, with no funds, works, or social services from the government, starting with their bare hands. They have been on their own—accepting, on their own terms, some irregular solidarity by people around the world. These folks were the teachers of the course.

The Structure of Freedom

The structures of political and legal procedures are integral to one another. Both shape and express the structure of freedom in history. If this is recognized, the framework of due procedure can be used as the most dramatic, symbolic and convivial tool in the political area. The appeal to law remains powerful even where society makes access to legal machinery a privilege, or where it systematically denies justice, or where it cloaks despotism in the mantle of show tribunals . . . Only the word in its weakness can associate the majority of the people in the revolutionary inversion of inevitable violence into convivial reconstruction. (Illich 1973, 109–110)

The word reigns in Zapatista territory, and it is openly used for the convivial reconstruction of society.

We observed a well-enforced state of law and a solid, peaceful social order in which all forms of violence have basically vanished (except, of course, the violence of paramilitaries and other people surrounding the Zapatistas).

If we consider that a state of law exists only for those societies in which all members of the social body know and accept the norms ruling their lives, and those norms are universally enforced with fairness and justice, then we must acknowledge that no society lives today under a state of law.[6] Except Zapatista society and probably many other indigenous societies around the world.

Zapatista norms are produced at three levels: the community, the municipality (a group of communities), and the *caracol* (a group of municipalities). Each of these bodies varies in size. A community can be a settlement of a few families; the bigger communities can have six or seven hundred families.

All members of a community participate in the decisions about the *norms* and the *accords* govern-ing life in the community. The norms are general rules of behavior and include the consequences for violating them. The accords establish the conditions to implement specific decisions concerning communal activities for the common good.

Norms and accords at the level of municipalities and *caracoles* are conceived and formulated by the common folk of the communities temporarily serving in positions of authority at the level of the municipality or *caracol*. The norms and most accords cannot be enforced unless and until they are accepted at the level of the communities—a bottom-up and universally shared (rather than top-down and elite) structuring of decision making and power relations.

There are norms for all Zapatistas: first, the seven principles of commanding by obeying, applied to all Zapatistas when they are in a position of authority, and second, the revolutionary laws.

The seven principles are:

- To serve, not to serve yourself (*servir y no servirse*);
- To represent and not to supplant;
- To construct and not to destroy;
- To obey and not to command;
- To propose and not to impose;
- To convince and not to win;
- To go down and not to go up.

These principles were conceived and formulated by common folk, widely discussed for a long time, and finally adopted consensually by all Zapatistas.

The revolutionary laws (about the land and about women) were formulated clandestinely before the uprising on January 1st, 1994, and were published that day. It is well known that many people participated in their formulation, and all Zapatistas know them pretty well, but it is not known how they were enacted. They are very simple and operate as general principles that are in continual revision. For example, the communities are currently discussing a proposal of thirty-three points about women, which will be a substitute for the ten points of the law of women if and when everyone agrees on them.

Given these conditions, the real norms and forms of enforcement vary widely in different communities, municipalities, and *caracoles*.

All the decisions on important matters require consensus in order to take effect, but for minor decisions, voting procedures can be used.

There are no police . . . and no need for them. The Zapatista communities, in spite of the external aggression they experience, are the safest place in Mexico and one of the safest in the world.

For some time, the most common violation of the norms was to become drunk, after a norm was established in every community banning alcohol and drugs.7 The first time a person violates this norm, he or she gets a warning and some advice and support. The second time, he or she must do some community work and get more advice and support. The third time, more community work. The person can be expelled from the community if he or she continues violating the norm.

The most serious crime committed in all these years, the only one deserving jail for the two men who committed it, was the cultivation of marijuana. The seriousness of the crime derives from the fact that it endangers the whole community and probably the whole social experiment, because it can give the government a pretext for repressing the Zapatistas, accusing them of drug production and trafficking.

Common folk also participate in different kinds of commissions to watch and control all functions of government and the implementation of communal projects. Transparency and accountability are totally ensured. A few cases of corruption have been discovered, and the offenders are required to engage in redemptive work for the communities.

Domestic violence has been basically eliminated, whereas prior to the uprising, beating women and children had been a daily event. As a result of these community-led transformations, children are showered with love and enjoy amazing freedom—a reality that is a palpable experience when you visit a Zapatista village.

Social Functions

Working

The Zapatistas work hard and for many hours a day. They all work in a wide variety of activities. There are three kinds of labor:

- Work for the sustenance of the family;
- Work for a communal project created by a collective or other group within a community, in which the participants get a portion of the outcome (in products or cash), and the rest is designated to recipients chosen in advance by the group, which could be: the group itself, a social fund, the community, etc. The members of the group agree upon the proportions before starting the activity or project;
- Work for the common good of the community, in which all the fruits of the work support the specific purpose decided by the community (a public work such as a bridge or a road, a communal bank, a clinic and its equipment, etc.).

Other "works" include attending meetings, serving in a commission or position of authority, serving in some social services, etc.

Eating

Most Zapatista families produce their own food and complement what they produce through some exchange with neighbors or through purchases in Zapatista shops, sometimes to procure what they are not able to produce (salt, oil, etc.) and sometimes to fill in a shortfall on occasions when they were not able to produce quite enough. As a group, they have a high level of self-sufficiency.

Learning

Everyone is learning all the time, basically from each other. The Zapatistas can be seen as a learning community. There is no compulsory education. Children participate in family activities but they are basically free until they decide to go to "school." Schools have no teachers. Young men and women are "promoters of learning" and they organize the learning process with the children. There are no standard curriculums, syllabuses, or grades. There are some general themes, such as history (of the community, the region, the ethnic group, the Zapatistas, Mexico . . .), approached in different ways in different areas. What dominates is learning by doing, but some folks like to read. "Mathematics" is a recurrent theme. One participant said: "At some point we will have our own mathematics, but for the time being we are using their mathematics." The word often alludes to knowing how to count.

Healing

Most Zapatistas live a healthy life. There are a lot of activities associated with what is usually called preventive medicine, implemented by young men and women serving as "promoters of health." Many women serve as *yerberas*, *hueseras*, and *parteras*—using herbs or massages or acting as midwives, without professionalization. They have clinics in the hands of trained local folks. They may use traditional remedies or modern equipment and medicines—x-rays, ultrasound, blood tests, antibiotics, etc. All *caracoles* have ambulances for the transportation of patients to non-Zapatista hospitals, when their health problems cannot be solved in their clinics. Non-Zapatistas, of nearby communities, often come to Zapatista clinics, given the poor attention they get in the government hospitals.

Settling

Zapatistas build their own houses, mostly with local materials. They use a wide variety of styles, sizes, materials, etc. They have good access to potable water, or means of making their water drinkable. Some of them use conventional latrines; many of them use ecological dry toilets. There are no homeless people or overcrowding.

Exchanging

They have a variety of forms of exchange among themselves, including barter. They also buy and sell in the open market, most of the time in groups: a community buys for the local shop, a group of coffee producers exports coffee, a *caracol* buys medical equipment for a clinic, etc. With the permission of the corresponding authorities, a man or a woman may leave the community for some time to work in other parts of Mexico or the United States.

Moving

Community members use their feet, horses, *burros*, boats, or bicycles to perform most of their daily activities. They have some communal vehicles for transportation of people and goods, and they may use public transportation. The main movements out of the community are for fiestas, political activities, serving as an authority, and visiting friends or family.

Property

The land recuperated through the uprising (250,000 hectares)[8] has been allocated to the communities as communal land.

There is no private ownership of the land or the means of production. All families have access to a piece of common land, of similar size and conditions. (A new couple will have access to another piece.) The availability of land for the families varies a lot in different *caracoles*.

Most families have some chicken or cattle, for direct consumption, for exchange (to get some income to satisfy daily needs), or as a saving for special needs.

In many cases, a group of families may have in common some chicken, cattle, a shop, equipment to produce something, etc.

More complex activities, such as a factory of boots, facilities to process coffee, etc., are owned collectively at the level of the community, the municipality, or the *caracol*. The workers in these activities, organized in a very horizontal structure, get a salary, and the surplus goes to a social fund.

There are several communal banks, providing credit at a very low rate of interest, for special needs of some families or productive projects.

The Pedagogical Experiment

The amazing organization was the first surprise of the *escuelita*. They were waiting for us in Unitierra Chiapas. With great efficiency they gave us our credentials, by which we could be identified as students of the *escuelita*, and put every one of us in the appropriate means of transportation to go to one of the five *caracoles*—more than ten hours of transportation from San Cristóbal de Las Casas, in some cases. In every *caracol* long lines of Zapatistas clapped as we arrived. After a warm and spirited reception, every one of us got a *votán*, a guardian (a man or a woman) who would take care of us twenty-four hours a dat, would be the interpreter (our hosts spoke in their own indigenous languages), and would support our studies (guiding us in the reading of the textbooks, for example) and answer questions. They guided us to the homes that were going to host us, sometimes after a long walk, a boat ride, or whatever was needed to reach the communities in which we were to stay for our learning.

The textbooks are a good illustration of the nature of the experience. There is frequent interaction and sharing in communities and municipalities, where they speak the same language and share the same culture. When the *caracoles* were created, they needed a lingua franca: Spanish (which is not mastered by everyone), because in each *caracol* there are people of different cultures. Since the people of the communities orient the *caracoles* from below, differences between them started to emerge. They needed to share the experiences of the different *caracoles* and learn from each other. In an effort that lasted several years, folks that had been authorities or had fulfilled different functions in the communities, the municipalities, or the *caracoles* began to openly discuss the experience, without fear or inhibitions, without reservations, examining mistakes or difficulties in order to share with others their experience. There was a moment in which they had accumulated a lot of materials, and someone imagined that it could be good to share those materials with other people, in order to sow outside their territory the seed of autonomy. That is how the *escuelita* was born.

The whole experience was very intense, convivial, and joyful. We shared in the activities of the family, including their daily work—in which our lack of the pertinent skills and physical condition was often very evident and produced a lot of laughter. We had time to read our textbooks, which are a collection of interviews with members of the five *caracoles*. We could ask any question and usually received enlightening answers. And of course we participated in many joyful activities, particularly the long, final fiesta.

In this course we completed only the first level (there will be more), but we learned a lot. We learned new categories created in the struggle for freedom. We learned that resistance, for example, was not something that started with the Zapatistas: their *abuelos* and *abuelas* (grandfathers and grandmothers) had been resisting for centuries and they kept that experience in their hearts. We learned that there is a Zapatista way, entirely transparent but difficult to understand or define, because it is a very *other* way, which cannot fit well in our mentality or our common way of understanding. We learned how autonomy is constructed, how the works are done, how authentic resistance is not only to endure things but to construct something new, what it is to organize, and more.

But we lacked words, because we were before radical novelties that did not come from books or ideologies, but from practice, and they are clearly enterprises of imagination. I believe there is no historical precedent, for example, for the process of orderly and coherent transfer of power from what the Zapatistas call *mandos político-militares*—those in political and military command before the uprising. The power the politico-military group had accumulated in that period, given to them by their "support bases" to organize and lead the uprising in 1994, had been gradually given back to the communities, as the people themselves, ordinary folk of the communities, step by step assumed all of the functions of government and of sociopolitical organization—such that currently it is the ordinary people who together control the decision-making and norm-setting processes at all levels of autonomy and government. A way of living and governing was constructed from below: political power and radical democracy are located where the people are, not above them. The *mandos* are still around, ready to offer support if it is required and occasionally consulting with the people on some initiatives.

Some of the students of the *escuelita* have already felt the temptation of translating what we learned into a formal course, transforming the experience into a package of knowledge and skills to transfer to others. But such an exercise would imply a betrayal of the meaning, style, and intention of the *escuelita*. We were not invited to be educated in a doctrine, and even less to be taught what to do. The Zapatistas shared with us a living experience whose substance can only exist in diversity, in a variety of forms. Every community, every municipality, every *caracol* had evident differences, because they have been created in freedom by different communities of people. They have many things in common, but the specific shape of those "principles" or "forms" corresponds not only to the natural and cultural diversity of the places in which people's lives have been organized, but also to the differential imagination of those participating in the process. The challenge is not to reduce the whole thing to a formal discourse, more or less technical, with some abstract categories, but to reproduce the experience in the personal style of every student through contagion. This requires, however, time to process the experience and prepare fertile soil in which the seed of autonomy can prosper.

On Saturday, August 17, when we were still bewildered by the emotions of the *escuelita*, we observed the arrival of hundreds of delegates of the National Indian Congress for an encounter convened by the Zapatistas. For many hours during the weekend, we heard the voices of indigenous peoples from the whole country, in what was called the Chair Tata Juan Chávez, homage to one brilliant indigenous leader, one of the founders of the Congress, who died two years ago. It will be a kind of nomadic chair, which can be organized in any place, to hear the voices of the indigenous peoples.

It was overwhelming to listen to the never-ending enumeration of plunder and aggression. The name of the protagonists and the matter of the plunder changed from one place to the other. But it was always the same crime: a war against subsistence waged by capitalist corporations, sometimes behind the façade of a local boss or a landowner, but always with the active participation and the open complicity of the government and the political parties.

It was even more impressive to observe the common denominator of most presentations: a combative, articulated, and vigorous resistance, waged with spirit and dignity; a battle in which they are not only defending their territories, ways of life, forms of self-government, and traditions, but also struggling for the survival of all of us.

In sum, exhausted after this intense, convivial, and joyful week that at times seemed interminable, overwhelmed by the weight of a learning that brings with it the moral obligation of sharing it, we came back to our places full of hope. We drank until slaked in this fountain of inspiration. We also learned that every one of us, in his or her own way, can do what we need to do, which will be as diverse as our worlds. We can construct a world in which everyone will be embraced. Inertias, paralysis, and fears will be dismantled. We are on our way.

Epilogue

I read and reread what I have written. I can see that I said nothing about the hard or exhausting work involved in constructing and defending autonomy and self-sufficiency, nor about the tensions and contradictions that still exist. As the Zapatistas recognize, reconstructing their lives after centuries of oppression is a long and hard process. It is sometimes possible to encounter residues of the old system, such as occasional instances of *machismo* or violence.

This is not a balanced account. But the fact is that these amazing folks, ordinary men and women, living in a "rebellious territory in resistance," have been able to transform one of the most unjust and miserable social conditions of the world into the materialization of their dreams of a decent society. I have produced a quick report in order to share with others the good news. Yes, it seems possible to find a way out of our current dead-ends, to create a valid alternative in the midst of one of the worst crises in human history. Perhaps others engaged in the search for such alternatives may find in this story some inspiration.

NOTES

1. No other movement has occupied a similar space in national and international media; in the number of books (tens of thousands) and articles (millions), with their materials or about them, published in a dozen languages; in their presence on the Internet: 5,620 active pages in 2002 according to the last formal counting. Neither the Web nor the texts, however, fully illustrate the importance and vitality of the movement. The mobilizations directly stimulated by the Zapatistas, from a few thousand in 1994 to the millions for the consultation in 1996 or the march of 2001, are living proofs of the echo Zapatismo finds among the people. But they are not enough to illustrate their importance. The only way to fully appreciate it would be to go directly to communities and barrios, in Mexico and the rest of the world. But no matter how much academics and activists attempt to do such exploration, it has become impossible. There is no way to count. What is most interesting in the search is that it always delivers results: wherever one tries to look, Zapatismo emerges, even in the most unexpected places.

2. Welcoming words by the *comandancia general* of EZLN, at the First Intercontinental Encounter for Humanity against Neoliberalism, spoken by the respected major Ana María, on July 27, 1996. The Zapatistas (1998, 24).

3. The figure is of course very impressive. It was estimated by adding the daily estimates published in the newspapers about the attendance at the Zapatista meetings in their journey to Mexico City.

4. *Escuelita* has a double meaning in Spanish: a small school or a dismissive statement about a school.

5. I am using for this essay my own experience and observations about the Zapatistas, the textbooks of the *escuelita*, and also the information and comments shared by thirty members of Unitierra who also attended the event.

6. In modern society, (1) only the experts, as a group, know the norms ruling society (and taken individually not even the experts know all of the norms); (2) the law itself, as well as all the rules produced by different levels of government and by corporations, are conceived and formulated by a small minority that does not represent the interests of the people; (3) those norms are increasingly formulated in such a way that a small group can violate them with impunity, while the majority are forced to obey and respect them (Foucault 2006); (4) the norms are not universally enforced and respected.

7. Alcoholism was a real problem. It was traditional in the pre-Zapatista regime for owners and managers to pay workers with money and *posh*, a very strong liquor. This fact and the dominant social conditions provoked extensive alcoholism and corresponding violence. Very soon after the uprising, the communities started to take a very firm stand on this issue, and they finally decided to establish the current rigid ban. This is of course a source of tension. One of the elements of the counterinsurgency strategy of the government is to organize fiestas with an abundance of alcohol and prostitution, to which some young Zapatistas are continually tempted to go.

8. The law of 1995 acknowledges the Zapatista occupation of the land. However, since the legal procedures to certify the property of the land have not been followed, non-Zapatista communities, with the support of the government, are continually trying to invade Zapatista territory.

REFERENCES

Esteva, G., & Prakash, M. (1998). *Grassroots postmodernism: Remaking the soil of cultures.* London: Zed Books.

Esteva, G., & Shanin, T. (2005). *Pensar todo de nuevo.* Oaxaca: Ediciones ¡Basta!. Reproduced in 2012 as Pensar todo de nuevo: Anticapitalismos sin socialismo. Una conversación con Teodor Shanin, *Bajo el volcán* 11 (18) (March–August 2012): 93–120.

Foucault, M. (2006). *Los anormales.* México: Fondo de Cultura Económica.

Hernández, N. L. (2004). Autonomía sin pedir permiso. *La Jornada*, September 7, 21.

Illich, I. (1971). *Deschooling society.* New York: Harper & Row.

Illich, I. (1973). *Tools for conviviality.* New York: Harper & Row.

JBG llama a los zapatistas a continuar construyendo sin miedo su autonomía. (2004). *La Jornada*, August 10, 21.

Subcomandante Marcos. (2004). Leer un video. *La Jornada*, August 20, 27.

Subcomandante Marcos. (2004). Leer un video. *La Jornada*, August 23, 28.

Subcomandante Marcos. (2004). La velocidad del sueño. *La Jornada*, October 2, 31.

Wallerstein, I. (2005). Los Zapatistas: La segunda etapa. *La Jornada*, July 19, 38.

The Zapatistas. (1998). *Zapatista encuentro: Documents from the 1996 Encounter for Humanity and Against Neoliberalism.* New York: Seven Stories Press.

Zinn, H. (2010). Rescatar las incontables pequeñas acciones de gente desconocida, la labor de Howard Zinn. *La Jornada*, December 30, 38. Translated by David Brooks, from Zinn, H. (1954), The art of revolution, in H. Read (Ed.), *Anarchy and order: Essays on politics*, Boston: Beacon Press.

The Accidental Activist Scholar: A Memoir on Reactive Boundary and Identity Work for Social Change within the Academy

Rob Benford

I would like to be able to tell you a heroic tale about myself as an activist scholar and how I conscientiously and strategically used my privileged positions within the academy and as a white male to set out to affect progressive social change in the world and thus to help those less fortunate than me. But that would be self-serving and not completely accurate. In reflecting on my activism across my academic career, I've reached the uneasy conclusion that my status as an "activist scholar" was somewhat accidental. Thus, rather than narrating a purely proactive story, I want to recount a few of my activist experiences from within the institutional context of U.S. state universities in terms that more accurately reflect their often reactive nature.

My auto-ethnographic account begins as a graduate student conducting participant observation research on a local peace and justice movement, and takes an unexpected turn into university credit-union activism. As I was pulled further into activist roles, my graduate career ended up hanging by a thread following my arrest during a campus anti-apartheid demonstration. After I completed my doctorate, my activist-scholar reputation contributed to a temporary retraction of my first academic job offer. Eventually, after repressing my activist-scholar identity for a few years in order to survive the tenure chase, I managed to negotiate the boundaries and overcome the constraints of three state universities to engage in a variety of activist roles within the academy. I conclude by offering a few reflections on the evolution of an activist-scholar career.

Participant Observation in the Austin Peace and Justice Movement, 1982–86

In May 1982, while a master's student at the University of Texas at Austin, I began an ethnographic study of the local peace and justice movement. Initially, I selected Texas Mobilization for Survival (TMS) as a site for a case study. I chose Texas Mobe not because I had a particular interest in them, but rather because they were focusing at that time on nuclear disarmament, and they had the reputation of being the vanguard group within the Austin peace movement. My interest in nuclear disarmament had little to do with my political identity or personal fears of Armageddon. Although I was sympathetic to the goal of nuclear disarmament, I had never participated in any antinuclear events or activities. In fact, I hadn't been active in any social movements up to that point, despite the fact that I was thirty-one years old and had grown up in a world rife with collective-action opportunities and a plethora of social movements. Rather than an ideological affinity for disarmament specifically, or peace and justice more generally, what drew me to that particular movement was an offhand yet intriguing remark a seminar professor had made. He had commented that the nuclear disarmament movement appeared to be the first genuinely global movement in history. Setting aside the dubiousness of that assertion (historically and empirically), I was curious about a cause that could unite people across cultures, classes, and continents. And I needed a thesis topic.

Entrée into the peace movement and thus my first foray into the activist-scholar role was straight-forward. In May 1982, Texas Mobilization for Survival was in the process of recruiting and organizing participation in the upcoming March for Peace and Justice in New York City.[1] A telephone call to the TMS offices elicited information regarding the next "orientation" meeting. During the introductions phase of that meeting, I informed the group that I was a graduate student in sociology conducting research on the peace movement, and that I was concerned about the "nuclear threat." I was warmly welcomed and began preparations for the trip to New York City.

On June 12 approximately three-quarters of a million people marched past the United Nations building to Central Park to attend a rally for peace and justice. While rally spokespersons and media emphasized the heterogeneity of the participants, neither the solidarity nor the unanimity of purpose was publicly questioned. By all outward appearances it seemed as though the peace movement had coalesced into a unified front. As a participant-observer, I perceived a collective feeling of social cohesiveness—a sense of "oneness"—binding the diverse gathering together. From the promotional literature distributed weeks prior to the event, it was apparent that the march and rally had been organized by a large coalition of some 150 to 200 social movement organizations (SMOs). Thus, from my vantage point, all indications pointed to solidarity within the "peace movement." But I was politically naive. Subsequent realization of my naiveté led to the formulation of a thesis question, a shift in methodologies, and the eventual adoption of an activist identity.

Before returning to Austin with the Texas affinity group, I began to detect signs of cracks in this unified wall. In Manhattan I overheard some participants complaining about the event's organization and leadership. Some felt that the event was "too organized" and "too structured." Others complained that the issues or grievances were too numerous, that the focus should have been *only* on achieving a nuclear-weapons freeze agreement between the United States and the Soviet Union. They contended that to add other issues to the agenda, such as calling for a halt to military interventions in Latin America or the redirection of military spending to meet human needs, only "confused" the "more urgent and crucial" issue—the threat of nuclear annihilation.

Still others objected to the planned civil-disobedience action scheduled to occur two days after the June 12th march. Not everyone who opposed the direct-action tactics did so based on the same grounds, however. A portion of the dissenters indicated that they were against employing such "confrontational," "illegal," and "disruptive" tactics as a means of attracting media attention. Several expressed fears that the planned acts of civil disobedience would detract from the positive image they believed had been projected by the large, "peaceful and law-abiding" demonstration two days earlier. Others were not opposed to civil disobedience per se. Instead, they argued that an isolated confrontation, divorced from an ongoing strategy, violated Gandhian principles. A few of the dissenters were also miffed that movement leaders provided those who had committed to participate in the civil-disobedience action with special accommodations in Manhattan and other status badges. Finally, I overheard a group of strangers complaining that the civil-disobedience planning was being conducted in an "undemocratic" fashion.

Subsequently, I learned that the June 12th Rally Committee had experienced a major schism that nearly prevented the occurrence of what to this day remains the largest protest and the largest civil-disobedience action in U.S. history. The primary point of contention had been the scope of their goals. One faction was adamant in maintaining that the march should be organized around a single issue—a nuclear "freeze." The other faction, equally steadfast in their beliefs, argued that the event should be organized around more general "peace and justice" issues. The focus, they contended, should not be solely on nuclear weapons, but should also call attention to racism, interventionism, and human needs, among other issues.

The single-issue advocates walked out. They decided that the public would be more supportive of a clearly stated, solitary political demand—"Freeze the arms race." Hence, they withdrew from the broader coalition and began planning their own march. Meanwhile, what remained of the original June 12th Committee continued to plan a "Peace and Justice" march. For a while, the groups were locked in a contest over which one legitimately owned the park and parade permits. There was confusion. The police and other officials did not know with whom they should deal. Two marches were being planned to occur at the same time and place.

Although the two factions reached an uneasy compromise and reunited prior to the march, the schisms and intramural differences regarding goals, ideologies, strategies and tactics, decision-making structures and leadership styles, collective identities, and representational issues—what I later referred to as "frame disputes" (Benford 1993)—underscored the fallacy of treating a particular social movement as a monolith. Returning to Austin after participating in both the June 12th march and the June 14th civil-disobedience action, I realized that I had been operating under the false premise that just because the various peace-movement groups shared the general goals of peace and ending the nuclear arms race, that each SMO would quite naturally strive to cooperate with the others to achieve these objectives. This realization prompted me to take a closer look at the Austin movement and to set aside my original assumptions. I soon discovered that, as with the national movement, the Austin peace and justice movement was characterized by intra-movement tensions. I decided to focus my research on interorganizational competition, conflict, and cooperation within the local movement.

Methodologically, this meant that I had to expand my focus from a case study of one SMO to an examination of the peace movement's multi-organizational field (Curtis & Zurcher 1973). Thus it was necessary to gain entrée into several local peace-movement organizations and coalitions and to attempt to attend events and encounters where interorganizational interactions were likely to occur. This not only resulted in a more time-consuming project than originally conceived, it also resulted in a deeper immersion into activist roles.

Initially, my level of participation in each SMO was minimal and fairly passive. I attended formal meetings and scheduled events. On occasion, I fortuitously discovered an informal meeting. However, since I was outside the members' social networks, such opportunities rarely occurred. My initial fieldwork role was essentially that of a novitiate, a novice in the double sense: a greenhorn recruit to the cause of nuclear disarmament and an inexperienced but gung-ho field researcher (who must have been quite an obtrusive sight, armed as I was with cameras and extra lens, a portable tape recorder, pens, and a reporter's notebook). Though I performed menial movement-related tasks, emphasis at this stage was on observation. I was clearly more of a scholar than an activist. The passive participation/novitiate role phase was characterized by feelings of marginality. I was not exactly an "outsider," yet I did not feel that I had been accepted as an "insider" either. Though I had succeeded in establishing rapport with several members of the SMOs under investigation, competing demands and a sense that I needed to remain "objective" led me to decline most opportunities to informally socialize with the core members.

As I became more comfortable with negotiating and managing the dual roles of participant and researcher, the sense of marginality gradually receded. By the early fall of 1982 (five months into the study), I had begun to achieve what I considered at the time to be an optimal balance between the two roles. Like other rank-and-file members, I participated in discussions and debates, volunteered to coordinate small tasks, and became more involved in movement friendship networks. Despite the greater sense of belonging associated with the rank-and-file role, I remained outside the boundaries of much of the movement's high-level decision-making processes. The "back regions" (Goffman 1959) had been penetrated. But the deepest quarters of those areas—the dressing rooms, to carry the Goffman analogy further—were beyond my observational range. Yet, because I was backstage, I had concluded that I was aware of everything significant that was happening within the Austin peace movement.

As was the case with much of my subsequent career as an activist scholar, a chance event stimulated me to radically shift from "balanced" to "active" participation, from a rank-and-file movement member to an ardent activist. In December 1982, while observing antinuclear activists testify, during an Austin City Council meeting, against the city's participation in a nuclear power plant project, one of the activists invited me to join other activists for dinner. The eleven activists present at this informal, impromptu meeting constituted the core leadership of the community's major peace and anti-nuclear-power SMOs. The meeting was significant to my research methods, subsequent level of activism, and evolution of my activist-scholar identity because the discussions that ensued at dinner were like no others I had witnessed during my regular SMO meetings or informal social gatherings. The core leaders engaged in frank discussions and negotiations regarding "turf," movement "image," and the efficacy of particular movement framing strategies and tactics. I learned more in those couple of hours than I had over the previous seven months regarding the interorganizational dynamics of the movement, the interpretive factors activists consider before publicly announcing and justifying their position on a specific issue, the social construction of meaning that occurs backstage, and the nature of frame disputes among movement groups.

Upon reflecting on that meeting, it became apparent that I had prematurely and mistakenly concluded that I had been "in the know" regarding the movement's internal workings and politics. The restaurant experience indicated that I knew a great deal about the public peace movement but little about the private one. I also realized that I lacked firsthand knowledge of what it was like to experience interpretive work and its associated challenges and dilemmas from the perspective of the activists. Finally, the realization that I was outside leaders' communication networks meant that the significant disputes, negotiations, and decision making pertaining to the movement's interorganizational dynamics were beyond my observational purview.

A change of research strategies seemed in order. Beginning in early 1983, I volunteered for tasks that required greater investment of time and energy than those I had previously been willing to perform. More responsibilities followed. Other movement leaders began to see me as more "committed." In a sense, I became an "ardent activist," a role and identity I would continue to embrace throughout the remainder of my MA thesis research and well into my dissertation fieldwork from 1984 through 1986.

In March 1983, the Austin Peace and Justice Coalition (APJC) began planning a statewide march to be held in Austin that October in conjunction with marches worldwide against the U.S. deployment of missiles in Europe. I volunteered and was accepted as a member (one of eleven) of the Texas March for Peace and Justice Coordinating Committee. For the ensuing eight months, I served on that committee as well as several subcommittees, attended two to three meetings per week, and coordinated the recruitment and committee assignment of some 350 volunteers. The phone rang incessantly. People dropped by my house at all hours to discuss politics, march organizing, and internal power struggles. The ardent activist role was all-consuming. But it gained me access to data I would never otherwise have gathered, including internal communications, national-level interactions, and activist experiences and emotions.

Following the October 22nd "Stop the Euromissiles" march and rally, I continued to volunteer for major roles. I received training as a peacekeeping trainer and trained others in peacekeeping, nonviolent action, and civil disobedience philosophy, strategies, and tactics. In the summer of 1984, I coordinated peacekeeping at two national events—the Pantex nuclear-weapons plant encampment and vigil near Amarillo, and the Republican Convention protests in Dallas. I sustained my activist-scholar work until the end of my doctoral studies in the summer of 1987, participating in the activities of University Mobilization for Survival, the Committee in Solidarity with the People of El Salvador, American Friends Service Committee, Austin Nuclear Weapons Freeze Campaign, Red River Peace Network, University Peace and Justice Coalition, United Campuses to Prevent Nuclear War, Jobs for Peace, Austin Peace and Justice Coalition, and Texas Mobilization for Survival, the SMO that was the site of my initial fieldwork.

In late April 1986, I was arrested for "disruptive activities" and "unlawful assembly" along with 181 other anti-apartheid protesters at UT who objected to the university's $850 million portfolio investment in companies that did business in South Africa. As I began my final year of doctoral studies, I received a letter from UT President Cunningham informing me that the university would hold a hearing to decide whether or not I would be expelled from the university. Progressive attorneys came to our rescue, pressing the university to honor our First Amendment rights to free speech and assembly. The university subsequently dropped the criminal and administrative charges against all arrestees and did what universities often do when an administration wants to cool out insurgents— they formed a committee to "study" policies related to campus protests. Meanwhile, UT's board of regents continued to refuse to consider divesting its South African portfolio. It wouldn't be the last time I encountered an intransigent university administration that didn't appear to appreciate activist scholars in their midst.

Shifting from Activism Outside the System to Inside: UFCU Board, 1984–86

In the spring of 1984, two years after entering the field to study the Austin peace movement, my "accidental" activism took a turn into a new domain. I had become increasingly frustrated by what seemed to me to be regressive policies practiced by the University of Texas Federal Credit Union (UFCU). For instance, the credit union instituted checking-account fees tied to rather large minimum balances, which of course tended to disproportionately affect students and the other low-salaried members of UFCU. This and other policies seemed to be out of alignment with the credit-union movement's core distributive-justice values of equality, and more in line with standard commercial-bank policies. Several fellow graduate students reported that they felt they were treated as undesirables, the lumpenproletariat of the credit union's membership. After my complaints to UFCU management were ignored or deflected, I'd had enough.

I decided that I would organize a protest of the credit union's policies. Taking a page from Alinsky's *Rules for Radicals* (1971) and Hailey's *The Moneychangers* (1975), I developed a plan to effectively shut down, or at least disrupt, the credit union for an afternoon by tying up the lobby and drive-through tellers with trivial, yet time-consuming transactions such as cashing and depositing small checks, changing and depositing coins, and so forth. I decided that it would only take around twenty volunteers continuously jamming the lines (i.e., returning to the teller lines after each menial transaction with yet another). A Friday that fell at the end of the month seemed to be the ideal time, given that it would be a double payday and thus would have the largest volume of business. I figured that after a couple of hours of disruptive collective action, I would hold a press conference to call attention to how UFCU mistreated its most economically disadvantaged members.

In the process of recruiting volunteers to join the protest, one of my fellow graduate students introduced me to two friends of hers who were leaders of the University Employees Union (UEU). They, too, had become frustrated by the credit union's shoddy treatment of students and working-class members. They asked me if I would run for the credit union's board of directors. They explained that National Credit Union Administration regulations provided for two avenues for becoming a credit-union board member: (1) be selected by the credit union's nominating committee to run and be declared "elected" by acclamation at the credit union's annual meeting, which few, if any, members attended, or (2) be placed on a ballot to run against the credit union's insider nominees by acquiring signatures from 1 percent of the total members of the credit union. To that point in UFCU's fifty-year history, there had never been an actual election for board membership. Nor had a graduate student ever served on its board.

My initial reaction to the suggestion that I run for the board was less than enthusiastic. I responded that I thought a collective-action strategy might more effectively succeed in cajoling or embarrassing the UFCU management into reconsidering some of their draconian policies. I added that I thought my plan would be "more fun" than collecting signatures and running for the board. They conceded the latter but pointed out that once we were on the ballot we could turn up the heat on the UFCU manager by attacking his policies publicly. They further noted that once the election was over and we had lost (everyone assumed we wouldn't stand a chance of actually getting elected), I could return to my Alinsky-style collective-action strategy. The UEU leaders finally convinced me to give the board-election plan a try and persuaded another graduate student from Library Sciences to run as well.

Collecting the requisite four hundred or so signatures was not difficult—just time-consuming for graduate students. Several of us, including grad students, UEU members, and Democratic Socialists of America activists stood in front of the credit-union building and asked members to support an actual election process by signing our petitions. We collected enough signatures for a slate of three candidates—two board members and one member of the Credit Committee, the only other office permitted to be elected from UFCU's general field of membership.

The campaign turned out to be more rewarding than expected. We were able to point out that despite UFCU's claims that graduate-student members tended to constitute a drain on the credit union's resources because of their low account balances but high service-activity demands, graduate students actually generated some of the credit union's highest and most consistent revenues. We learned that UFCU not only earned substantial revenue from processing, administering, and brokering student loans, this income involved virtually no risk, because the federal government guaranteed the loans. Either because they never regarded us as a legitimate threat to their control of the credit union, or because they were unable to fashion a resonant counterframe (Benford & Hunt 2003; Snow & Benford 1988), UFCU management failed to muster a defense of their policies. To our surprise, we won all three credit-union offices.

Initially, UFCU's manager and several board members appeared mortified that we were joining the board of directors of one of the nation's largest university credit unions. They set out to co-opt us, apparently assuming that they could eventually bring us around to their way of thinking. The manager brought my newly elected colleague and me in for "orientation." He began by handing us UFCU's organizational chart. I interrupted his patronizing lesson by commenting that the chart was inaccurate because it listed the board of directors at the pinnacle. He responded that the board had the final say in all matters and thus the chart was in fact accurate. I then reminded him that the members belonged at the top of the chart, above the board, that this was what distinguished credit unions from banks, and that UFCU management's apparent failure to understand that structure was what a number of members found to be problematic. Thus, it was apparent from the outset that co-optation might not be the credit-union management's best approach to dealing with two insurgents on their board. But their worries soon seemed to subside once they did the math: five of them to two of us.

As a minority on a board otherwise comprised of UT administrators, business professors, and a social-work professor (who ironically seemed oblivious to the needs of poor students and staff), we weren't able to radically change the credit union. However, we did identify an occasional ally on the board—a woman who served as the director of financial aid for UT. And a year later we were able to maneuver adding a Marxist-economics professor to the board, thereby giving us a tenuous majority during the latter months of our tenure. Subsequently, we were able to affect the realignment of a number of UFCU's policies so they were more consistent with the credit-union movement's ideals.

Although the service on the credit-union board was onerous and tedious, I found it to be more intrinsically rewarding and empowering than my peace-movement activism. In contrast to the ambitious, amorphous, often unreachable global goals espoused by the peace movement, our goals at the credit union were modest, focused, local, and achievable. In short, I felt a sense of efficacy in my credit-union activist role, despite the bureaucratic constraints, that I rarely felt as a peace activist.

Downplaying an Activist Identity within the Academy

Following graduate school, I landed my first continuing academic position at the University of Nebraska Lincoln (UNL). As an untenured assistant professor from 1987 to 1992, I primarily kept my head down while seeking to ensure that my record would be strong enough to earn tenure. After all, my initial hiring at UNL had nearly been sidetracked by the College of Arts and Sciences associate dean John Peters.[2] Shortly after receiving an offer from the Department of Sociology, the department chair called me to inform me that they were retracting their offer due to a "hiring freeze." The late Louis A. Zurcher, one of my mentors, contacted his former colleague and friend at UNL, who in turn intervened on my behalf. It turned out that there was no hiring freeze. Rather, Peters had concluded that I was "more of an activist than a scholar." My half dozen publications, including a coauthored paper in sociology's preeminent journal, *American Sociological Review*, seemed irrelevant to the associate dean. He evidently felt that my fieldwork on the peace movement demonstrated that I was just "a peacenik." Fortunately, my future colleagues at UNL managed to convince the dean that I had emerged from a national search as *the* "scholar" whom they wanted to hire. Thus, throughout my untenured years, while I occasionally joined protests such as those against local environmental degradation, apartheid, and the Persian Gulf War, I primarily sought to avoid being viewed by my colleagues and UNL administrators as an "activist."

Getting Sacked by SAC: Fighting the Cold War Collective Memory Wars, 1992–95[3]

In March 1992, shortly after receiving word from Dean Peters that my tenure had been approved, I received a call from the Strategic Air Command Museum's executive director, Jim Bert, who explained his new vision for the SAC Museum. He wanted to expand it from a purely military operational history to one that also examined SAC's and the Cold War's cultural and social impact. He asked me to serve on a committee of scholars, museum curators, and exhibit designers dedicated to transforming the museum's narratives.

Concerned that any museum changes might, at best, only perfunctorily represent nonmilitary perspectives and, at worst, trivialize the concerns raised by peace activists, I hesitated at first. Located on a closed section of an adjacent Offutt Air Force Base runway, the museum primarily celebrated U.S. air power and military might. The museum's main attractions were thirty-one aircraft and a few missiles, most of which were on loan from the U.S. Air Force.

But Bert seemed genuinely committed to the vision of creating a more holistic, and thus unique, military-history museum. With the Cold War's end and with SAC stepping down, he felt the museum could also change. Peace activists cautioned me to be wary of Bert's "true motives," urging me to avoid the SAC Museum like the plague. Nevertheless, I accepted the invitation to work with the SAC Museum. The history of SAC would be told by someone. Why not include the voices of its critics as well as its supporters in the telling? While I remained skeptical about fundamentally altering the museum's central "white knight" narrative, I worked with other committee members to write new storylines, design new exhibits, and apply for funding. In September 1992, we obtained a small grant from the Nebraska Humanities Council and began writing for larger grants from the National Endowment for the Humanities. We drafted scripts for exhibits portraying Cold War culture, the social construction of evil ("mirror images of the enemy"), duck-and-cover drills, the bomb shelter craze, the peace movement and disarmament campaigns, and the Cold War's aftermath, including the economic, political, and environmental effects on U.S. and Soviet societies.

The further we progressed with our designs, the more often I raised questions with Bert about whether these exhibits actually had a chance of ever being displayed. "What about the generals?" I asked, referring to the retired SAC generals on the Strategic Air Command Memorial Society board, which had governed the museum since 1991. Bert would always reply, "Rob, let me worry about the generals." Who I should have also asked Bert about were the "captains"—the captains of industry, that is.

Unknown to the public, some of Omaha, Nebraska's most powerful business leaders were working behind the scenes with retired SAC generals and others to raise $26 million to construct a new SAC Museum. Once the plan was unveiled, the leaders claimed they were trying to preserve the deteriorating aircraft by building a new museum large enough to move them all indoors. The new museum would be located closer to the interstate highway so it could eventually become self-supporting through admission fees. No doubt the captains of industry and the generals really wanted to preserve the aircraft. But they also wanted to preserve the museum's narrow narrative focus on SAC as "America's Shield." In the words of the Omaha business leader spearheading the new museum's fundraising campaign, "Adults can learn about SAC's role in defending the country."

Before the new plan was unveiled, Bert struggled with the generals over the museum's transformation. One of them questioned Bert's patriotism, claiming he was from the wrong generation—the Vietnam War generation. This particularly frustrated Bert, who had volunteered to become a U.S. Marine Corps officer during the Vietnam War. The situation further deteriorated when the shock waves from the Enola Gay controversy hit.[4] As Bert explained to me in an interview: "Immediately after the Enola Gay controversy, everything we started to do toward the new exhibits became super secret . . . Plans were not allowed to circulate." The SAC Museum board "became increasingly superfluous" as power shifted to the "money people in Omaha." "It was very much a power issue," Bert lamented.

In September 1995, Bert quietly resigned from his position as SAC Museum director. He had come to realize that neither the generals nor the captains appreciated his expertise or his vision of a more holistic museum. And I retreated back into my occasional and often accidental activism within the confines of the university. My final act related to the SAC Museum involved participating in a protest with various members of Nebraskans for Peace at the museum's grand opening in 1998.

Gun Free Zone Movement: A Reaction to Gun Violence at UNL, 1992–94[5]

I was not always exclusively concerned about violence on a global scale such as that represented by the nuclear threat. As a father of two young daughters and a professor on a large campus, my attention was sometimes diverted toward more immediate threats of violence. From the fall of 1992 to the fall of 1994, a series of events unfolded on or near UNL's campus that amplified my fears concerning the proliferation of guns and thus the increased chances of gun violence. The first and most dramatic incident occurred on October 12, 1992, when a graduate student walked into his actuarial-science class, pointed a semiautomatic assault rifle at students, and pulled the trigger. Fortunately, the gun jammed; as he slammed the rifle's butt against a desk trying to unjam it, the students managed to pin him against the wall with a desk and escape.[6] The attempted killer, who had two 30-round clips of ammunition, was later caught, arrested, and convicted of second-degree attempted murder, but found not responsible by reason of insanity. He remains in state custody.

I recall thinking how lucky we were as a campus community that the would-be mass murderer's gun had jammed. Several more incidents involving guns on or near the UNL campus made me wonder how long our luck would hold. A year after the near massacre, a student brandished a weapon at a campus police officer while driving his car on a road adjacent to campus. When the officer attempted to apprehend him, the student wounded the officer. After his arrest, campus officials revealed that campus police had previously confiscated the same weapon from his dorm room on the grounds that he violated university housing's prohibition against having guns in the dorms. However, citing the Second Amendment, a judge ruled that UNL officials were required to return the gun to him.

A few months later, a third gun-related shooting incident involving a student heightened our growing concerns. A University of Nebraska football star was arrested for firing two shots at another moving vehicle from the car he was riding in near campus. The shooting was a continuation of an earlier dispute involving college and professional football players that had begun at an off-campus party. The shooter pleaded no contest to a felony charge of unlawfully discharging a gun and to misdemeanor assault, served a few months in the Lancaster County Jail, and went on to star in the National Football League.[7]

Whereas the three gun incidents involving students heightened my concerns, it was the results of systematic data-gathering by another student that prompted me to take action. In the spring of 1994, Kelly Asmussen, a doctoral student, conducted a survey in my two large introductory sociology classes. A few months later, Asmussen provided me the general results from his survey. I was stunned at what the data revealed and their implications: 14.2 percent of the male students and 4.6 percent of the female students admitted that they had carried a gun or knife to campus. And though the percent indicating that they had actually carried such weapons to classes was smaller—6.9 percent for males and 1.0 percent for females—I was even more disturbed by those reports. I did the math. Given that approximately 300 students (of 350 enrolled) attended each of my two sections of Introductory Sociology each Monday and Wednesday morning, I could expect that there could be a dozen weapons present in each class.

As I thought about the shooting incidents and Asmussen's disturbing findings over the summer break, I decided to float the idea of a "gun free zone" among colleagues. I borrowed the idea from my studies of the nuclear-disarmament movement. A number of small island countries, as well as a few municipalities around the world, had declared their jurisdictions to be "nuclear free zones" during the 1980s (Benford 1988; Pitt & Thompson 1987). Why not apply the same logic to our campus and not allow guns within UNL's borders?

When classes resumed in the fall of 1994, I first approached my friend and colleague Jack Siegman. Drawing on our knowledge of social movements and complex organizations, Jack and I decided that in order for the Gun Free Zone movement to be successful, we would need to mobilize campus leaders, including not only UNL administrators, but representatives of various constituency groups on campus. We thus held a series of meetings with representatives and directors of student affairs, housing, police, judicial affairs, Greek affairs, student government, faculty senate, office professionals, and professors representing several departments.

One of the first things we realized was that not everyone agreed that guns on our campus constituted a social "problem." Hence, we spent time in our initial meetings convincing others that we were sitting on a powder keg and that they should join our Gun Free Zone movement. Fortunately, we enjoyed immediate support from most campus leaders, perhaps most significantly from UNL's police chief, Ken Cauble. He indicated that among the items most frequently reported stolen from students' vehicles were guns, including hunting rifles students stored in their cars and trucks.

We surveyed other Big Eight Conference schools regarding their firearms policies, and used these to help write a new student policy for UNL. We recommended that the student code of conduct be revised so as to not permit guns on campus and, in the interest of fairness and equality, sought to extend the policy to all members of the UNL community including faculty and staff. After considerable debate, our recommendations were adopted by UNL's student government and the board of regents, and put into effect the following fall. A year later, the gun ban was extended to faculty and staff.

It became apparent not only from Chief Cauble's remarks but from a variety of quarters that we should address the needs of hunters. Some pro-gun folks argued that we were trying to take their guns away and that we were ignoring hunters' rights to pursue their preferred recreational activities. Chief Cauble volunteered a solution. He offered space in the police station where hunters' guns could be kept in lockers. This would get the weapons out of students' vehicles and decrease the likelihood of accidental shootings, and shootings carried out by persons under the influence of alcohol or drugs, or in a fit of anger. The gun locker option also allowed us to claim that we were not seeking to revoke the Second Amendment. The gun locker proved to be quite popular. One year after we started our Gun Free Zone movement, fifty-four lockers were full of guns and ammunition and the police had expanded the program.

As with my credit-union activism, the Gun Free Zone movement was gratifying because we were able to achieve tangible results that had the potential to improve the quality of life within the university community. The fact that we were able to effectively negotiate within the boundaries of UNL's bureaucracy, and mobilize some of its officials and other university resources while sustaining our activist scholar identities, was also significant.

Activism in "The Belly of the Beast": Challenging Intercollegiate Athletics, 1993–2004[8]

My accidental activism took yet another unexpected turn at UNL that would lead to a dozen-year odyssey in and out of intercollegiate athletics—what I later came to refer to as "the belly of the beast." My initial involvement with athletics emanated from my interactions as a faculty member at Nebraska with athletes and members of the Athletic Department. Several experiences led me to the not particularly profound conclusion that most UNL athletic administrators and coaches valued athletics over academics. Two such interactions remain etched in my memory. In the fall of 1993, my afternoon honors seminar was suffering sustained disruptions from deafening noises coming from Memorial Stadium. We literally could not hear each other due to the intermittent noises. Upon investigation I discovered that head football coach Tom Osborne[9] had ordered artificial crowd noise piped into the stadium at maximum decibel levels during afternoon practices in order to simulate game-day crowd noise. The sound could be heard from miles away. I mentioned the problem to my department chair, who suggested I call the Athletic Department. When Coach Osborne and athletic director Bill Byrne refused to respond to my phone calls, their staff routed me to Al Papik, senior associate athletic director. While on hold for Papik, replays of the previous week's gridiron contest along with the Husker fight song blared through the phone. Finally, Papik came on and wanted to know what my problem was with the stadium noise. When I responded that the racket interfered with the learning environment, he replied that Coach Osborne had ordered the simulated crowd noise (as though invoking his eminence should suffice to deter me from going any further with my complaint). Papik said he could not do anything about the crowd noise; instead he offered to move my class to a soundproof room in South Stadium, the bunker area within the bowels of Memorial Stadium. I asked him whether or not he could also accommodate the scores of other classes taught during football practices. He responded that I was the *only* professor who had complained about the noise. He made it patently clear that my values were askew if I thought that student learning was more important at Nebraska than contending for a national championship in football.

A second incident that led me to conclude that athletics took precedence over academics occurred in the summer of 1995. Over the previous few years, interactions with the academic-advising wing of Husker athletics demonstrated their propensity to treat athletes paternalistically and to expect other members of the faculty and staff to make special accommodations on their behalf. Academic "advisors" and "tutors" called me on behalf of "student" athletes. They selected classes for the athletes, helped resolve problems they encountered with their instructors, and generally ran interference through the university bureaucracy like a fullback clearing a hole for a Husker I-back. They ushered athletes to classes and monitored their attendance, thereby contributing to the athlete's "learned helplessness" (Seligman & Maier 1995). While I found this pattern of "academic support" problematic and counter to the Athletic Department's goal of preparing athletes for the future, I was not particularly disturbed by the process. When the process involved covering up academic dishonesty, I grew more concerned.

Two Husker football players submitted identical incorrect answers to a ten-part methods class assignment.[10] I confronted them separately, and each denied wrongdoing but suggested the other was to blame. I gave them the choice I give all students who engage in acts of academic dishonesty: either write a ten-page essay on academic honesty or roll the dice with the student judicial board. I failed to realize that the date I confronted the students was the last day they could drop the course without consequence. They both left my office and dropped the course. I subsequently reported both cases to Dennis Leblanc, associate athletic director for academic and support services; Coach Osborne; and James Griesen, vice chancellor for student affairs. None of them acted on my complaints. I repeatedly contacted Griesen, who promised me he would look into it. Had any of the UNL officials acted on the complaint, they might have saved the university considerable embarrassment, given that both athletes committed highly publicized crimes. Once again, it was apparent to me that the UNL administration's actions (or lack thereof) demonstrated that winning football games took priority over academic integrity.

While my observations and interactions with Husker athletics and UNL's administration led me to question their commitment to academics, their handling of a spate of cases involving football players' violence toward women generated my next round of accidental activism. Between 1991 and

1995 several women reported that Nebraska football players had sexually and/or physically assaulted them. A few of the cases generated considerable national publicity, casting the University of Nebraska in a disgraceful light. Although not as deplorable as the violent acts, the lack of an appropriate institutional response tended to reproduce the extant rape culture. In each of the cases, Coach Osborne conducted investigations himself. Most anywhere else in the United States, private citizens who engaged in the activities in which Coach Osborne engaged would have been charged with tampering with witnesses, evidence tampering, and obstruction of justice (Benedict 1997).[11] With few exceptions, the accused perpetrators received no sanctions from Coach Osborne, the Athletic Department, or UNL. The victims, on the other hand, frequently found it necessary to flee the university, their jobs, and even the state, as rabid Husker fans blamed the victims for their gridiron heroes' violent acts.

In the fall of 1995, UNL women's groups publicly condemned a decision to reinstate one of the perpetrators (Benedict 1997). Several women faculty members and students engaged in one of the most courageous acts of protest ever undertaken in Lincoln, Nebraska. They gathered in front of Memorial Stadium to protest UNL's failure to address the Athletic Department's "epidemic of violence" as 76,000 red-clad Husker fans poured through the gates. In the face of the Big Red fans' vicious threats, vulgar insults, and constant taunting, they stood firm in their support of the assault victims. For various reasons I did not attend the protest. However, inspired by the women's courage, outraged by the lack of an appropriate institutional response to the escalating violence, and, by this juncture, enjoying the job security afforded by tenure, I became more vocal in my criticisms of the Athletic Department and UNL's administration. Eventually, my outspokenness contributed to the faculty senate appointing me to the Intercollegiate Athletics Committee (IAC).

It became apparent immediately that the IAC functioned to provide legitimacy to the Athletic Department, rubber-stamping virtually all decisions in support of the Husker status quo. Growing increasingly frustrated by the charade, at the final meeting of the 1997–98 year I muttered audibly that we not meet the ensuing academic year, adding, "We could instead just email our rubber stamps in." Although my remarks were sarcastic (albeit sincere), I had not intended them to be taken as a campaign speech. Nevertheless, my colleagues nominated and elected me as the IAC chair for the 1998–99 year.

My service on the Nebraska IAC (1997–2000), particularly the year as chair, provided me a window into bigtime college sports that few outsiders are afforded. It also led to other opportunities and additional activist and fieldwork roles, including attending the 1999 founding meeting of the National Alliance for College Athletic Reform (NAFCAR), which later changed its name to The Drake Group, serving on its first executive council (2000–01), and being invited as panelist and presenter to the 2003 National Institute for Sports Reform Summit at Lake George, New York.

Soon after moving to Southern Illinois University Carbondale (SIUC), I managed to get pulled back into intercollegiate athletics when the faculty senate appointed me to serve on the Intercollegiate Athletics Advisory Committee (2002–04). Although the Saluki beast was considerably smaller that the Husker behemoth, the problems were similar. SIUC's gender climate, like UNL's, was deplorable.[12] And as in Nebraska, administrators—including the majority of the members of its board of trustees—placed athletics ahead of academics. Moreover, shared governance was practically nonexistent at SIUC.[13] Whereas most intercollegiate athletics committees are under the auspices of faculty senates, SIUC's serves at the behest of the chancellor. Needless to say, I found my time on the IAAC frustrating but illuminating as I sought to traverse and negotiate the boundaries of the academy and bigtime college sports.

Activist Pedagogy: Southern Illinois University and University of South Florida, 2008–12

Not long after I grew weary of intercollegiate athletics' apparent imperviousness to reform efforts, I rediscovered the efficacy of scholarly activism in an undergraduate classroom. Semester after semester, I had experienced a gnawing sense that there was a disjuncture between classroom focuses and the world out there. It seemed that the largest disconnect between understanding a field and developing skills to apply that knowledge occurred in my upper-level social movements course. Students completing the course could identify, compare, and critically assess various social movement concepts, theories, and research. But I remained unconvinced that by semester's end they could organize lunch, let alone a social movement. This gap became all the more problematic in light of the current state of affairs. Clearly, our dying planet, troubled nation, and neglected communities need talented and trained activists to lead effective movements for progressive social change. So in the fall of 2008 I decided to shift the focus of my social movements course at siuc from one of preparing students to become the next generation of movement scholars, to preparing them to become the next generation of community activists. This transformation was realized by fashioning an active learning environment in which students could develop community-organizing and activist skills.

Following a three-week-long process during which the students completed individual and group assignments and discussed and debated the relative merits of organizing a movement to ameliorate various specific local and global injustices, the class elected to organize a renters' rights movement. It was the first renter's rights movement ever formed in that slumlord-dominated college community. Calling themselves TAPT (Tenants Are People Too), the class spent the next couple of weeks gathering and analyzing data regarding the history of other renters' rights movements; local renters' experiences; city, county, and state laws pertaining to the landlord/tenant relationship; and redress mechanisms available to renters. The class designed and administered a survey of tenants and analyzed approximately 250 completed surveys. Drawing on their research as well as assigned activist handbooks, students developed movement goals, a mission statement, strategies, tactics, and publicity materials. The students then publicly launched their movement, using a variety of print and electronic media, and organized a series of educational, recruitment, and direct-action events focusing on educating, assisting, and empowering renters in the region.

The results of that initial foray into activist pedagogy exceeded my aspirations. The class goals were realized beyond expectations. Take-home exams, assignments, and occasional mini-lectures ensured that students mastered basic social-movement concepts and theories. But more importantly in terms of their futures, the students gained hands-on experience in all facets of organizing a social movement. They were empowered and learned valuable lessons about civil society. They learned how to work more effectively with others. They honed their communication skills and exercised their sociological imaginations. And perhaps most significantly, students established a sustainable social movement organization—one that continued for several months after the class was over. Two students summarized the class's activist accomplishments in *The Engaged Sociologist* (Moran & Richter 2009).

Since arriving at the University of South Florida, I have continued to teach the Mobilizing for Change course. In the spring of 2012, after considering a number of social injustices the students found problematic, the USF class decided to focus on the classist, racist, and other damaging effects of federal, state, and local drug laws and policies. They formed Tampa Students for Sensible Drug Policy (SSDP-USF) and obtained official student organization status. Students worked with university officials to formulate and implement a "Good Samaritan" policy, which ensures that students who have a crisis, or report a fellow student having a crisis, associated with drug or alcohol use are held harmless (administratively and criminally) upon seeking help from health-care workers and/or other university officials. They also forged official linkages with the national SSDP organization. More than a year after the class concluded, SSDP-USF was still quite active. They hosted the 2012 statewide convention and have continued to work with university administrative, health, and public-safety officials to affect campus policies related to drugs. The USF Mobilizing for Change class was so gratifying that I can't wait to see what injustices the next cohort of students decides to take on next semester.

Concluding Reflections on an Activist Scholar Career

As the foregoing accounts suggest, when I entered the academy I didn't set out to try to change the world or even the small corner of it around me. Rather, the bulk of my activism within the academy was born out of reactions, my colleagues and my own, to apparent opportunities and perceived injustices that appeared from time to time on my radar screen. My initial foray into the field to study the peace and justice movement was primarily happenstance, as was my deeper and deeper immersion into the peace-activist role. My subsequent activist work, including the credit union board, the SAC Museum exhibit design collaborations, the Gun Free Zone movement, the Intercollegiate Athletics Committee service, and The Drake Group sports reform activities, was only moderately strategic in a proactive sense. The lion's share of my activism did not entail developing an a priori plan to effect change. For the most part I reacted to various contingencies and constraints as they arose and as I understood them.

The academy is perhaps more open than other workplaces to its employees, particularly faculty and students, engaging in activism. Clearly, academics have more discretionary time, a condition social movement scholars have identified as conducive to engaging in various forms of collective action (McCarthy & Zald 1977). Scholars also tend to be embedded in extensive social networks that are likely to yield exposure to issues that are often the bases of activism, as well as opportunities to be recruited to and join movements (Snow, Zurcher & Ekland-Olson 1980). Moreover, campuses tend to be hotbeds of a plethora of social causes. Finally, the norm of academic freedom can provide scholars greater freedom, perceived or actual, to exercise their voices in the face of apparent injustices within the academy and the world beyond.

Yet, as my biography illustrates, academic identity concerns, career considerations, and administrative pressures constrain scholars' activist opportunities and choices. Not only was my initial academic position as an assistant professor jeopardized by my earlier activist research, I felt that I needed to temper my activism during my probationary period until tenure was achieved. Later in my career when I served as department chair at SIUC (2000–03 and 2008–10) and USF (2010–13), I found it necessary to once again set aside activist proclivities in the interests of the department. While I never felt that administrators at USF would retaliate against my department if I took up the "wrong" side of an issue, such as seeking to reform intercollegiate athletics, I was fairly certain that a few powerful administrators at SIUC would engage in such wholesale retaliation, especially if the target were one of their sacred cows such as athletics. A few colleagues in the sociology departments at both SIUC and USF made it clear that as long as I was department chair, I should avoid being publicly associated with politics and I should keep my political opinions to myself. For the most part during my service as chair, I was able to set aside my activist-scholar activities and identity to accommodate my colleagues' wishes.

Despite the institutional and interpersonal constraints, my career as an activist scholar has had efficacious moments. The credit union and Gun Free Zone experiences stand out as particularly gratifying. However, the most effective and rewarding efforts have been related to activist pedagogy. Helping students develop the activist and collaborative skills needed to effect progressive change, and witnessing them become empowered, has been exhilarating and energizing. Hopefully, many of them will go on to mobilize their fellow citizens to confront injustices they encounter in their communities, workplaces, and the world. And perhaps a few will go on to become scholar activists themselves.

NOTES

1. The June 12, 1982 March for Peace and Justice was organized to coincide with the United Nations' Second Special Session on Disarmament.

2. The year after I started at UNL, John Peters became the dean. He subsequently served as provost at the University of Tennessee and president of Northern Illinois University.

3. This section is a slightly revised excerpt from a paper I published in *Peace Review* (Benford 2006).

4. In early 1994, veterans' groups attacked the proposed Enola Gay exhibit script (commemorating the B-29 that dropped the atomic bomb on Hiroshima) at the Smithsonian Institution. They claimed that the exhibit would memorialize Japanese war casualties and trivialize U.S. losses. Scores of politicians, including House Speaker Newt Gingrich, entered the fray to support the veterans, generating threats to cut the Smithsonian's annual $750 million budget if the exhibit was not changed. The political firestorm raged for nearly a year, through five script revisions, before Smithsonian secretary Michael Hyman succumbed to the pressure. A few weeks later, the Air and Space Museum's embattled director, Martin Harwit, resigned.

5. This section is a revised version of a section I published (Benford 2011) in Korgen, White & White's *Sociologists in action: Sociology, social change, and social justice* (Sage, 2013).

6. For a description of the incident, see Asmussen & Cresswell 1995.

7. "Green Bay Packers' Tyrone Williams sentenced to six-month jail sentence," *Jet*, December 9, 1996.

8. This section is a revised excerpt from my 2006 Midwest Sociological Society Presidential Address, which was published in the *Sociological Quarterly* (Benford 2007).

9. Tom Osborne served as UNL's head football coach from 1973 through 1997. He served in the U.S. House of Representatives from 2001 to 2007 from Nebraska's Third Congressional District. In 2007 he returned to UNL to serve as its athletic director until 2013.

10. The Family Educational Rights and Privacy Act (FERPA) precludes me from revealing the identities of the students who cheated. But as Jon Ericson, The Drake Group's founder and first executive director,

frequently points out, FERPA does not protect university officials who refused to do anything about the reported academic dishonesty.

11. In one instance, Coach Osborne locked a gun in his drawer, for several days, that he knew the police were looking for in connection with a drive-by shooting committed by a Husker football star (Benedict 1997, Farber 1995).

12. In September 2000, the Department of Education's Office of Civil Rights began investigating a Title IX complaint regarding the lack of facilities for the softball program and athletes. In order to get the OCR off their backs, SIUC eventually agreed to build a softball facility, but claimed they had planned to build it all along. Assistant athletic director for compliance Nancy Bandy publicly questioned whether or not SIUC ever intended to build the facility, suggesting that the longstanding neglect of women's athletics vis-à-vis men's programs was discriminatory (Cusick 2000). Shortly thereafter, SIUC terminated Ms. Bandy, who had been a strong advocate for women athletes at SIUC for several years.

13. My conclusions regarding the lack of shared governance at SIUC are derived from my experiences and observations throughout the six years I served on the faculty senate, including a term as vice president (2003–04) and a term as president (2005–06). They are also based on comparisons of shared governance at other Illinois institutions I gleaned from attending the Council of Illinois University Senates on two occasions.

REFERENCES

Alinsky, S. (1971). *Rules for radicals: A pragmatic primer for realistic radicals.* New York: Random House.

Asmussen, K., & Cresswell, J. W. (1995). Campus response to a terrorist gun incident. *Journal of Higher Education* 66: 575–591.

Benedict, J. (1997). *Public heroes, private felons: Athletes and crimes against women.* Boston: Northeastern University Press.

Benford, R. (2011). A campus gun free zone movement. In K. O. Korgen, J. M. White & S. K. White (Eds.), *Sociologists in action: Sociology, social change, and social justice,* 120–126. Los Angeles: Sage/Pine Forge Press.

Benford, R. D. (1993). Frame disputes within the nuclear disarmament movement. *Social Forces* 71: 677–701.

Benford, R. D. (2007). The college sports reform movement: Reframing the "edutainment" industry. *Sociological Quarterly* 48: 1–28.

Benford, R. D. (1988). The nuclear disarmament movement. In L. R. Kurtz, *The nuclear cage: A sociology of the nuclear arms race,* 237–265. Englewood Cliffs, NJ: Prentice Hall.

Benford, R. D. (1996). Whose war memories shall be preserved? *Peace Review* 8: 189–194.

Benford, R. D., & Hunt, S. A. (2003). Interactional dynamics in public problems marketplaces: Movements and the counterframing and reframing of public problems. In J. A. Holstein & G. Miller (Eds.), *Challenges and choices: Constructionist perspectives on social problems,* 153–186. New York: Aldine de Gruyter.

Curtis, R. L., & Zurcher, L. A. (1973). Stable resources of protest movements: The multi-organizational field. *Social Forces* 52: 53–61.

Cusick, C. (2000). Title IX complaint filed against SIU. *Daily Egyptian* 86 (11): 1.

Farber, M. (1995). Coach and jury: Nebraska players charged with crimes have a steadfast ally in the man who runs the program, Tom Osborne. *Sports Illustrated* 83 (13): 31–32, 34.

Goffman, E. (1959). *The presentation of self in everyday life*. Garden City, NY: Doubleday.

Hailey, A. (1975). *The moneychangers*. New York: Doubleday.

McCarthy, J. D., & Zald, M. N. (1977). Resource mobilization and social movements: A partial theory. *American Journal of Sociology* 82: 1212–1241.

Moran, A., & Richter, M. (2009). Student sociologists in action: Anthony Moran and Mike Richter. In K. O. Korgen & J. M. White (Eds.), *The engaged sociologist: Connecting the classroom to community*, 2nd ed., 96–99. Thousand Oaks, CA: Pine Forge Press.

Pitt, D. C., & Thompson, G. (Eds.). (1987). *Nuclear-free zones*. London: Croom Helm.

Seligman, M. E. P., & Maier, S. F. (1995). *Learned helplessness: A theory for the age of personal control*. New York: Oxford University Press.

Snow, D. A., & Benford, R. D. (1988). Ideology, frame resonance and participant mobilization. *International Social Movement Research* 1: 197–217.

Snow, D. A., Zurcher, L. A., & Ekland-Olson, S. (1980). Social networks and social movements: A microstructural approach to recruitment. *American Sociological Review* 45: 787–801.

Can Development Bridge the Gap between Activism and Academia?

Cristina Espinosa

This short article is not a research paper but rather a reflection based on my personal experience, sharing some insights on this interesting discussion about the gaps and synergies between theory and practice, in particular between activism and academia.[1]

Our perceptions and our knowledge are not universal, neutral, or objective, but rather particular, subjective, and situated, as well presented by Nazarea (2006). And this is reflected in the different ways each of us experience either activism or academia or both, and how our views evolve according to our different positioning. In my case, my experience in both during the last five decades tells me that there are different activisms and different academies.

When I was completing studies for my BA in social sciences at the Universidad Católica in Lima in the 1970s, there were strong links between academia, social movements, and the New Left. Even though most faculty members were not directly involved in the New Left, they were its supporters on ideological or more practical grounds. For instance, while not organically linked to the New Left parties, they might express sympathetic views in regard to their ideology or programmatic plans or even support their actions in logistical or financial terms. Politics was on the streets, in the after-meal discussions at home, on the news, in the street demonstrations, and of course at school. The topics discussed in class, the readings, the academic papers, the discussions on the patios, the invited speakers, student street demonstrations, and our participation in the street demonstrations of miners, schoolteacher unions, and other social movements, everything was closely related and there was a passion to learn, to understand, and to change our society. There seemed to be no real gap between activism and academia, at least not for me.

Then everything changed when I joined a group of students to do fieldwork in Cusco. The Student Union organized this fieldwork, responding to an invitation of the Federation Campesina del Valle de La Convención y Lares.[2] Living for a month or so with a poor peasant family, visiting a different family from the village each day, working in their coffee fields, meeting at night to help these peasant men and women to read and write, and discussing their problems, eating their food, sleeping in their homes, sharing their stories, their poverty and suffering, all that radically changed me. This experience made me aware of the class divide and ignited my desire to overcome it. The prospect of graduating and starting a career in academia, with that loose and easy support of the New Left parties and of social movements, was no longer attractive to me, because I was eager to play a more direct role in bringing change to a country where most people lived disenfranchised, exploited, and marginalized. I was clearly aware of the abyss separating classes in Peru, and I was no longer comfortable with my privileges as a member of the upper middle class. I accelerated my graduation and decided to burn my bridges. I left Lima and joined the rank of activists working in the provinces as militants preparing the political conditions for the masses to organize and conduct revolution.[3] When I took this radical decision, my view of academia became more critical because my experience in Cusco had given me a sense of urgency that I did not have before. So, it was not that academia had changed that much—rather I had changed, and after my experience in Cusco, my sense of timing, my need to become more engaged, to detach myself from my bourgeois life and practice, all that had given me other lenses to perceive academia and its contribution to social change. Following the argument presented by Nazarea (2006) my viewpoint, my social and political positioning had changed; therefore my point of view did as well.

There were some factors contributing to isolate me as an activist from research and academic debate. My life as an activist did not leave much room to conceptualize or to document my experience. There was immediacy in terms of timing and resources, and like most activists I operated in conditions of high uncertainty and risk. In addition, in those pre-computer and pre-Internet days, activists working in the provinces were pretty much isolated from academia, which was mostly concentrated in the capital; this isolation from academic debates or publications was important, discouraging activists from writing a piece that could transcend pure activism. The role of technology in overcoming this isolation is a very important factor these days and should be considered when discussing the possible links and synergies between activism and academia.

Nevertheless, there are always moments of pause between one campaign and the next, and when trained as a social scientist, it is difficult for an activist to avoid some critical thinking. While still a militant in the 1970s, I was in disagreement with the prevailing Leninist theory for party-building (this idea that the party should be a small vanguard operating on behalf of the masses) and was intrigued by Gramsci's emphasis on democratic participation of the masses and their agency. My discomfort with patriarchal gender views and practices within the group was building up on top of my discomfort with the paternalistic ways in which peasants and workers were treated by the party local leadership. Finally I had to question the prevalent blindness about ethnicity and indigeneity in favor of class analysis in a country where most of the rural population was indigenous or of indigenous descent and discriminated against on this basis. These ideological discrepancies coincided with my motherhood and my absolute need to provide for and protect my family, so I left my life as an underground activist. Being proud and stubborn, I did not return to Lima to take refuge with my parents. I stayed in the province of Chiclayo on the northern coast of Peru and worked really hard to make a living as a freelance researcher and consultant. After almost ten years I returned to Lima, to my own place. I joined a large development program focused on improving small husbandry for poor farmers in different parts of the country to make their livelihoods more sustainable: the Small Ruminant Research and Support Program (SR-CRSP) coordinated by the University of California-Davis. I had been a freelance researcher for them while I was in Chiclayo, and in Lima I became the manager for one research program component. That job started a long segment of my career combining applied research and program management within the field of sustainable development.

This program combined field research with interventions; it offered me the opportunity to design, conduct, and supervise research and to have my first publications, first as part of their technical report series and then as articles submitted to academic interdisciplinary journals. At this time there was a confluence of researchers from different disciplines, some belonging to academia and some to NGOs and GOs,[4] and there was an extraordinary platform in Peru to share research results and discuss issues and concerns: SEPIA–Seminario Permanente de Investigación Agraria (Permanent Seminar on Rural Research), supported by the Ford Foundation, which held biannual nationwide conferences and published papers presented there. SEPIA became such an important platform, first to unify researchers from different disciplines inside and outside academia, but also to include some activists who did not consider themselves researchers but intellectuals. The difference between these two categories at that time had to do with your institutional affiliation: researchers were affiliated with universities or with research NGOs and were part of research teams funded by grants; intellectuals were a broader group that could include researchers, journalists, and even activists who independently of their affiliation or professional training were engaged in the systematic analysis of current affairs, with critical views voiced through publications, radio, or TV debates or interviews. They were influencing not only their peers but also public opinion by expressing their dissent, revealing hidden, relevant facts or research findings. Intellectuals played an important political role at that time in Latin America, and they were in some ways bridging the gap between activists and researchers, a role that is usually overlooked.

It is interesting to note that after I left the political party, I never defined myself as an activist[5]—even though I was engaged in projects and programs aimed at bringing social change, improving the livelihoods of poor peasants, women, and indigenous communities; even though I was challenging some common wisdoms about development and the role of small farmers, women, and marginalized groups, despite the long hours of hard work, low pay, and strong personal commitment. I always considered myself an applied researcher, even though I was outside academia, sometimes as a freelance researcher and consultant, sometimes attached to an NGO implementing or coordinating a development project/program.

The most important reason for not defining myself as an activist was that I was being paid for my job—first poorly and then not so much. My positioning in terms of class was not the same I chose after my experience in Cusco. I had a family to support and my jobs were allowing me to become a better provider, and that meant for me that somehow I had reentered the world of the bourgeoisie—I was back into my own world, even though not exactly in the same place of privilege I left. Basically, the high personal costs in terms of security risk, being blacklisted for a job, isolation, poverty, vulnerability, and uncertainty due to one's priority commitment to "the cause," were all gone. I felt, therefore, that I did not deserve to be identified as an activist. While I felt safe in that regard, I was not truly back into my bourgeois world because it was never the same. You pay a price for being "out": you lag behind, compared to what your peers have accomplished in the ten years or so that you were "outside" academia, and you are also transformed by the experience of being an activist.

The fact that I never considered myself an activist after I left the party raises the question of who is and who is not an activist. I think it is important in our discussion to differentiate between two types of activism. One is an activism that is done within a class/ethnic positioning that coincides with those subaltern and oppressed groups who we aim to support and empower, and with whom we commit to share the present and the future—as good or bad as it might be. The other is an activism that is done within the boundaries of our own class positioning—which is different from those we aim to support and empower. This second activism has become more popular both in the global South and also in developed countries, thanks to the exponential growth of NGOs and grassroots organizations and, to a large extent, to the role of development institutions, discourses, and practices. These are important distinctions to make. One option is to share the "field conditions" for a few months or more, knowing that you have the protection of being a scholar and/or a citizen from the United States or Europe if anything goes wrong, and knowing that after this experience you are returning to a safe life. Another option is to share the same risks and vulnerabilities local people you are working with face, without any protection, and furthermore to embrace the fact that your future career might be compromised by your activism, especially in situations where the academy is dominated by nonprogressive points of view.

This distinction I propose between different types of activisms is quite important because of the growing number of scholars and development professionals who claim to be activists. While I am not proposing a normative prescriptive approach to this issue—ultimately each one has the right to define ourselves as we choose—having clarity on the issue of positioning can help us to better explore the gaps and bridges between activism and scholarship. The distinction I propose is also important to honor the men and women who are facing violence, poverty, and discrimination because of their activism while we are not, and in this regard it aims to bring some sense of justice to the discussion: are the costs and benefits of being engaged in activism equally shared among all of us? Since this is not the case, it makes sense to differentiate in terms of how the costs/risks and benefits are distributed among different types of activism.

There is another element to consider and that is the role of what I call here "enabling activism," which complements the direct action of activism. For instance, any mobilization requires not only those directly involved in the organization and participating in the actions; it requires also a broad range of support, from the local to the national and to the global. That provides quite a demand for what I call here the "enablers," those activists who are not on the front lines but who perform a series of actions that allow campaigns and struggles of oppressed people to succeed against all odds. There are several examples of local struggles that were able to obtain some political leverage thanks to the support they received from global campaigns. In this regard, if we use a more inclusive concept of activism, we can recognize the important role played by activists of the second type supporting the work of activists of the first type. We could not only understand the differences between them in a more integrated way, but also value the way they complement and support each other.

Activism can be further differentiated according to the subaltern group engaged, for instance along the axes of gender, class, ethnicity, racial constructions, sexual orientation, and so on, since each group brings a different type of agency and practice. Further elaborating on this differentiation is beyond the scope of this piece, since I am not interested in proposing any form of typology.

Academia is neither the same everywhere nor is it static. Academia has also been influenced by the emergence of development. As well-presented in Escobar (1995) and So (1990), this new and expanding field of intervention in developing countries after World War II—in the midst of the Cold

War and anticommunism—required new professionals with expertise on societies characterized then as "traditional" and poor. The "problematization of poverty" (Escobar 1995) gave legitimacy for intervening in fields like public health, demography, education, agriculture, and economics, and that intervention required "expert knowledge" from developed countries, the sites where modernity was already occurring.[6] While this new field of development was instrumental in keeping developing countries underdeveloped and dependent, it also transformed academia by creating new programs and by influencing the research agenda through substantive grants. Area studies were instrumental in this transformation. While applied research and applied and interdisciplinary academic training were looked down upon by most faculty members housed in traditional discipline-based departments, funding gave leverage to those working in new applied/interdisciplinary programs. Even though it still exists, this divide between pure and applied science and research has become more subtle. Depending on where you are, you can witness a more or less active war between the discipline-based departments and the interdisciplinary or transdisciplinary centers or programs. Having been part of area studies centers like the Center for Latin American Studies (LATAM) at the University of Florida and the Institute for the Study of Latin America and the Caribbean (ISLAC) at the University of South Florida, I have experienced both scenarios. There is also variation within disciplines; for instance, having being trained as a social scientist and as an anthropologist and having worked with economists and historians, among others, I feel that not all disciplines have the same flexibility and openness in regard to other disciplines and to nonacademic voices. Anthropology is the only discipline explicitly addressing the cultural divide between researcher and researched and devising methods to minimize that gap, recognizing through the notion of cultural relativism that no culture is superior to others. Without ignoring the historic legacy of colonialism shaping this discipline and its role in "othering" subaltern groups, it has also offered conceptual, methodological, and practical spaces to overcome the gap between researcher and researched and between research and activism. Anthropology tends to be more applied and friendly to non-anthropologists, with inter/transdisciplinary programs/research, and with actors/voices from outside academia. Through my teaching at graduate programs focused on Latin American/ Latino studies and sustainable international development, I have experienced the distrust of some faculty members who do not consider publications outside the major discipline-based or strictly academic journals to be scholarship. This has been an issue among colleagues from the departments of anthropology where I have also been affiliated faculty.

When it comes to the relation between academia and activism, it seems to me that the more inter- or transdisciplinary the academic setting is, the more inclusive it is towards nonacademic voices and perspectives. If the tendency within academia to become more applied and inter/ transdisciplinary continues, we can expect a more favorable scenario for academia to become more inclusive and willing to incorporate nonacademic knowledge, perspective, and agency within its operation. This would be a positive development that would be more conducive to bridging the gap between research and academia.

There are other issues that affect academia and those working within it. It has to do with its patriarchal and ethnocentric bias, expressed in the resistance to accept more diversity not only in terms of its faculty and student body but also in terms of perspectives, topics, and methodologies. Many times when diversity is discussed within academia[7] it refers to issues of racial inclusion or religious tolerance, but it tends to ignore other important dimensions like class or the triple burden women face outside academia and how it might affect their scholarship; or the lack of recognition of activist work and related publications for faculty members who have closer links with activism. Another challenge to consider is the need to recognize that the value of scholarship cannot be only measured by the recognition obtained from mainstream academia or professional associations. Many times critical perspectives and research closely linked to activism fail to be recognized by these institutions despite their significant contribution made to grassroots activism. Some research might be highly instrumental and relevant to activism and at the same time ignored by academia. Finally, but not less important, is the narrow definition of the scholarly field, usually limited to the United States and/or Europe, leaving out of the rest of the world. Perhaps the fact that too many American scholars don't speak a second language explains how unaware they are of important contributions and debates led by "Third World" scholars and activists. This is usually shown in the review process for faculty rank promotion when publications not in English or in major American or British journals are not considered as part of the scholarship to be reviewed. Here again, there are many academic programs where this bias is lessened by the direct engagement of American scholars with scholars or grassroots organizations from developing countries. Many American social scientists have developed strong and wide partnerships with scholars and activists in developing countries that empower local people and local researchers.[8] Nevertheless, the point I want to make here is that junior faculty members whose careers have a strong component of activism or practice outside academia, with important publications outside the United States, usually face resistance and/or discrimination from peers whose careers have only been within academia and/or within the United States.

Having a broad field of expertise is also considered a disadvantage within academia since most scholars develop a tunnel specialization and expertise and therefore distrust less specialized expertise with the same hostility offered to interdisciplinary and transdisciplinary scholarship and to the association of scholarship with activism.

We need to remember that the academy was born sanctioning the basic division between manual/physical labor and intellectual pursuit, reinforcing the very Western dichotomy between doing and thinking. The creation of this institution devoted to learning/teaching in Europe in the twelfth century was promoted by scholars to further develop their secular scholarship and to train new scholars—and in this regard it perpetuated the division of labor between those doing physical labor and those doing nonphysical labor. However, the academy was also born as an independent space for intellectual inquiry,[9] and here resides its potential to contribute to social change: its capacity to protect and encourage critical thinking, to conduct research, and reflect on experience without the urgency and immediacy of activism. This is an important characteristic of the academy that we need to keep in mind as we explore the links between activism and academia.

Academia, however, is not monolithic or static. Reflecting this process of change and of differentiation are some academic programs that include nonacademic experience, knowledge, and perspectives as part of their academic practice. Usually these programs are interdisciplinary and applied and operate outside the discipline-based departments, using the spaces created by development within academia, such as area-studies centers. One example is the Tropical Conservation and Development Program (TCD), hosted at the Center for Latin American Studies at the University of Florida. The TCD program is a collaborative research and training program that brings together faculty and students from the social and biological sciences, as well as researchers, development/ conservation practitioners, and activists from the global South who are working on conservation and development issues in the tropics. While this program was originally focused on Latin America, it has grown to become a global network linking small and large NGOs, universities, and activists/ advocates from all over the world. This program has a tremendous impact on the people and institutions in the tropics, but it has also influenced its academic host: TCD has been behind the recent creation of the School for Natural Resources Management at the University of Florida, which has a strong interdisciplinary and applied focus. While I am not familiar with them, I know there are other collaborative initiatives in areas like health and policy research; there is an interesting literature discussing community-based participatory research and policy research as advocacy, as emerging strategies to overcome the gaps between research and activism (Nyden & Wiewel 1992; Weiss 1991; Nyden 2003; Stahl & Shdaimah 2008).

Considering what we have so far discussed about activisms and academies, it is important to review if there is room for synergistic collaborations between activism and scholarship: Can scholars reflect and analyze the reality and experience of activists and this way support their work? Or does this option reflect a paternalistic view that reproduces stereotyped views of what is activism and what is scholarship? Can activists reflect on their own experience and the social reality they try to change while doing the urgent tasks demanded by their social and political commitment? Should scholarship be radically redefined by repositioning it in intimate connection with practice? We might respond to these questions differently since there might be divergent perspectives for defining the links between activism and scholarship.

The field of international development has played an important role in this tension between activism and academia. It is true that development was born after World War II as a field of intervention to control former colonies, as is well explained by Escobar (1995). In the context of the Cold War, development became both a discourse and a practice justifying this political and economic control, and reshaping the way the global South was perceived: as a crippled region in need of aid from Western and Northern countries to emulate their development. It is important to note that this perception was also internalized within developing countries, demobilizing and neutralizing their agency for autonomy.[10] Academia played a very important role in this process—for instance, providing the rationale for development interventions through the modernization theory that obscured the imperialist and neocolonial nature of these interventions and of the development narrative. The professionalization of development strengthened the links between development and academia, creating new areas of studies and supporting new required areas for research and training through substantive grants. It also funded thousands of professionals from the global South to obtain advanced degrees, and this has contributed to making academia in the global North more diverse and international, as much as it has empowered professionals from the global South. In this regard, development has influenced academia and transformed its structure while relying to a large extent on certain hegemonic paradigms produced by academia.

Despite its negative effect increasing the dependency and vulnerability of countries of the global South and increasing global, national, and local inequalities, international development has also opened some opportunities for social change and some new spaces for activism, if we accept the second type of activism as valid. The hegemonic development paradigm of modernization was not to remain unchallenged. First, the modernization theory was challenged by the dependency theory, a new paradigm that took a critical view of development from the perspective of developing countries.[11] The legacy of colonialism and postcolonialism and the imperialist connotation of development were unveiled, same as the structural processes and links that explained the "development of underdevelopment" (Cardoso & Faletto 1979). The second challenge to hegemonic or orthodox development came mainly from the North, after the realization of the environmental limits for economic growth, increasing instability, and unsustainability of capitalist development, in a context of expanding global interdependence. Apocalyptical scenarios were to affect not only the global South or the North, but both (Redclift 1987). For the first time, the triumphalism of modernization theory was challenged from the perspective of human life survival on earth. The alarm rung by environmentalists—in the context of the oil crisis and the vulnerability of modern agriculture—was enough to produce a paradigmatic shift towards sustainable development. It was, however, not strong enough to change the basic nature of development as a field of intervention to control the global South and secure the process of capitalist accumulation on a global scale.

Even though "sustainable development" never really became the new orthodoxy, it did a good job showing the limits and contradictions of capitalist development. The public admission that there was a development crisis opened spaces for alternative development paradigms, which provided a justification for other type of praxis within the development field or apparatus, especially at the community and/or grassroots level. Participatory methodologies, pro-poor-oriented interventions, the propagation of human-rights approaches to development, women's rights, minority rights, etc., provided a buffered space to support different types of activism that in many cases helped to strengthen civil society and social movements.

While I can remain skeptical about the long-term impact of these new initiatives on addressing the structural roots of poverty or inequalities, I cannot deny their critical role in holding some buffered spaces for activism and the defense of human rights, especially under authoritarian regimes. Noteworthy is the role of international NGOs and international cooperation missions to hide and get out of the country so many political and social activists facing persecution and death. (I know that was the case for Chile and El Salvador; I am sure there are many other examples.)

There is another unintended consequence of development. It brings a first-hand local experience of developing countries to new generations within developed countries, which facilitates a process of awareness and critical thinking about the status quo. For instance, thousands of American youth have participated in programs like the Peace Corps, which place them in a poor village setting within a developing country for a year or more. Of course these programs have been the subject of much debate, but the point I want to make here is that such an experience usually deeply transforms the views and perceptions of the youth involved and sets a process of personal change for them, which connects them with the broader process of social change both locally and globally. Many of these youth enroll in college—usually in applied and interdisciplinary programs or departments such as anthropology, sociology, political sciences/international affairs, or international development[12]—and end up working in the development machinery, while others immediately engage in activism working with domestic unions, cooperatives, and grassroots organizations. Those becoming part of the development machinery usually start working at the local level in participatory local programs. Like many development practitioners working at the local level, they might after a while share discontent and frustration with the ways development operates; they might feel first in their idealism that "development is not working," and some might later realize that development is working but not solving the problems it was supposed to solve.

What I want to highlight here is the effect that this type of development volunteering practice has on the youth of hegemonic countries; thousands of young women and men can experience firsthand life in remote corners of developing countries, become aware and critical of the hegemonic role their country plays, and be willing to engage in social change to reverse dependence and poverty. If they look for a career in development, they perceive it as a form of activism, a venue for putting their commitment into practice. This is important because when we discuss the links between activism and academia, most development practitioners would identify themselves as activists. Their claim would fit into the second definition of activism provided earlier in this piece. Now, being part of the development apparatus long enough might bring disenchantment and critical views not only on hegemonic development discourses and practices but eventually on the concept of development itself. How far this disenchantment will go might depend on so many factors, like the specific organization where the individual is working, her/his academic training, peer and/or family pressures, personal attitudes, and so on, which might explain why some quit, some conform to this machinery, and some decide to stay and use it in a sort of strategic pragmatism.

Another factor to consider is the differentiation of the development machinery after the emergence of alternative paradigms like sustainable development or the capabilities/rights approach to development.[13] The 1980s witnessed a process of differentiation within the development apparatus, even though the hegemonic discourse and practice remained in place. Some organizations—for instance the Ford Foundation, the Inter-American Foundation, or OXFAM—have been more focused on participatory community development and supporting grassroots organizations, especially those organizations and potential leaders from disadvantaged groups. Others have been more committed to human rights and using the capabilities approach—for instance, the UN system developing the Human Development Index that aims to replace the GDP as the exclusive measure to compare progress made by individual countries towards development, and/or provide institutional support to human-rights frameworks and to the global struggle for indigenous peoples' rights. Even institutions like the World Bank, promoting and imposing the orthodox hegemonic development paradigm, have programs generating documents and practices that do not fit within hegemonic discourses—for instance in the case of the World Bank, their programs dealing with indigenous peoples. Another feature of development after the 1980s is the donors' preference to work with NGOs and grassroots organizations instead of the GO, which explains the exponential global growth of NGOs, a sector that offers a lot of space for activism of the second type.

This differentiation within the field of development makes it more difficult to answer the initial question "Can development bridge the gap between activism and academia?" since there is no single one but many developments, the same way there is no single one but many activisms and many academies. While this heterogeneity speaks of the contentious nature of these spaces, it also reveals multiple spaces for individual positioning, and more opportunities to work within the system against hegemonic discourses and practices. I am not delusional at all about development. I am well aware of its ultimate political aim to control the people of the "Third World," manipulating governments and elites to control the masses to prevent an autonomous democratic process that could lead to their own model of development, finally cutting the bonds of dependency for which they fought so hard during the independence wars. We all know that sixty-plus years of development have not reduced poverty or inequalities either at the local or global levels, nor have they offered ways to reduce dependency and postcolonialism.

In this regard, development can be perceived as a bureaucratic intervention that inhibits the growth of local autonomy, local forces, and visions that can reverse/reduce/eliminate the causes of poverty, inequalities, economic stagnation, and so on—an intervention that enables conditions necessary to keep the process of capitalist accumulation on a global scale. I have seen how the expansion of development at the local level can demobilize social and political activism, especially if their agendas are compatible (for instance addressing the immediate needs of poor city dwellers). When the agendas are compatible, development can depoliticize and demobilize activists working with grassroots organizations, first by reducing their focus to the immediate needs or goals that fit within the priorities of development agencies to fund a project. The strategic needs and goals, the contestation, their own broader paradigm, their level of autonomy to make decisions and remain critical, all these aspects tend to lose weight or disappear when activists or grassroots organizations come under the influence of, or depend on, donors and global development organizations. Furthermore, they might lose key leaders who might be recruited to work in the local, national, or international NGOs.[14] Excessive focus on "projects" and on the planning, implementation, and evaluation of these projects according to donors' demands and priorities can further restrict the work of activists so their operations become more bureaucratic and less able to respond to their base, their constituencies. In this regard development could be perceived as a self-reproducing apparatus that inhibits activism as a local autonomous praxis towards liberation. In some cases we can see how the expansion of development can elicit virulent forms of fundamentalism rejecting Westernization and modernization promoted by development, affecting women's agenda as part of universal individual rights, and the work of local activists.

At the same time, development can be understood as an apparatus that is internally differentiated, with some institutional spaces able to support processes, organizations, alternative views, and praxis that can be conducive to a local shift towards autonomic alternative democratic liberation and well-being. By supporting the expansive growth of NGOs and grassroots organizations, development has increased spaces for the second type of activism, as discussed earlier. This contribution becomes more relevant in contexts that are more authoritarian where the respect for human rights is in question. Providing a buffered institutional space and a legitimate rationale for local participation, for more democratic practices, for more egalitarian participation under the umbrella of development can be important to support and expand all types of activism and this way push for more democratic reforms in governance.

As we have seen, development has different meanings in different contexts, and as such it plays more than one role affecting activism and academia. It has transformed academia, bringing scholarship closer to practice. In regard to activism, development has many times been a controlling, castrating apparatus that inhibits autonomous activism. It has also created some safe spaces for activism and democratic reform to unfold. It has shown the good, the bad, and the ugly when it comes to affecting local people. Whether development can provide some institutional spaces and resources to bridge the gaps between activism and scholarship will depend on how we position ourselves in this divide, and whether we are willing and able to use these institutional spaces provided by development to advance social change.

By bringing research closer to activism, we might help to reduce the epistemological exclusion that is tied to and reproduces the social exclusion that characterizes globalization, as well presented by Appadurai (2000), who highlights the role of imagination in social life as "a positive force that encourages an emancipatory politics of globalization" (6). By expanding the circle of legitimate knowledge to include those outside academia, we should also be redefining the parameters of academic epistemology, the topics we study, and how we do it to better reflect the extreme diversity of perspectives and interests that exist outside academia. While doing this, we might as well expand our imagination to envision alternative future realities without the limits of our current epistemologies, cultures, and pragmatism—and in this process learn from subaltern visions. This process can enrich and expand the quality of academic inquiry, and empower alternative visions of development, bringing academia and development closer as they become more useful to activists engaged in bringing social change.

NOTES

1. This reflection is based on my personal experience first as a militant of Vanguardia Revolucionaria in Peru, then as a researcher and development program manager in Peru with institutions like the Instituto de Estudios Peruanos (IEP), the SR-CRSP Program coordinated by the University of California, the Instituto Interamericano de Cooperación para la Agricultura (IICA), and in Switzerland leading the Social Policy Global Program of IUCN, The World Conservation Union. My experience within American academia has been shaped by my affiliation with the University of Florida, the University of South Florida, and Brandeis University; the Society for Applied Anthropology, the American Anthropological Association, and the Latin American Studies Association; and by discussion with colleagues and friends from other American universities on this topic. It is also informed by debates on development paradigms and the postmodernist critique of development, closely related to my graduate teaching.

2. This peasant union was one of the strongest and most combatant peasant unions in Peru; after suffering extreme exploitation from landlords in the 1950s, they occupied lands in a very politicized regional movement that forced the first Land Reform Law in Peru around 1962 to contain the peasant movement and to neutralize insurgent guerrillas of De la Puente and Lobatón, which were operating in the area with local support.

3. The group I joined did not subscribe to militarist but to political strategies to prepare a popular insurrection.

4. NGO refers to nongovernmental organizations and GO to governmental organizations.

5. I stopped being a militant around 1976 and a "simpatizante" around 1983, when I cut any organic or ideological link with Vanguardia Revolucionaria and the New Left.

6. The field of international development, as well-presented in Escobar (1995), arose as a hegemonic discourse that disempowered local power, local agency, and local perspectives and voices and established the legitimacy of "expert knowledge," the new professionals in planning, sociology, demography, economics, anthropology, public health, etc., who were in charge of tracing the route for developing countries to follow the path of the United States and Europe through modernization.

7. Being a member of the Brandeis Provost's Steering Committee on Campus Diversity since 2009 has
allowed me to learn how different American universities address the issue of diversity.

8. I can think of Helen Safa, an anthropologist who pioneered studies on gender, race, and class in Latin
America and the Caribbean, and who supported so many women researchers from the region to obtain
advanced graduate degrees and establish themselves as researchers and/or policy makers; or Marianne
Schmink, who did the same supporting so many of us involved in gender, tropical conservation, and
development; or Alan Burn, supporting Mayan activists and researchers—just to mention some committed scholars I was lucky to meet while doing my doctoral studies at the University of Florida.

9. While "studium generale" (university) and "universitas" (corporation of students or teachers) existed
before 1231, after the Parens Scientiarum papal bull in 1231 was issued for the University of Paris, other
universities attained similar status, and since then autonomy became a defining feature of the university
system; see Rashdall's (2012) erudite exploration of the creation and evolution of universities in Europe.

10. This is not to ignore important mobilizations protesting this intervention, but to highlight some level of
internalization that perceives development intervention as necessary or unavoidable.

11. While the dependency theory never got full recognition or acceptance, especially from economists, it
certainly was an important critique of the modernization theory and had a large impact on scholars,
activists, and policymakers from the global South, and to a lesser extent on Northern scholars studying
issues related to development. Its critical view of development came out at a time when the global South
was articulating alternative views on the agency of the poor and on paths to social justice and social
inclusion, for instance Liberation Theology or the Pedagogy for Liberation.

12. I had the opportunity to meet many of these students at UF, USF, and Brandeis, and learning about their
experience and their personal transformation broadened my perspective on programs like the Peace
Corps.

13. The modernization paradigm never gave up its power despite being challenged by different groups
presenting different arguments—for instance, the dependency theory, the environmentalists, the
capabilities approach, and so forth. For instance, while at the Rio Conference of 1992 important agreements were signed under the new paradigm of sustainable development, the modernization theory was
still dominating the discussion on education policies for developing countries at the Jomtien 1990 World
Conference on Education for All (WCEFA), especially the argument that providing access to education for
girls would not only reduce gender inequalities, but reduce fertility rates and act as a powerful tool for
developing countries to reduce population growth. This argument is assuming that education will bring
girls into modernity and overcome traditional practices that persist due to ignorance. A good critique of
this simplistic and patronizing argument has been backed up by research in different settings that prove
that the gender gap in education reflects gender hierarchies within the household, the school, and the
community at large, which explains why reducing gender gaps in access to education is not enough to
transform the reproductive behavior of young women, especially when they have no autonomy to decide
on the timing of their marriage, on their husbands, and on controlling their fertility. See Heward and
Bunwaree (1999), Unterhalten (2005), or Arnot & Fennel (2008) for this discussion.

14. This has been also addressed for the case of women's movements in Latin America by Alvarez, Dagnino, &
Escobar (1998).

REFERENCES

Alvarez, S. E, Dagnino, E., & Escobar, A. (1998). Introduction: The cultural and the political in Latin American social movements. In S. E. Alvarez, E. Dagnino & A. Escobar (Eds.) (1998), *Culture of politics, politics of culture*. Boulder, CO: Westview Press.

Appadurai, A. (2000). Grassroots globalization and the research imagination. *Public Culture* 12 (12): 1–19.

Arnot, M., & Fennel, S. (2008). (Re)visiting education and development agendas: Contemporary gender research. In S. Fennel & M. Arnot (Eds.). (2008). *Gender education and equality in a global context: Conceptual frameworks and policy perspectives*. London: Routledge.

Cardoso, F. H., & Faletto, E. (1979). *Dependency and development in Latin America*. Berkeley: University of California Press.

Escobar, A. (1995). The problematization of poverty: The tale of the three worlds and development. In A. Escobar, *Encountering development*. Princeton, NJ: Princeton University Press.

Heward, C. (1999). Introduction: New discourses of gender, education and development. In C. Heward & S. Bunwaree (Eds.), *Gender, education and development*. London: Zed Books.

Nazarea, V. D. (2006). A view from a point: Ethnoecology as situated knowledge. In Haenn & R. Wilk (Eds.), *The environment in anthropology: A reader in ecology, culture, and sustainable living*. New York: New York University Press.

Nyden P. (2003). Academic incentives for faculty participation in community-based participatory research. *Journal of General Internal Medicine* 18 (7): 576–585.

Nyden, P., & Wiewel, W. (1992). Collaborative research: Harnessing the tensions between researcher and practitioner. *American Sociologist* 23 (4): 43–55.

Rashdall, H. (1895/2012). *The universities of Europe in the Middle Ages*. Vol. 1. Oxford: Clarendon Press.

Redclift, M. (1987). *Sustainable development: Exploring the contradictions*. London: Routledge.

So, A. Y. (1990). *Social change and development: Modernization, dependency, and world-system theories*. Newbury Park, CA: Sage Publications.

Stahl, R., & Shdaimah, C. (2008). Collaboration between community advocates and academic researchers: Scientific advocacy or political research? *British Journal of Social Work* 38: 1610–1629.

Unterhalten, E. (2005). Fragmented frameworks? Researching women, gender, education and development. In S. Aikman & E. Unterhalten, *Beyond access: Transforming policy and practice for gender equality in education*. Oxford: Oxfam.

Weiss, C. H. (1991). Policy research as advocacy: Pro and con. *Knowledge and Policy: The International Journal of Knowledge Transfer* 4 (1 & 2): 37–55.

Leaving the Field: How to Write about Disappointment and Frustration in Collaborative Research

Ulrich Oslender

A phenomenologist must tell everything.

—Gaston Bachelard, *The Poetics of Space*

Collaborative research is back on the agenda these days. It has certainly become more accepted in mainstream academia than back in the 1970s, when Orlando Fals Borda and others developed what came to be known as Participatory Action-Research (PAR). Research councils are increasingly interested in funding collaborative research proposals, seemingly willing to listen to and learn from the experiences of subaltern groups. Surprisingly, maybe, much collaborative research reinvents itself today without reference to the pioneering work of Fals Borda and others. One of the lacunae of methodological engagement is the lack of addressing issues of *fracaso*, or failure, where the academic-activist him/herself has experienced deep disappointment or frustration in the way the research situation unfolded on the ground. In this chapter, I want to reflect on a collaborative research experience that I have been involved in, and critically think through those situations that resulted in personal disappointment, as I was facing the limitations in the field of my maybe too naive approach to collaborative research. I have so far refrained from writing about these issues, as they pose significant ethical problems in possibly identifying research partners, who are part of this story of disappointment. However, I believe that it is only through critically examining and addressing the failures and frustrations of collaborative research agendas that those disappointments may be avoided in the future. *How* to write about these failures—or if to write at all about them—is a question not easily answered.

Meeting Don Agapito

It was already getting dark as I climbed the steps of a wooden ladder that led to a small platform from which I entered the house of Don Agapito. He was waiting for me, rocking back and forth in his armchair. It was a hot and humid afternoon in the tropics. I was only just beginning to get used to this climate. "Buenas tardes, Don Agapito," I greeted my host and stretched out my hand to shake his, immeasurably larger and firmer, as befits a peasant farmer and fisherman who at eighty-plus years old still seemed fit and strong.

I had come to talk with Don Agapito about his life growing up along the riverbanks of the Colombian Pacific Coast region. Recent legislation had opened up channels for rural Afro-descendant populations in this region to apply for collective land titles. This had triggered widespread political mobilization throughout the myriad of river basins that make up the Pacific lowlands. As a new territorial regime was introduced, discussions ensued over how to demarcate the lands to be titled. In countless meetings and workshops—formal and informal—the collective memory of local populations was mobilized to reflect on past ways of occupying their territories and what these might hold for future strategies of territorialization. The elderly—traditionally respected in those communities—were seen as rich sources of knowledge about land, customs, and history. Most of this information was passed on through generations in the oral tradition. And this was precisely what I wanted to explore with Don Agapito: his relationship to the land and the river, and what he thought about the exciting new political possibilities that were opening up, and around which a growing social movement of black communities was forming in Colombia. At the time, in the mid-1990s, I was beginning to examine what I would later call the "geographies of social movements" and how these were informed by and constituted through local epistemologies and everyday practices surrounding the "aquatic space" in that region (Oslender 2002, 2004, 2007).

I sat opposite Don Agapito, a cup of *agua de panela* in my hand, which his wife had offered me during her brief appearance, upon which she disappeared again behind a curtain that presumably led to the kitchen. As Don Agapito kept rocking back and forth in his armchair, he began to tell me about his life as a boy fishing in the rivers and accompanying the elderly (*los viejos*) on their at times long trips into the hinterland (*el monte*) where they went hunting. On these journeys in their dugout canoes, they spent their time challenging each other in ritual storytelling that often took on the form of *décimas*: poems with a fairly complex rhyming structure. In fact, Don Agapito loved to perform these *décimas* throughout his life. I was fortunate, as he still remembered them and was quite happy for me to record them on my at the time rudimentary recording device.

I was thrilled of course at this opportunity that had come up quite by chance (and I think we need to theorize this element of chance in our fieldwork and research methodology much better, as it opens up these often unsuspected channels of encounters—those "chance encounters" that end up impacting significantly on our understanding of a particular research situation; see also Benford in this volume on "the accidental activist scholar"). A few days earlier I had visited the local office of the biodiversity conservation program Biopacífico. There they had mentioned Don Agapito as being one of the recognized elders in town, respected *decimero*—or poet of the oral tradition. Two days later, then, I sat in his living room, enchanted by the wealth of his stories, his capacity to recite long poems, and in general his gusto to talk about those days past (while frequently complaining about the current state of his health).

All of a sudden a group of three young people (well, they were my age at the time) came into the room and asked me in no uncertain terms who I was, what I was doing there, and who had authorized my presence. I was flabbergasted. Who were these people? And what right did they have to storm into Don Agapito's house and ask me all these questions? I didn't know what to say or how to react. I looked over at Don Agapito. He kept rocking back and forth in his armchair as he had done for the last hour. The expression on his face did not change a bit. I was shell-shocked. It was then that one of the gang of three stepped forward and explained that they were members of the regional community organization of black communities; that they should be informed if anyone wanted to do "research" in their community; that all those gringos had wreaked enough havoc already in the region; that times were changing.

I immediately realized my mistake. I really should have known better. I knew of a number of community organizations active in town and should really have contacted them beforehand. In fact, I had intended to do so, but was so thrilled by the opportunity to talk to Don Agapito that I had put this concern momentarily aside. What followed was my attempt to explain my situation: who I was, where I was coming from, and with what objectives—doing ethnography—and that no, I was not one of those dodgy gringos coming to exploit local knowledges to then sell those on. It was an awkward situation.

However, as time went by, the initially slightly aggressive tone underlying the conversation subsided. Don Agapito's wife had entered the room again and brought more cups of *agua de panela* for the visitors. It turned out that the woman in the group was in fact Don Agapito's granddaughter. We had all sat down by then, and suddenly I found myself talking to them about the University of Glasgow (where I was doing my PhD studies at the time). They were particularly interested in hearing about the growing signs of devolution in Scotland and if that was the first step for independence from the UK. And they told me in return about attempts by some to push for the devolution of the Pacific Coast region from the Colombian state, an argument based on the region's strong cultural specificity due to its ethnic composition, with almost 95 percent of its population Afro-Colombians. In sum, our initially awkward encounter turned into a friendly and animated discussion, exploring common links and experiences, connecting local realities in the Colombian Pacific lowlands (territorial reorderings and cultural politics) to wider global processes of political change. My interlocutors were young and educated former university students themselves, keen on understanding the intersections of local and global processes to better place their own *lucha* in the wider history of minority rights, land, and peasant struggles.

It was in this first discussion—which was followed by many more in the days to come—that the idea emerged of doing a more collaborative kind of research. I felt that my own research questions could be usefully drawn upon in the communities' project of a "recovery" of their collective memories, as they called it. To me, my own research interests acquired a potential relevance for the political project of the social movement of black communities that I had not foreseen until then. The initial encounter with these three activists had clearly forced me to rethink my fieldwork strategy, but it also opened up new channels of doing research that I felt were exciting. Again, it was this coincidental encounter that set off this process, and I would argue that fieldwork is often made up of experiences of this kind and of "chance encounters." As far as I know, nobody has so far tried to theorize these relations in any great depth; after all, theorizing about chance—*el azar*—is a difficult and, to many in the social sciences no doubt, an "unscientific" procedure.[1] How do we want to hold something in place for long enough to construct a theory of it, if it is based on randomness and nothing graspable? We might as well concur with the philosopher Patrick Suppes's view that the universe is essentially probabilistic in character, or, to put it in more colloquial language, that the world is full of random happenings (Suppes 1984, 27).

Yet, I believe we should embrace these random happenings as part and parcel of the fieldwork experience. We should address them head on as a constructive force in research, and not just shy away from them as if we had to be embarrassed to acknowledge the presence of elements of chance in our ways of "doing research." From this view, owning up to the chance elements in fieldwork could be a rebuff to the well-rehearsed critique—coming mostly from the quarters of the quantitative converts of number-crunching teleology—that qualitative research methodologies are "unscientific." I also object to the many attempts to make qualitative methodology more "scientific" by force-feeding us more technological gadgets that would somehow streamline and discipline what are by nature very messy affairs. Anyone who has ever submitted a funding application to a research council knows what I am talking about. The last decades have seen the emergence of a "tyranny of methodology" in the research councils, often dominated by the disciples of quantitative monotheistic religion, where any kind of qualitative research increasingly has had to "justify" its means and scientific worthiness by incorporating discourse-analysis software programs and other technological gadgets to streamline and control the one thing that makes qualitative research so powerful and rewarding: personal, in-depth reflection and analysis, often stretched out over time.

As a result of this "trying to please" and "beg to be considered relevant" trend, all kinds of supposedly new research methodologies have sprung up. Nowhere does this seem to be as obvious as in the field of collaborative research. Surprisingly, however, much collaborative research reinvents itself today without even the slightest reference to the pioneering work of Colombian sociologist Orlando Fals Borda and others in what came to be termed Participatory Action-Research (PAR)—known as *Investigación Acción Participativa* (IAP) in Latin America. It may appear that in the heat of being "new," the "old" is just left by the roadside.[2] Referring to a large gathering in Cartagena, Colombia, in 1997 that celebrated the twentieth anniversary of the global launching of the PAR movement, for example, the Colombian anthropologist Arturo Escobar tellingly states that "these more third world–oriented gatherings tend to go unreported in northern accounts of the global justice movement" (2008, 365). It is therefore useful to briefly review PAR in the light of this "trend to forget," and to reflect on reengaging some of its central proposals.

Participatory Action-Research (PAR)

In Colombia PAR has become mainly associated with the Colombian sociologist Orlando Fals Borda, who regards "the participatory action-research approach as an original input from the world periphery, a dialogical research oriented to the social situation in which people live" (Fals Borda 1987, 336). Another of PAR's leading figures, Mohammed Rahman, describes the theoretical stance of PAR in these words:

> The basic ideology of PAR is that conscious classes and groups, those which at present are poor and oppressed, will transform their environment progressively via their own praxis. In this process other people can play a catalytic and supportive role, but they will not be able to dominate the process. (Rahman 1991, 23; my translation)

PAR was initially conceived in the 1970s as a response to

> the miserable situations of our societies, to the excessive specialization and the void of academic life, and to the sectarian practices of a great part of the revolutionary left. We felt that transformations of society as well as of scientific knowledge, which had generally remained in the Newtonian era with its reductionist and instrumental orientation, were necessary and urgent. To begin with, we decided to embark on the search for adequate answers to the dilemmas of those who had been victims of the oligarchies and their politics of development: the poor rural communities." (Rahman & Fals Borda 1991, 39; my translation)

Until 1977 PAR was characterized by activism and even anti-professionalism. Gustavo Esteva (1987, 128) stresses the ambiguous positionality of the activist and researcher, and promotes the idea of a "de-professionalized intellectual" as the only way of working with oppressed groups and against established academic models and paradigms. In his contribution to this volume (chapter 2), discussing his own experience of sharing time at a community school in Chiapas, Mexico, Esteva shows what the interactions between a de-professionalized intellectual and oppressed groups in resistance may look like. Many of the early PAR activists actually renounced their academic posts as they became more deeply involved with PAR projects.[3] The early efforts of PAR were strongly influenced by other participatory research methodologies such as *intervention sociologique*, promoted by the French sociologist Alain Touraine (1988), and the concept of *conscientização*, developed by the Brazilian educator and advocate of critical pedagogy Paulo Freire (1971). The latter in particular—understood as a process of learning to perceive social, political, and economic contradictions and to take action against the oppressive elements of reality—provided the basis for a more clearly articulated methodology in PAR: one in which the traditional division between researcher (subject) and the researched (object) was substituted by a subject/subject relation, wherein a dialogue with the people about their actions was to take place (Freire 1971, 38–39) and mutual trust would exist between researcher and the subjects of the study (46–47), leading to a reflective participation on the part of the people (52). Such a process also implied the "rebirth" of the researcher him/herself (47), a notion that has consequently been developed both by Spivak (1996), who insists on the need to unlearn one's own privileges when conducting research, and Esteva (1987, 141), who stresses the need for unlearning the language of domination. Freire was mostly concerned with a new "pedagogy for the oppressed," rejecting the traditional "banking concept of education," which feeds students with information in a teacher/subject–student/object relation without encouraging critical thinking, thereby serving the interests of oppression (Freire 1971, 64). He advocated a "problem-posing education," which would respond to the essence of consciousness in the student as intentional historical subject, taking historicity as a starting point.

PAR took these considerations a step further by emphasizing the factor of "action" in the dialogical research between oppressed groups and researchers. The International Symposium on Research Action and Scientific Analysis, which took place in Cartagena, Colombia, in 1977, provided a first international space of reflection on the advances of PAR in the theoretical and methodological fields, as well as a first measurement of its practical implications and success. Some seventy-five researchers and activists from different parts of the world analyzed the advances of their participatory research methodologies as applied in the field. These exchanges and discussions resulted in two volumes that came formally to constitute PAR. As Rahman and Fals Borda state retrospectively:

> We began to understand PAR as a research methodology with an evolution towards a subject/subject relation in order to form symmetrical, horizontal and non-exploitative standards in social, economic and political life, and as a part of social activism with an ideological and spiritual commitment in order to promote (collective) popular praxis. (Rahman & Fals Borda 1991, 40; my translation)

These aims were further articulated during the Tenth International Congress of Sociology in Mexico in 1982. As a result of the collective exercise of self-reflection on the part of the researchers and activists involved, a wider field of action was explored, transcending the initially somewhat restricted peasant and communitarian questions to include dimensions of urban, economic, and regional life.

PAR thus developed into a "revolutionary science," which "becomes a real possibility, not only a felt necessity" (Fals Borda 1987, 330). It now implies a demystification of research, not conducted any longer exclusively by detached "expert" academics, but as collective research where researchers and the subjects of the study work together in defining the aims and methodology of the study. Fals Borda conceives of PAR as contributing to a "people's power":

> the capacity of the grass-roots groups, which are exploited socially and economically, to articulate and systematise knowledge (both their own and that which comes from outside) in such a way that they can become protagonists in the advancement of their society and in defence of their own class and group interests." (Fals Borda 1987, 330)

People's power hence acts as a "countervailing power exercised against exploitative systems" (Fals Borda 1987, 331).[4] The emphasis on action differentiates PAR from other forms of participatory research such as Touraine's (1988) *intervention sociologique*. It shares with these research methods the view that the outsider/researcher is crucial in setting off and guiding processes of self-reflection of the subordinate, suppressed groups or social movements, and of providing contexts that go beyond the immediately visible implications for any one group: "Catalytic external agents play a crucial role in linking up the local dimension to regional and, at a later stage, to the national and the international levels" (Fals Borda 1987, 334).

An objection can be raised to this claim of the outsider/researcher setting off processes of self-reflection in the subordinate, in that it seems to imply that the subordinate cannot make their own connections and reflections, and that the role of the researcher is one close to an intellectual vanguard. There is a danger that PAR gives a priority to the role of the researcher by denying the self-reflective capacities of the people. However, rather than rejecting the researcher's possible contribution in these self-reflective processes altogether, we should stress his/her potentially, although not necessarily, positive impact by adding a dynamic and giving some kind of orientation to these processes.

Four points have been identified as major supporting columns of the emerging edifice that is PAR:

1. *collective research on a group basis*. This process implies a conscious dialogue between the

researcher and the people that allows for a social validation of objective knowledge and is regarded as a service to the community. It takes the form of meetings and workshops, which the researcher organizes and where locals are encouraged to engage in a process of articulated self-reflexivity. This is intended to raise awareness and consciousness of their situation (the process of conscientization, *conscientização*). The researcher acts here as the catalytic agent to stimulate and to contribute to this debate.

2. *critical recovery of history.* The aim is to tap into the collective memory of communities, which at times may be invisible or buried. Traces can often be found in the oral tradition, especially with the elderly, in the form of stories, poems, and legends. These stories are rich in symbolisms and metaphors. Furthermore, they are commonly place-specific in that they are rooted and grounded in particular environments, with references to specific places, customs, and people. The recovery of a community's collective memory in this respect has been argued to function as a "grass-roots corrector of official history" (Fals Borda 1987, 341).[5] It makes practical use of the concept of "memory as a site of resistance" (Foucault 1980), in that new visions and alternative projects can be imagined and put into practice based on a people's historical experiences.

3. *valuing and applying folk culture.* Closely connected to the previous point, aspects of local folk culture such as traditional music, dances, storytelling, and religious beliefs are actively applied in the articulation of a people's struggle:

All these elements of oral culture may be exploited as a new and dynamic political language which belongs to the people . . . Feelings, imagination and the sense of play are apparently inexhaustible sources of strength and resistance among the people. These three elements have a common basis which cannot be ignored in the struggle to promote mobilisation and people's power in our countries: religious beliefs. (Fals Borda 1987, 343)

4. *production and diffusion of new knowledge.* As a final step there has to be a systematic dissemination of the knowledge derived from dialogical research. As Fals Borda (1987, 344) stresses, "there is an obligation to return this knowledge systematically to the communities and workers' organizations because they continue to be its owners." Fals Borda himself has proposed and practiced an interesting form that this systematic return of knowledge could take. In his well-known *Historia Doble de la Costa*—a project published in four volumes between 1979 and 1986—the presentation and diffusion of research findings constitute a "double history" that applies two different narrative styles parallel to one another—one for academic purposes and another one for local consumption. In the publication, the left page narrates, analyzes, and explains the research and its results in an academic vocabulary, whereas the right page uses a more colloquial language explaining to the academically uninitiated reader the content, context, and analysis of the problematic.

This kind of presentation of research results has been criticized by some, however, as exposing a patronizing attitude that PAR may develop, and also the lack of a closer identification of the researcher with the subjects of the study. This is because there is still a differentiation in the language chosen, thus emphasizing the perceived intellectual superiority of the researcher. At the same time PAR has been, and still is, criticized by the reactionary elements in the academy as "nonscientific" and subjective. These elements, of course, hide behind claims of objective scientific research, untenable in any case, and simply do not engage with the subjects of their study. Knowingly or unknowingly, they promote the "continuation of a hierarchical idea of knowledge that falsifies and maintains structures of domination," as the African American feminist critic bell hooks (1991, 128) would say.

PAR, "Chance Encounters," and Frustrations

I don't intend to go into the various critiques that PAR has been confronted with over the years. Of course, its very language may seem to some pertaining to a different age, rooted in structuralist thought that didn't give a damn about postmodern uncertainties. Others may find a perceived hierarchy troubling, in which the external researcher as "catalytic agent" seems to play a deterministic, possibly patronizing role. However, what does stand out in PAR is the serious and systematic engagement with local knowledges (the "folk culture" in point 3 above) and the critical role of collective memory. It is in my opinion not that far removed from the "decolonizing option" that adherents of the Modernity/Coloniality/Decoloniality framework propose today (Escobar 2008; Mignolo 2005); yet they hardly ever mention PAR.

To me it was clear that I could not stamp a PAR project out of the ground like that. Particularly point 1—collective research on a group basis—requires an enormous amount of preparation and discussions before embarking on a formal PAR project. However, on a more informal basis, it became apparent in the conversations with community activists that our respective interests overlapped and could be mutually beneficially pooled together. My research thus became more collaborative as it went on. I accompanied movement leaders on their trips to river communities. I held workshops on "social cartography" (exploring territorial perceptions with local communities that were drawn upon in the demarcation of lands to be titled collectively). We had hours and hours of meetings and discussions.

One of my concerns was what I perceived to be a lack of cooperation between the various community organizations active in the region. I had introduced myself to all these groups and began to propose collaborative research relations. Yet, clearly there were divisions between these groups, and I increasingly felt this to be a real hindrance in the advancement of what seemed to me the principal political goal: namely, the territorial empowerment of local communities vis-à-vis the state and capital-driven exploitation of their lands. I addressed these concerns with the various groups and made it pretty clear that I thought this lack of cooperation to be extremely destructive. I realized that personal issues between movement leaders played a part in the animosity with which they confronted each other. I got increasingly desperate with what appeared to be petty divisiveness. As a last act of trying to help to reconcile the different groups—what made me think that I could do that in the first place?—I invited movement leaders to a dinner in my house . . . alas, no one showed up. This situation was no doubt the largest frustration of my attempt at collaborative research, as it quite painfully showed up the limitations of my potential as "external catalytic agent" (in PAR speech).

I never wrote about this frustration before, and I am still not sure I should. After all, what good can come of it? Would it be harmful to the movement to be portrayed in my writing as one where internal bickering took precedence over the "real" issues of representing community interests in relation to the Colombian state? Would my story of divisiveness not be counterproductive to the construction of a people's power that Fals Borda claims as one of the central objectives of PAR?

In the end, time went by, and now, some fifteen years later, I am less traumatized by what happened. Was it really as bad as it felt at the time? (Yes, it was.) Is it not natural for differences to occur in all social mobilization processes? (Yes, but did they have to be so destructive?)

So what could be learned from this *fracaso*? First, it taught me to be humble in my approach to fieldwork. To accept the limitations. To not see myself as a "catalytic agent," but rather a friend who accompanies the political process with whatever modest contributions are at my disposal. Being a friend of the process also means to accept the imperfections of political mobilization; to work on them, yes; but to despair over them? No. Quite the contrary, the limitations and failures themselves can be mobilized in future collaborative work in order to better define expectations and possibilities. Second, it taught me to recognize the process of political mobilization for what it is: a process. A process that goes through various phases. Today, fifteen years later, new alliances have built in the region; previously antagonistically opposed movement leaders work together (God knows how they got it sorted out!) and they have moved on. They always do. With or without me. Again, humbleness helps.

In one particular incident, what felt like a frustration at the time has turned into a positive outcome—with time. In 1999, I suggested to a group of activists that we change the name of the local airport in a direct action event. At the time the airport was named after Julio Arboleda. If asked who this person was, those people in Colombia who had actually heard of him would answer that he was a well-known poet. In fact, Julio Arboleda was one of the country's most cruel slave owners. He was from the town of Popayán and owned a number of gold mines in the Pacific Coast region. Shortly before the official abolition of slavery in 1851, he sold 99 adult slaves and 113 child slaves for 31,410 pesos to Peru (Mina 1975, 40–41), thereby not only defying the ideas of abolition but also acting illegally since it was then already against the law to sell slaves abroad.[6]

Irony has it that Julio Arboleda should be widely known as a recognized poet, even in the area of the Pacific Coast by the descendants of the very enslaved he mistreated and sold. To me it seemed incomprehensible that the local airport was named after this man, in a town where the population consists of over 90 percent Afro-Colombians. Yet, even leaders of black communities remembered Julio Arboleda as a poet and not as a cruel slave owner. Julio Arboleda has entered official history as a respected poet, and his blood-stained hands and heart have been whitewashed by collective amnesia and dominant historical representations.

As we sat around the patio of my house, reflecting on a necessary name change of the local airport, some proposed to name it after a local female educator. The next day we painted a banner with the new name, which was to cover the "letters that said slavery" at the airport, agreed on a time for the event to take place, and arranged for the local radio station to cover the direct action live. However, at the last minute some leaders retracted their support for the idea and argued that it might be better to discuss the issue with the mayor instead of using direct action. It was probably a wise decision not to go ahead with the planned action, as an already nervous police force, alert to the presence of guerrilla forces in nearby river basins, might have reacted in a hostile manner, which to assess was clearly beyond our planifications. Nevertheless, I felt frustrated over what I perceived as a failure at the time to make a potentially significant statement in the "critical recovery of history" (point 2 in the PAR model). Catalytic agent or not, I was very happy to hear from my friends that in 2005 the incoming municipal administration made the name change of the airport one of their priorities. Today the airport is in fact named after the local historian and practitioner of folk culture Juan Casiano Solís. It seems that PAR's third point—valuing and applying folk culture—has been adhered to in the renaming process.

Concluding Remarks

The universe is essentially probabilistic in character. The world is full of random happenings. Chance encounters frame our everyday lives. They equally impact on our ethnographic fieldwork experiences, often opening up hitherto unsuspected channels of examination. Chance thereby becomes a constitutive element of fieldwork. We should embrace this possibility as an essential characteristic of human interaction in the world and not ignore it or hide behind some ill-conceived conceit that only if we control the research situation completely by eliminating coincidence, do we "do science."

At the same time, frustrations and failures form part and parcel of the experience of collaborative research. Rather than trying to ignore them, or keeping quiet about them, we should embrace them as constitutive of the research process. The ethics of collaborative research would caution us against exposing our research partners in a negative light. Yet, admitting to frustrations, failures, or internal dissent within a social movement, for example, does not necessarily have to be a destructive impulse or treason. Quite the contrary, it can help improve our understanding of always messy research constellations on the ground, and perhaps help us avoid making the same mistakes again. *How* to write about these failures—or if to write at all about them—is an altogether different question and one that I have still not answered, and maybe never will.

NOTES

1. I am discounting here the efforts in philosophy, as they have been found to be unsatisfactory, mostly geared towards the "mathematics of chance" and often blurring the boundaries between objectivist and subjectivist views of chance, such as in Richard Johns's (2002) "causal theory of chance."

2. As a case in point, and just to illustrate this wider trend, Rachel Pain in her three-part "review of action-oriented research" in the prestigious journal *Progress in Human Geography* does not mention once Fals Borda (Pain 2003, 2004, 2006). In her only mention of PAR, she somewhat bizarrely states that "participatory action research [is] more common in high-income countries" (Pain 2004, 653). Worrying also is Geraldine Pratt's (2000, 574) assessment that "Participatory action research is a research process that emerged out of feminist and humanistic geography." It didn't do that at all. PAR has been used in feminist and humanistic geography, but it emerged "as an original input from the world periphery" (Fals Borda 1987, 336). I do not intend to single out Pain or Pratt for their omissions and misrepresentations, but rather to stress the more general amnesia that has befallen much of the debates about action research. For a welcome exception, see Breitbart (2010), who discusses PAR in some detail. Incidentally, and while usually taken with a pinch of salt, the Wikipedia entry for PAR is excellent: http://en.wikipedia.org/wiki/Participatory_action_research.

3. Similarly in the late 1960s, with the emergence of radical geographies, U.S. geographer William Bunge

argued against the "tyranny of professionalization" in the academy and quite literally took geography out into the streets of Detroit to apply the discipline practically in attempts at solving real and tangible social problems (Bunge 1977).

4. Again a comparison can be drawn between the PAR approach and debates in geography in the late 1960s, when calls for a *people's geography* were made by early radical geographers who lamented the disjuncture between an established academic geography and real-world socioeconomic problems and struggles. To them, a people's geography would study these problems with an eye to devising viable solutions in a way that included the ordinary people who were subject to those problems and solutions. Reminiscent of earlier debates on geographical activism that can be traced back to the anarchist geographer Pyotr Kropotkin (1899/1995), radical geographers wanted research to focus on politically charged questions, in which geographers themselves became involved with the people and communities under study to work together on solution-finding processes. One of the most original attempts at such a people's geography can be found in William Bunge's "Geographical Expeditions" in Detroit (Bunge 1977).

5. Some may worry about this suggestion that there exists a truer or more authentic account of history. However, I believe that there *is* in fact a more authentic history to be recovered from other voices, and that it is a postmodern conceit to think that this is not the case, and that we should not think in these terms. The notion of a "corrector of official history," rather than an argument for a complete replacement of official history by a "people's history," stresses the need to take seriously those "other voices," and to uncover those previously unheard, ignored, or silenced histories that shed a new light on and thus "correct" official versions of History with a capital H.

6. The Law of Womb Liberty from 1821 states in article 6 that "it is rigorously forbidden to sell slaves outside of Colombian territory," and article 7 prohibited all kinds of negotiations with slaves.

REFERENCES

Bachelard, G. (1958/1994). *The poetics of space.* Boston: Beacon Press.

Breitbart, M. (2010). Participatory research methods. In N. Clifford, S. French & G. Valentine (Eds.), *Key methods in geography*, 141–156. London: Sage.

Bunge, W. (1977). The first years of the Detroit Geographical Expedition: A personal report. In R. Peet (Ed.), *Radical geography: Alternative viewpoints on contemporary social issues*, 31–39. London: Methuen.

Escobar, A. (2008). *Territories of difference: Place, movements, life, redes.* Durham, NC: Duke University Press.

Esteva, G. (1987). Regenerating people's space. *Alternatives* 12: 125–152.

Fals Borda, O. (1979–1986). *Historia doble de la costa* (4 vols.). Bogotá: Editores Carlos Valencia.

Fals Borda, O. (1987). The application of participatory action-research in Latin America. *International Sociology* 2 (4): 329–347.

Foucault, Michel (1980), *Power-knowledge: selected interviews and other writings 1972–1977*, Brighton: Harvester Press.

Freire, P. (1971). *Pedagogy of the oppressed.* New York: Herder and Herder.

hooks, b. (1991). y*earning: race, gender, and cultural politics.* London: Turnaround.

Johns, R. (2002). *A theory of physical probability.* Toronto: University of Toronto Press.

Mignolo, W. (2005). *The idea of Latin America.* Oxford: Blackwell.

Mina, M. (1975). *Esclavitud y libertad en el valle del Río Cauca.* Bogotá: Fundación Rosca.

Oslender, U. (2002). The logic of the river: A spatial approach to ethnic-territorial mobilization in the Colombian Pacific region. *Journal of Latin American Anthropology* 7 (2): 86–117.

Oslender, U. (2004). Fleshing out the geographies of social movements: Colombia's Pacific coast black communities and the aquatic space. *Political Geography* 23 (8): 957–985.

Oslender, U. (2007). Re-visiting the hidden transcript: Oral tradition and black cultural politics in the Colombian Pacific coast region. *Environment & Planning D: Society & Space* 25 (6): 1103–1129.

Pain, R. (2003). Social geography: On action-orientated research. *Progress in Human Geography* 27 (5): 649–657.

Pain, R. (2004). Social geography: Participatory research. *Progress in Human Geography* 28 (5): 652–663.

Pain, R. (2006). Social geography: Seven deadly myths in policy research. *Progress in Human Geography* 30 (2): 250–259.

Pratt, G. (2000). Participatory action research. In R. Johnston, D. Gregory, G. Pratt & M. Watts (Eds.), *The Dictionary of Human Geography* (4th ed.), 574. Oxford: Blackwell.

Rahman, M. A. (1991). El punto de vista teórico de la IAP. In O. Fals Borda & M. A. Rahman (Eds.), *Acción y conocimiento: Cómo romper el monopolio con Investigación-Acción Participativa*, 21–35. Bogotá: Cinep.

Rahman, M. A., & Fals Borda, O. (1991). Un repaso de la IAP. In O. Fals Borda & M. A. Rahman (Eds.), *Acción y conocimiento: Cómo romper el monopolio con Investigación-Acción Participativa*, 37–50. Bogotá: Cinep.

Spivak, G. C. (1996). *The Spivak reader: Selected works of Gayatri Chakravorty Spivak* (edited by Donna Landry and Gerald MacLean). London: Routledge.

Suppes, P. (1984). *Probabilistic metaphysics.* Oxford: Blackwell.

Touraine, A. (1988). *The return of the actor.* Minneapolis: University of Minnesota Press.

Invisible Heroes

Eshe Lewis

> I am invisible, understand, simply because people refuse to see me.
>
> —Ralph Ellison, *Invisible Man*

European intellectual traditions dominate the mindsets and frameworks of scholars and intellectuals all over the world. The people who produced these frameworks are well known. Their lives and thoughts are transmitted from generation to generation in textbooks and novels, their images reproduced by the media. There are, however, many unsung heroes—people whose ideas could help others, providing them with alternative frameworks for thought and analysis, whose lives could inspire by example, because their work for justice and equality has impacted many lives in their own countries. The lives and works of most of them remain unknown to the world in many cases because they do not communicate in English, or because they are part of a culture that relies strongly on orality, so that they have not published their thoughts. They are rendered invisible through an active process of "invisibilization" in which Western culture mutes their voices (Gordillo & Hirsh 2003). Women and nonwhites are the foremost victims of this invisibilization, due to prevailing legacies of racism, sexism, and (neo)colonialism that continue to venerate and normalize white, male, Western dominance in most parts of the world.

Latin America has a rich history of opposition to colonial domination and, in the face of the extreme inequality that characterizes the region, of rebelling against oppression, and struggling to construct better, more inclusive societies (Moraña, Dussel & Jáurequi 2008). In fact, dire circumstances marked by great social and political hostility have borne powerful discourses of liberation and revolution during which Latin American and Caribbean thinkers have shared their visions of equality and hope for social change with the rest of the region and the world (Gilroy 1993). The twentieth century alone has witnessed profound writings by exemplary figures such as Cuban ex-president Fidel Castro, the Argentine revolutionary Ernesto "Che" Guevara, Liberation theologists from Peru (Gustavo Gutierrez) and Nicaragua (Ernesto Cardenal), the Mirabal sisters of the Dominican Republic, and the Martinican authors and thinkers Aimé Césaire and Frantz Fanon. Their words, ideologies, and actions have inspired millions and sparked movements that have had profound effects on their own nations and others around the world.

While the aspirations of some of these figures are known at the national, regional, and international levels, others who have contributed selflessly and continue to fight tirelessly in the name of social justice, equity, and equality remain anonymous. In the interest of bringing the work of a few remarkable individuals to light, this chapter introduces six influential minority-rights leaders of Latin America. All of them are very well known and respected in their own countries, even as some are not officially recognized by their own governments, and are rendered invisible by the mainstream media. Their international invisibility, however, is paramount. They are African descendants, members of the largest marginalized group in Latin America that consistently experiences disproportionately high rates of racial, cultural, political, and economic discrimination, and extreme rates of poverty and illiteracy fostered by a lack of basic public services and infrastructure (Morrison 2007; Telles 2007). In the face of adversity, and eclipsed by the dominant discourses and power of Europe and North America, as well as those of the white and mestizo upper classes in Latin America, these leaders denounce the structural and everyday racism that forms the core of most Latin American national ideologies about race and citizenship (Andrews 2004; Whitten & Torres 1998; Minority Rights Group 1995).

The black leaders, advocates, intellectuals, writers, speakers, and organizers introduced below are thus of great importance to their countries—Colombia, Peru, Bolivia, and Ecuador—and the region. Their struggles for justice and equality are not only heroic, as some of them have faced death threats and continue to put their lives on the line for their cause, they are also epic, as the well-being of some 150 million Afro-Latin Americans critically depend on their ability to organize and press national and international governing bodies to implement changes that will improve their quality of life and future opportunities. Thus, the individuals introduced here all play key roles in this monumental collective effort aimed at justice, equality, and brotherhood—promises that have been systematically denied to African descendants of the Americas.

The interviews upon which this chapter is constructed were conducted in Panama City, Panama, in May 2012. The University of South Florida's Institute for the Study of Latin America and the Caribbean (ISLAC) invited these six leaders to a conference and planning meeting in order to define the contours of a joint project: the Frantz Fanon Summer Training Institute for African Descendant Community Leaders of the Americas. The six participating community leaders were part of a working group, which also included ISLAC staff, a small number of academics with experience in this field, and a few funding-organization representatives. The community leaders represented a larger group of twenty-five black community-based organizations from different Latin American and Caribbean countries. All of these organizations have created educational projects in their respective countries, targeting their African-descendant populations. The working group had met several times before the 2012 meeting in Panama, and they had already decided that they wanted to join forces and share their experiences, build networks among themselves, and thus benefit from each other's experiences. ISLAC provided the necessary institutional framework for this joint effort.

Through survey research, ISLAC staff were able to map the priorities of the twenty-five black organizations that responded to this survey, and detected that academia could also play a role in this networking effort of Latin American and Caribbean black community organizations. Most surveyed organizations expressed a wish to learn from the experiences of other, similar groups, operating in different countries. They also wanted to gain access to formal academic titles and integrate university-level content into the curriculum—a strategy aimed at balancing out the informal certifications that are common among their young activists. ISLAC thus took on the role of an institution able to facilitate this interchange and to coordinate the effort to marry academic and grassroots knowledge in order to respond to the local needs of African-descendant communities of the Americas. This, in turn, resonated with previous efforts by the coordinator of this project at ISLAC, Bernd Reiter, who had already organized a conference in 2010 aimed at sharing academic knowledge with local communities of African descent (see Reiter and Simmons 2012).

The idea of a summer training institute for African-descendant community leaders was created to satisfy the need for an exchange between academia and grassroots activism. It would serve to build networks and share experiences among local black community and advocacy groups; allow organic, local knowledge to receive official recognition; and facilitate the sharing of knowledge produced in academia to allow academics to give their research practical relevance and meaning beyond narrow academic procedure. In May 2012, this working group gave final definition to the launching of the Frantz Fanon Summer Institute.

I was invited by the organizers to attend as an observer and record keeper—a role that allowed me to conduct interviews with the participants and record meeting notes. As a doctoral anthropology student working on issues of race, racism, and gender in Latin America, and with special interest in Peru, I was well acquainted with most of the people present at this meeting and was familiar with the organizations they represented. I conducted and audio-recorded all of the interviews in Spanish over the course of the Panama conference. The transcriptions were sent to the interviewees for verification and transparency, and upon receiving their final approval, I translated them into English. The transcripts have not been altered apart from shortening the quotations that appear below in some cases. To provide further context, I give some biographical information on each interviewee and a summary of their work in the organizations that they have either founded or currently direct.

In the context and anticipation of the opening of the leadership school, these interview excerpts provide an opportunity to learn more about the hopes, dreams, knowledge, and visions of leaders who will be at the forefront of the project. This is a chance to learn from them as they describe in their own words what they strive to achieve, and what they hope to pass on to another generation of Afro-descendants who will join them in a collective regional effort to improve the reality of African descendants in Latin America.

Percy Paredes

José Percy Paredes Coimbra was born in Bolivia on October 24, 1967. A lawyer and communicator by profession, Paredes currently serves as the vice-minister of public safety, and the general director of the free identification program (*carnetización gratuita*). He is also an advisor to Representative Jorge Medina Barra, the first Afro-Bolivian member of assembly in the Movimiento al Socialismo–Instrumento Político por la Soberanía de lo Pueblos (Movement for Socialism–Political Instrument for the Sovereignty of the Peoples, MAS-IPSP), led by the current president of the Plurinational

State of Bolivia, Evo Morales. Inspired by his Afro-descendant mother, Paredes began to dedicate a substantial amount of time and effort to the Afro-Bolivian movement in 2000 after having contributed indirectly in earlier years. He joined el Centro Afro-Boliviano para el Desarrollo Integral y Comunitario (the Afro-Bolivian Center for Complete Community Development, CADIC) during this period as well. CADIC is an organization that strives to promote and strengthen Afro-Bolivian identity, to increase awareness and education within the Afro-descendant communities of Bolivia through educational programs and development efforts, to contribute to the healthy growth of the nation, and to strengthen the relationship between the government and the Afro-Bolivian community (CADIC 2013).

The results from el Censo National de Población y Vivienda (the National Census) of 2001 indicate that there are more than 40,000 Afro-descendants in Bolivia, the majority of which are located in the northern region of La Paz, and in the Sucre, Santa Cruz, and Cochabamba departments (CADIC 2013). As an activist, Paredes works within a national system that continues to facilitate racism, to ensure the enactment of public policies that will allot much needed resources to Afro-Bolivian communities. Although he asserts that the problem of inequality will be resolved gradually in society, he is adamant that the government and the law must comply with their obligations to eradicate racial injustice. These obligations are reflected in the plethora of laws that protect the rights of Afro-Bolivians and other ethnic minority groups, such as Law 045, which identifies racism and other forms of discrimination as crimes punishable by law. Paredes carries out the majority of his work through CADIC and his government position. His approach to battling racism consists of carrying out community work that strengthens individuals and smaller collectives, and working within the national government to contest and denounce exclusionary structures in order to better the quality of life of Afro-descendants and all Bolivian citizens.

This leader frequently speaks of President Morales and the important, impactful changes he has made, referencing the new articles in the constitution that pertain specifically to Afro-Bolivians; however, he also recognizes that much work remains to be done in order to increase visibility, improve access to resources and political spheres, and ensure that Bolivia continues to strive to become an equitable country. Paredes has participated in a wide array of important conferences throughout his country and the Latin American region, and lectured about the condition of the Afro-Bolivian people. He stresses the importance of respecting individuals, but puts great emphasis on community effort as a mechanism for bringing about important changes in Bolivia and throughout Latin America.

A short time after arriving in Panama, Paredes spoke to me about the focus of his current projects within the Afro-Bolivian movement:

> At this moment we [CADIC] are working on the political aspect of the movement. Many of the resources that the community receives are dictated by political structures. It is not a question of organizations providing for them, it is the state that distributes those resources, so we've decided amongst ourselves to address this problem at the structural level to make sure that resources reach the community. You have to look into everything from adequate water conditions, light, telephone service, basic necessities, to larger issues, you know? So the organization helps us to continue to work in the community while we also put pressure on political structures with the intent to consolidate the organization and bring in public resources.

He spoke with optimism about recent successes, crediting them in part to the Morales government, and calling attention to what remains to be done:

> Some historic things have happened since Evo Morales became president, and they have allowed us to advance, I would say about 60 percent. We still have 40 percent of the work left to do, but what are left are details, details surrounding public resources . . . We are constructing a new state and we will be able to include these improvements in this new state, the state that we [Bolivians] will build together.

Paredes notes the social changes that have resulted from the work of antiracism groups and legislation like Law 045:

> Bolivia continues to be a racist country, but since the passing of that law, the levels of racism have decreased. For example, no one will say "fucking black person" to you, which was very common some time ago. So now, at least those things have begun to diminish, people are beginning to understand that being a different color does not imply that you are less [human]. You have the same level of intelligence, the same feelings, everything is the same it's just that you are another color, that's all. So we are succeeding in getting through to people and we have done work to increase the visibility of these problems in order to get these stereotypes out of people's heads, you know? About the indigenous peoples, about Afro-descendants, about peasants, about women.

When I asked him about the importance of a regional school for Afro-descendant leaders, the activist responded by providing national perspective, and reflected on the experiences of the Bolivian leadership schools:

> We have achieved something that many Afro-descendants in Latin America have not. We have four, five articles in the constitution that pertain to the Afro-Bolivian people. They say "this corresponds with the Afro-Bolivian people" and they take us into account as a distinct collective within the Bolivian state. Being incorporated into the constitution presents us with the opportunity not only to make ourselves visible as a people, but also to incorporate ourselves into politics. We need what has happened on the macro scale to happen on the micro scale as well. In our training school we have focused on developing projects specifically with women. We know that there is still inequality between men and women and although we have passed the one-year point with the women's training project, we want to make sure that there are female leaders who can be union leaders, community leaders, and mayors. We think that it is very important [to achieve this] if this school is going to help us with this education project. What is taught to the men and women will help us attain equal conditions and to fight to maintain them. This process of inclusion will be more organized and inclusive.

Paredes reflected on the most critical aspects that the regional school should incorporate so that students will be as prepared as possible for their future endeavors:

> I think the school should have different levels. The basic level should promote increased [identity] consciousness. Another level should be reserved for people who are already professionals, it could

be on-line, in person, maybe half and half, we will have to see what options we have, that will help us to increase their capacity. There should be a specialization in conflict resolution, a master's degree in human rights. As I've said, we have been able to get Afro-descendants in different state structures: in different departments, in labor unions, in municipal politics. There are individuals who are present in these positions now, but our priority is to ensure that those people have good quality training and are not just there to fill the seats. It sounds terrible to say this, but those people, if they are not of good caliber then they are no good to us. Achieving this goal is only going to be possible if we can provide training, academic training, the training that university provides. That is what permits you in some way to increase the level of participation.

Juan de Dios Mosquera Mosquera

Juan de Dios Mosquera Mosquera is the director of el Movimiento Nacional por los Derechos Humanos Afro-colombianos "Cimarrón" (the "Cimarrón" National Movement for Afro-Colombian Human Rights, or Cimarrón), a movement that was founded in 1982 and has more than thirty years of experience in human- and ethnic-rights advocacy and development for the Afro-descendant people of Colombia. According to the data from the national census of 2005, 10.5 percent of the 41,468,384 registered inhabitants of the country self-identify as Afro-Colombian, *palenquero*, *negro*, or *raizal*. All of these terms denote African ancestry and have been incorporated into the race and ethnicity portion of the census since 2005 to provide a wider range of culturally appropriate choices for self-identification (Ministry of Culture 2009). Although Afro-Colombians reside in all parts of the country, some regions have large populations, including the Pacific coast, the Caribbean coast, and the departments of Antioquia, Risaralda, Caldas, and Quindío (Ministry of Culture 2009).

Mosquera Mosquera was born in Santa Cecilia in the municipality of Pueblo Rico, located in the Risaralda Department. In addition to a number of different activities, he has dedicated more than thirty years to social activism on behalf of the Afro-Colombian communities. He completed a bachelor's degree in social science and history at la Universidad Tecnológica de Pereira before traveling to Mexico to obtain a master's degree in sociology at la Universidad Iberoamericana de México. This community leader became involved in activism in 1976 when he created el Círculo de Estudios de la Problemática de las Comunidades Negras de Colombia "Soweto" (the Soweto Circle of Studies of the Problems of the Black Communities of Colombia, or Soweto) along with other Afro-descendant university students in Pereira. These youth felt the need to learn about their African ancestry, their history, and the African-descendant people in their country. They also sought to understand the roots of the racism and discrimination that Afro-Colombians experienced, manifested as numerous kinds of exclusion and poverty.

Six years later, Mosquera Mosquera and his colleagues founded the Cimarrón movement, which continues to be a protagonist in the struggle against racism and discrimination in Colombia. Among its contributions, the movement has succeeded in organizing various sectors of the Afro-Colombian community. Mosquera Mosquera has since left his position as a university professor to dedicate the majority of his time to Cimarrón. On two occasions he has been in the running to serve as a political candidate representing Afro-Colombians in the National Congress (Bravo 2010). His political campaigns have brought important themes such as the protection of communal lands and the need for more public resources to the forefront (Bravo 2010). This activist oversees a series of permanent projects, including a campaign against racism and discrimination that features protests for racial diversity, as well as la Escuela Nacional de Liderazgo Afro-Colombiano "Nelson Mandela" (The Nelson Mandela National School for Afro-Colombian Leadership). The school has a variety of training programs for youth, women, and children that center around issues of identity and leadership.

Mosquera Mosquera dedicates a great deal of his time and the movement to politics, identifying the need for a political party that represents the interests of the Afro-Colombian people as a major goal. He has taken this idea to the regional and international levels, and maintains that the political organization of Afro-descendants will be crucial to their ability to bring about social, political, and economic changes that will ameliorate the quality of life for people of African descent.

After dinner, Mosquera Mosquera accompanied me to the sitting room in our hotel to explain

> Well, this process began in 1976 when we, a group of Afro-Colombian students, decided to create el Círculo de Estudios de la Problemática de las Comunidades Negras de Colombia "Soweto." We wanted to learn and to understand what it meant to be Afro-Colombian, we wanted to learn about our history, about the importance of African communities in the construction of the nation of Colombia and the world, what racism and discrimination meant in Colombia, and why the majority of Afro-Colombian communities were alarmingly poor. We developed the fundamental methodological concepts that allowed us to understand the Afro-Colombian reality and the commitment that we needed to make in support of our organization, of the mobilization, and the political empowerment of the Afro-Colombian people. In 1982 we founded el Movimiento Nacional por los Derechos Humanos Afro-colombianos Cimarrón.

Mosquera Mosquera continued, reflecting on the significance of the name of the movement—Cimarrón—and its purpose:

> The Spanish used the word "cimarrón" to refer to wild animals, and when our ancestors arrived imprisoned and kidnapped in America, fighting for their freedom, they ran to the mountains and created their maroon communities called "palenques." They were defending their freedom. We discovered that they [the Spanish] called our ancestors "cimarrones" because they were considered escaped livestock, livestock without a mark, without a brand. In memory of the struggle of our maroon ancestors we named the movement "Cimarrón." And the goal of the movement was to fight in Colombia to win our dignity, ethnic rights, ethnic identity, and political power for the Afro-Colombian people. This is a fight against racism and discrimination, a fight against the consequences of slavery in Colombian society, a fight against the disarray of our community, a fight for the creation of political power, for political organization that allows us to represent ourselves and make ourselves visible by way of our own votes and our own leadership.

Since a national school for Afro-Colombian leaders already exists, I wanted to know why Mosquera Mosquera thinks an international school is important. His response illustrates the hope he has for the project:

It means creating a groundbreaking asset that will allow us to strengthen the political and ideological capacities, leadership skills, and social and political capacity of the leaders and organizations of the region. If we are able to train and provide leaders with an outlook, with an organizational methodology and political capacity they will strengthen their organizations and they will strengthen their communities.

I asked him to name the most important aspects of the school in question, and he alluded to many, from imparting knowledge about identity to politics:

First off, for me, the most important aspect is the construction of a vision and a conceptualization of the history of the Afro-descendants of the Americas. That is the foundation. After that, we need to have a clear idea of the reality of these communities as a result of slavery. Third, we need to clearly explain what ethnic rights we have and how they have come out of the history and the perseverance of Afro-descendant communities. Fourth, we need to identify strategies for development, ethno-development of the Afro-descendant populations of the Americas. Fifth, we need to learn to develop political power.

Since Mosquera Mosquera was the first activist that I had spoken with who placed significant emphasis on the subject of politics, I was interested to know how—according to his vision—politics would help the Afro-Latino movement. He responded:

We need to understand the significance of political power. It means organization. Our communities have not been organized enough to participate in political debates in our countries, and because of this we have not had political power. So we have to develop this, we have to organize the Afro-descendant peoples for political participation, for all nations. We need this. And while we do this we need to develop training methods for leadership, leadership skills, and we need to train [youth] to carry out strategic planning in organizations.

Mosquera Mosquera summed up the importance of the new school, expressing his hopes in a few final words:

All of this will create the possibility for the political empowerment of our communities, to improve our living conditions and increase our economic, social, cultural and political progress.

Gregoria Jiménez

Honduran activist Gregoria Jiménez Amaya was born on August 14, 1970, and currently holds the position of secretary of educational affairs in the Central Board of Directors for the Organización de Desarrollo Étnico Comunitario (Organization of Ethnic Community Development, or ODECO), a not-for-profit organization created in 1992. ODECO's motive is to contribute to development and to support the needs of the Afro-Honduran population, which consists of the Garífuna who are peoples of African and Carib descent, *criollos* (creoles) whose ancestors came from the English-speaking Caribbean islands to work in Honduras, and the *coloniales* (colonials) who are the descendants of the enslaved Africans who were brought to Honduras during the colonial era (ODECO 2013).

According to the World Bank, 10 percent of the national population is Garífuna and 2.8 percent is *criollo* or colonial (González 2006). The majority of the Garífuna communities are located in the department of Atlántida, while the majority of *criollos* live on the Bahía islands (González 2006). Other Afro-descendant communities can be found in the departments of Gracias a Dios, Colón, and Cortés (González 2006). The organization realizes the majority of its work in the areas of the country that correspond with this demographic. ODECO runs numerous projects that raise awareness among members of this community, teach leadership skills, and provide empowering educational information about civil and human rights so that members can recognize and denounce the violations that they suffer as part of a marginalized and excluded population, with the intent to facilitate the creation of an inclusive multicultural society (ODECO 2013).

Jiménez, who holds a degree in social work and is currently enrolled in a master's program in project administration, decided to join ODECO in 1998 because of her concern about the lack of postsecondary education opportunities for Afro-Hondurans, who face numerous obstacles as they attempt to obtain university education as they strive to develop themselves and give back to their communities. In response to this problem, she has participated in and led various projects related to education, community training, health, and politics. Jiménez is the head of la Escuela de Formación de Líderes Afrodescendientes en Derechos Humanos (the Human Rights Training School for Afro-descendant Leaders, or EFLADH), an initiative that resulted from a series of youth encounters that ODECO had hosted since its inception. In 2006 EFLADH received its first cohort, and it has since expanded to include a variety of courses and opportunities for extension work so that participants may acquire the necessary technical and theoretical skills to later hold leadership positions, and to strengthen Afro-descendant individuals and communities in Honduras and throughout Central America (EFLADH 2012).

Under Jiménez's leadership, ODECO has provided educational training to over six hundred young leaders from Honduras as well as other Latin American countries such as México, Guatemala, Belize, Argentina, Costa Rica, Nicaragua, and Chile. This activist has also taken part in important efforts that have successfully obtained rights and public resources for Afro-Honduran communities. She has also participated in a variety of national meetings and conferences, including las Encuentros Nacionales de la Juventud Afro-hondureña (the National Afro-Honduran Youth Encounters), and los Encuentros Nacionales de la Mujer Afro-hondureña (the National Encounters of Afro-Honduran Women). At the regional level, she has represented ODECO at momentous events like el Segundo Simposio Internacional sobre Interculturalidad y Educación Superior (the Second International Symposium on Interculturality and Postsecondary Education).

Sitting on the bus on the way to a meeting in Panama City, Gregoria told me about her work in ODECO. When I asked her about her current projects, she spoke with excitement about a few that she was working on:

> We are always working on issues of education and health . . . We are developing a project about chronic illnesses specifically in Garífuna communities with the American Health Organization and the Pan-American Health Organization, and in 2013 that project will receive financial contributions from the Secretary of Health. We are also working in the political sphere to resolve some community land issues and to defend human rights. There are some people who have had problems in the tribunals and we

are offering them free legal services. We are also working on micro-finance initiatives with the help of donations, specifically for women's and youth groups. The International Year of Afro-descendants just passed and we helped to create the first world summit for Afro-descendants that put forth concrete ideas and goals. We are hoping that in this decade we will have more economic opportunities that will help to better the community.

With respect to the School for Afro-descendant Leaders, this leader provided a basic explanation of the initiative and its format:

In 2006 the idea for the Human Rights Training School for Afro-descendant Leaders came about. The program consists of four months of in-class work and then during the remaining weeks the youth carry out their extension work in their communities, applying the concepts and lessons that they learned in the school. They are also required to conduct investigations and to report to us on the state of the communities. All of this provides us with information that we can present to the government when we ask that more public resources be implemented.

Jiménez commented on the courses offered in the program, but furthermore, she discussed the goal of the school:

The main goal is to teach [students] about [their] history so they can understand their identity. That is the main objective of the course about Afro-descendants in the Americas. The second course covers philosophies and theories of human rights and leadership, in the third we discuss the struggles of the organizations that fight on behalf of Afro-descendants, and the final course addresses issues related to the Garífuna community because we have made a number of advances with respect to land—more than 3,200 hectares of land has been registered as communal land that belongs to the Garífuna. The goal in this training process is to show youth that they can be leaders, that they can empower themselves, and that they can be a part of political changes in their municipalities and local governing bodies, as well as at the national level.

Changing the focus, Jiménez shared her thoughts with me about the process of creating a regional school for Afro-descendants. She conveyed the importance and value of the school, specifically because it would allow opportunities for collaboration with other countries, organizations, and institutions:

First, there will be the opportunity to share experiences with other countries like Colombia that has a similar school, with other allies in Ecuador who have also been working hard and have made advancements, to let youth see what others have done, you know? The University of South Florida has a lot of expertise, it is a very prestigious university and that will help us to gain more knowledge. For us it is important that we are here [planning the school] because our organizations need a lot of support to ensure that we can provide continued support for the youth who come out of the school, right? What will our strategy be? What tools will we use, what techniques? We know that the university [USF] can help us with these questions, that it can be an ally in this process of human rights and leadership development.

This activist expressed the importance of looking into the possibility of providing accreditation—an international certificate—to the participants so that they might have better opportunities in the future:

> We need to discuss the possibility of providing an accreditation, something that is more noteworthy than what our national schools can provide. It will allow students to have something else to add to their curriculum vitae and will perhaps give them the opportunity to get a job or better access to [further] education, to a post-secondary, master's or doctorate degree. It is very important because there are not as many opportunities for our Afro-descendant youth to access a quality education, a higher education, it's very difficult. We dedicate ourselves to this goal, and so it is also part of this process.

Finally, Jiménez stressed the importance of ensuring that the school would have a political focus:

> For us as activist organizations that have made demands over many years, it is very important that everything that we are going to discuss takes politics into consideration. The youth are going to think that this is an opportunity to come to visit Panama or to develop themselves, but this is important work. We want the school to teach political content, and to have the resources that will enable the project's success.

Leonardo Reales

Leonardo Reales Jiménez is an Afro-Colombian historian, political scientist, activist, and leader. Born in the city of Santa Marta on the Caribbean coast of Colombia in 1974, Reales became interested and involved in issues pertaining to Afro-descendants after multiple discriminatory experiences, and taking note of the complex and grave reality of Afro-Colombian communities. After taking on this new focus, he met Juan de Dios Mosquera Mosquera, a veteran activist and the director of el Movimiento Nacional Afro-Colombiano "Cimarrón" (the "Cimarron" National Afro-Colombian Movement, or Cimarrón) who became his mentor. Reales's experiences served as a driving force not only for activism but also for his studies; he earned a bachelor's degree in political science and history from la Universidad de los Andes, for which he wrote a thesis on the politics and history of the nineteenth century with a focus on Afro-descendant communities. This strengthened his opinion about the importance of the African presence in the country, which has not been valued. He graduated in 2005 from the master's program in Political, Economic and International Affairs at la Universidad Externado de Colombia, and is currently a doctoral candidate in political science at The New School for Social Research in New York, where he continues to study issues of identity and political participation. Reales has completed various international programs about human rights and development. Participation in these programs has allowed him to travel to countries throughout the Americas and Europe, where he has given presentations about Afro-descendants in the Latin American region and specifically in his country, in which the internal armed conflict and racial discrimination continue to greatly affect Afro-Colombian communities (Afrolatinos 2011).

This scholar-activist has directed his academic and community work towards helping the Afro-Colombian movement. Once he joined Cimarrón, Reales's dedication and hard work allowed him to take on greater responsibilities, and eventually led him to an administrative position. He worked as the coordinator for Cimarrón for more than ten years and maintains a strong relationship with his mentor Juan de Dios Mosquera Mosquera. His studies have been published in books, and both national and international academic journals (Afrolatinos 2011). Reales is also a gifted storyteller. He took note of the abundance of racist jokes in comedic routines and took a stance against this practice as well. Recognized as one of the most important storytellers in Colombia, he always takes advantage of any opportunity to share and comment on his subject of interest in-country, abroad, and in front of diverse audiences, where he shares his knowledge in the four languages he speaks: English, French, Spanish, and Portuguese. Reales has continued to write and disperse useful information through the documentary *Afrolatinos: The Untaught Story*, a project that has allowed him to travel throughout all of Latin America in order to produce a film that contributes to the process of making visible the cultures, histories, socioeconomic conditions, and the barriers that Afro-descendant peoples in the region face (Afrolatinos 2011).

Over the lunch break, Reales briefly told me about the experiences that caused him to become an activist:

[From a very young age] I was always thinking, analyzing, but really I became an activist, a very active, strong, almost radical activist because of two situations or encounters. In the first I was in the army in the Presidential Guard Battalion. We were in charge of protecting the president . . . A captain who was in charge of the soldiers said: Okay, Private Rodríguez . . . Private Gómez, black man . . . " and I said "wait a minute, I am also a soldier," and he said, "that's an order, do you have a problem with that?" "No, no, it's fine." At that time I wasn't as aware of my identity but I always remembered that moment. I left the army and began university and it was there that a professor said to me: "You are black and Indian, you are screwed on both sides." And that's really when I said, "No, something is wrong here," and I decided to investigate on my own. Finally, I found other professors who studied Afro-Colombians, and I also found Cimarrón.

While talking about his current projects, he mentioned and described a few, including the *Afrolatinos* documentary:

As an academic I am finishing my dissertation on ethnic identity and political participation, and as an activist I work with different NGOs as a human and ethnic rights advisor. I am also one of the advisors for the Afrolatinos project. We participate in conferences, we put on workshops all the time and not just in Colombia, but also in other countries in Latin America and the Caribbean, and it's a project that is very ambitious and important. We are looking for more funding. It's a great project. Aside from the problems and obstacles we have been able to do very interesting things. Obviously the activism is more regional, and by regional I am referring to Latin America and the Caribbean, and I, of course, continue to work permanently in Colombia. I do this through informal education; that is to say, workshops with community leaders and youth activists.

He spoke about the structural obstacles that Afro-descendant communities face:

Well, there are some structural problems, it's all a cycle . . . and it's extreme precisely because of these structures. We have social exclusion, marginalization and racism. The two principal problems . . . are:

racism and racial discrimination, one, and the negation of these problems [two]. We also have a problem that impedes community advancement. On a smaller scale, though it also exists, is endo-racism. It is strong in all of Latin America for many historical reasons. The other problem—although everything is connected—is the issue of . . . the absence of opportunities to access political power and opportunities for progress, and also services and social programs in health, housing, education, culture . . . Finally, we have an education system that is totally exclusive, that ignores, omits, denies or eclipses the Afro-descendant contribution to the construction of the Latin American nations. And when you deny these contributions, the people, the children and the youth do not have any reason to be proud of their own history because they don't know about it, it doesn't exist, they don't know who their ancestors were and so they have no reason to be proud of them.

Reales also commented on common discriminatory attitudes and perspectives that are influenced by the media, and that affect the new generations of Afro-descendants by hindering their development through the use of common stereotypes:

What the [Afro-descendant] children want is to be like everyone else . . . because of the media where important figures continue being racist and exclusionary, and where they laugh at [our] communities in television shows, in the news, everywhere . . . So the youth, the children want to be what they see on TV, and what they see on TV in Latin America is not black people as celebrities, in fact, it's the exact opposite. They are always domestic help or working in unskilled positions, so many want to be like them when they are older. They do not want to be engineers, lawyers, doctors, scientists, etc. [The two spheres] where the Afro-descendant population is successful are sports and in music . . . It is much more difficult for a person of African descent to become a scientist, an engineer, an architect, a lawyer, than it is for a white or mestizo person in Latin America. Obviously there are white and mestizo people who are also poor in socio-economic terms, but without a doubt, poverty in Latin America has a color and that color is black.

Given his previous comments, I asked his opinion on the regional leadership school. He responded succinctly:

It is very important [to have this school] for two reasons. First, training teachers guarantees a multiplier effect in the entire region. That is to say, we are going to reach more people because of what we do as activists and teachers, and this generates an immediate multiplier effect, which is necessary because people need more education, both formal and informal. On one hand, much like what the University of South Florida is doing, we will guarantee in some way that these two kinds of education are available. The other reason why this is important is because the leaders and teachers need to broaden their knowledge base in order to continue creating Afro-descendant thought in a consistent fashion . . . We are still in the process of creating stronger, more consistent Afro-descendant thought that will reach all of the spheres and all of the levels in all of the countries of Latin America. And this school will allow this to happen, it will allow this to happen because it is going to train teachers who are already working on these problems and will simply strengthen their knowledge so that it can reach other people who in turn will do exactly the same thing—increase the knowledge to empower all of the Afro-descendant people of Latin America and the Caribbean.

Oswaldo Bilbao

Oswaldo Bilbao Lobatón, a Peruvian activist born in Lima on September 19, 1959, to a mother from Chincha, a city famous for its African heritage, has been the director of el Centro de Desarrollo Étnico (the Center of Ethnic Development, or CEDET) since its creation in 1999. Bilbao's working-class family valued education and inspired him to get a postsecondary degree. He worked in the Ministry of Agriculture as a farm worker while studying at el Instituto Técnico de Administración de Empresas, where he graduated with a bachelor's degree in business administration. Later, he completed another bachelor's degree in accounting at la Universidad Inca Garcilaso de la Vega. Bilbao continued his work with the Ministry of Agriculture in the general management of forestry. When he left this position he began to focus his efforts on ending the social inequality, racism, and marginalization faced by Afro-Peruvians.

Bilbao became increasingly militant upon joining a leftist group in his community, where he began to question the complete lack of attention given to ethnic diversity in general, and to Afro-descendants in particular in the political agendas of the Left. In 1992 he participated in el Primer Encuentro de Comunidades Negras del Perú (the First Encounter of Black Communities of Peru), organized by el Movimiento Negro Francisco Congo (the Black Francisco Congo Movement, or the MNFC). That same year he became a member of the MNFC and continued to fight for the rights of the Afro-Peruvian population. As a part of the MNFC, this activist worked to bring about important changes at the national level—for example, he took part in the effort to make the Peruvian state officially recognize peoples of African descent as "Afro-descendants" or "Afro-Peruvians" instead of "blacks," and he took part in lobbying efforts that resulted in a national day that celebrates Afro-Peruvian culture. In 1999, in the wake of then-president Alberto Fujimori, Bilbao and some other MNFC members decided to separate from the movement because of political differences and formed CEDET. This nongovernmental organization (NGO) conducts and publishes studies and literature, and organizes workshops in Afro-descendant communities with the intent to strengthen cultural identity, recognize and value the invisible contributions of Afro-Peruvian people and communities, and contribute to the promotion of training and necessary initiatives designed to help Afro-descendants in Peru develop their own communities (CEDET 2011).

According to CEDET's studies, the Afro-Peruvian population constitutes between 6 and 10 percent of the nation, the majority of which live in urban centers in the coastal region, and in areas that have historically been inhabited by Africans and their descendants (CEDET 2008). Peru has one of the highest levels of inequality in the world, and statistical data on poverty, employment, income, and expenditures that compare Afro-descendants to the rest of the Peruvian population serve as evidence that Afro-Peruvians continue to be victims of this extreme inequality. Among the most worrisome data trends is the indication that development for Afro-Peruvians has stagnated between 2001 and 2010, while the rest of the population has seen improvements in this same period (PNUD 2012). CEDET's expertise and successful projects have resulted in the production and dissemination of important literature and numerical data about Afro-Peruvians, which have been incorporated into various United Nations documents. The recommendations that this NGO makes with regard to bettering the quality of life of Afro-Peruvian communities are also based upon this data. As the director, Bilbao has been able to travel in order to educate the public and advocate for the African descendants of Peru at various national, regional, and international conferences.

After a long day in the conference room, Bilbao told me a bit about how he came to be involved with the MNFC:

> I had a career, I was the sub-director of personnel in the Ministry of Agriculture . . . and when I applied for another position the union leader wanted to know why I had the position I held at the time, and one of the highest ranked members of the union said: "hey, black man, how do you expect to get that position? I don't think you are smarter than the other person who is applying." . . . I had held . . . that position for ten years; no one knew the job better than I did. I was a professional, why would someone who had never held that job know more about it than me? So, that is when I began to realize that racism was structural . . . So I had to leave the ministry, and somewhere over those next few years the first encounter of Black communities in Peru was held, and that is when I became part of the Afro-Peruvian social movement.

He also spoke about separating from the MNFC and the creation of CEDET, an independent organization:

> That was the time when Fujimori was going to be re-elected, and Fujimori infiltrated the movement, the MNFC. He was attracting people from the movement, saying: "Look, come with me, I will make you a member of congress, etcetera," so that is when the friction started. Those of us who became CEDET started asking: "How can we support a corrupt government that violates human rights, etcetera? We can't be part of this," and so we decided . . . not to participate in the group . . . and that is where the movement split. There is one group that is still the MNFC, and we became CEDET because our work is founded upon the respect for human rights and we say that there was evidence that Fujimori's government had violated those human rights, so that was the problem for us. That is where the movement broke, and that is why we could not go back, because of ideological problems.

Bilbao also elaborated on CEDET's national contributions and participation in regional efforts for Afro-descendants:

> There have been some important contributions, for example, I think that in the last two United Nations reports, all of the references and the recommendations about what should be done to help the Afro-Peruvian population were influenced by a document that we presented with Makungu for Development (an Afro-Peruvian youth group). We have also presented another alternative document for the periodic universal report that also creates recommendations. I think we have addressed Afro-descendants in Peru, but in a more technical way, that is not just so that we are seen as a social movement, but also as a collective that can debate on equal grounds about public resources, about human rights, about a number of issues at the technical level. I think that that is what is different. And the topics as well, we have advanced the subject of Afro-descendants in Latin America in the last 10 to 12 years after the Durban conference1 . . . everything came out of Durban thanks to our own efforts. Afro-descendants, primarily

the introduction of the word "Afro-descendant," we coined it. This was important because it brought this recognition to all of the Latin American states and to the world.

The veteran activist reflected on the significance of the leadership school and the ways in which the participants would be able to contribute to the process of development that will benefit Afro-Latino people:

> I think there are a number of motives, first, the lack of training within our social group, we need to find new leadership, new foci and regional visions. It is true that we need to focus on what is happening at the national level, it is important to look at it from the outside, that is one side, but the other side is that it [the school] will be a point of encounter and discussion. Yes, there will be national schools where you can work at that level, but in this school [students] will have to examine the whole picture, and that will be a source of strength. A third point is that it will allow for professional exchanges and let us look for new, logical leaderships in the face of new challenges in Latin America and the Caribbean . . . I think that everything has to do with a political perspective . . . in order to gain power democratically you have to be prepared, you have to know what to do, [you have to have] social networks, etcetera, because without them you won't advance. And the idea is to start to construct a new model of democracy, a new model of development . . . from our perspective for everyone, because we also can't cut ourselves off. We are starting this so that they can become people who can contribute to the development of their countries . . . these aspects are important to me. This needs to be about developing a perspective about development, but also a perspective about politics.

José Chalá

José Franklin Chalá Cruz is an Ecuadorian anthropologist and an activist. Chalá was born in the city of Ibarra on May 11, 1963, and spent his childhood in the Chota Valley in the La Concepción y Salinas community, one of the most readily recognized regions in the Republic of Ecuador for its historic and present-day Afro-descendant presence. The seventh national census conducted in 2010 indicates that 7.2 percent of every 100 Ecuadorians self-identify as Afro-Ecuadorians, which translates to 1,041,559 individuals out of a national population of 11,483,499 (INEC 2012). Afro-descendants live throughout the country, but notable concentrations are located in the Guayas, Esmeraldas, Pichincha, Manabí, Los Ríos, Santo Domingo, Imbabura, and Carchi provinces. The regions mainly recognized for their historic African presence are the Chota Valley, and the Imbabura, Carchi, and Esmeraldas provinces. The inhabitants of these communities experience racial, social, and economic discrimination, and have low levels of access to public resources and political representation, all of which are recognized by activist organizations as violations of civil and human rights (CODAE 2010b).

Due to recent activist efforts, the national constitution of 2008 now includes a series of individual rights and twenty-one collective rights that pertain directly to Afro-Ecuadorians. This has been recognized as a great advancement for the nation and for Afro-descendant citizens who, until these changes were made, were invisible in society and deprived of the rights that are afforded to other social, racial, and cultural groups (CODAE 2010a). Chalá was one of the protagonists that helped ensure that these rights were enshrined in the constitution. Influenced primarily by his family, this academic and activist learned at a young age to value and protect his culture and identity, and above all to recognize Afro-Ecuadorians as citizens with rights and voices that need to be heard. In grade school he began to question teachings that excluded the influences and contributions of Africans and their descendants in Ecuador. He decided to study anthropology in order to conduct more profound investigations about the sociocultural practices and legacies of his community. In 1983, he founded el Centro de Investigaciones Familia Negra (the Center for Black Family Studies, or CIFANE) with other Afro-descendant youth from the Chota Valley, all of whom were eager to learn more about their own history. His anthropological studies led him to activism, and he began to focus on civil rights, citizenship, and human rights, and the role of the state.

Chalá holds a master's degree in anthropology and culture, degrees in applied anthropology and education science, and another graduate degree in government and resource management (CODAE 2010b). He is the director of CIFANE, a member of la Federación de Comunidades y Organizaciones Negras de Imbabura y Carchi (the Federation of the Black Communities and Organizations of Imbabura and Carchi, or FECONIC), and la Alianza Estratégica Afro-latinoamericana y Caribeña (the Strategic Afro-Latin American and Caribbean Alliance), and is the executive secretary of la Corporación de Desarrollo Afroecuatoriano (the Corporation of Ecuadorian Development, or CODAE) (CODAE 2010b). He continues to contribute to important efforts to demand more rights and resources that will help to better the lives of Afro-Ecuadorians. One of these efforts has resulted in the implementation of higher-education resources for Afro-descendant youth, who can now continue their studies and obtain master's degrees because of an agreement between CODAE and the Latin American Social Sciences Faculty (FLASCO). CODAE has taken on the task of permanently organizing forums, discussion sessions, and public debates that teach society and encourage citizens to denounce racist and discriminatory practices. Chalá is involved in conference planning and program development that includes information about the individual and collective human rights of the Afro-Ecuadorian people (CODAE 2010c). He has also developed antidiscrimination teaching materials for the national police force that center on human rights.

Reclining in a chair after a long but fulfilling day of planning for the regional leadership school, Chalá affirmed that his family and primary-school environment were the two key factors that sparked his interest in Afro-Ecuadorians:

Essentially, it was my family. My grandfather, my parents, my older brothers, those are the people who began to talk about the need to be social actors because we are people with rights, we have a rich culture which gives us purpose, we are part of the African diaspora, we have a history that has not been valued by the nation or the world. They were the first to make me reflect, to help me gradually understand the importance of our reality as humans, our existence as citizens with physical attributes and culture that were different from other sectors of Ecuador, but that at the same time we were the same, we held the same rights as citizens, Ecuadorians, to enjoy our civil rights that we hold according to the constitution as individuals and as the collective that is the Afro-Ecuadorian people. My father, Salomón Chalá Lara always told us: "Education makes us free, culture and identity make us strong and invincible." With this environment at home, in my community and in primary school I developed social consciousness and militancy.

He explained that local and collective perspective of Afro-descendants was an integral part of the fight for the rights that are now incorporated into the national constitution and other important legislation:

> What has helped me to immerse myself in the knowledge of the Afro-Choteños is the fact that I have discovered that our knowledge is more than epistemology, it is our life. This has helped me rediscover who we are as Afro-Choteños. We are part of everything and we are responsible for each other. That is our philosophy. This re-discovery of the knowledge of our maroon ancestors makes our identity discourses stronger throughout the country, and it encourages us to demand recognition and respect of our inalienable civil and collective rights that are written in the constitution of the Republic of Ecuador.

With respect to his current work, Chalá told me of the efforts and projects that he is developing in academia as well as in the political sphere:

> I have finished a research investigation about maroon knowledge in the Chota region that will be published soon. I hope that this study will be used as pedagogic material for Afro-descendant youth and children in the Chota Valley, and for all Afro-Ecuadorians . . . This study allowed me to decipher the discourses that had been kept hidden, encoded. The wise men and women of the community transmitted their knowledge and discourses orally, through myths, stories and social games, through mythical characters, through music and dance, but as time passed new generations do not have a clear understanding of the meaning of those transcendental discourses . . . After approximately two decades of research, I have recovered the foundation of that knowledge.

Chalá conceptualizes the regional school for leaders as a space where students will have the opportunity to reflect upon community knowledge and visions that can aid with the internal development of Afro-Latin American communities in order to effectively respond to their needs:

> This project that we are starting with the University of South Florida allows us to break free of the Euro-centric civilizing process that began in the 16th century, with a totalizing vision that presented Western reason, science and technology to us as though it were the only and absolute truth, and we know that this is not true . . . I consider this a great opportunity, in which knowledge that is a product of diversity, from all the different communities can be in conversation . . . I think that by establishing this school, we will have the opportunity to construct a curriculum based on a philosophic Afro-diasporic vision. It will create the possibility to generate other discourses based on our symbols and environments . . . If our children are not effectively empowered by this knowledge they will continue to think from the perspective of other cultures without valuing what they are. When we truly understand our knowledge and we value it we will become true citizens of our countries and of the world.

This scholar-activist insists that the focal point for students attending the school should be Afro-diasporic culture and history:

Every aspect of the process of Afro-diasporic teaching and learning is important, however I think that in terms of methodology the pedagogic process must begin with critical learning, reflection on Afro-diasporic learning, knowledge, philosophies and cosmo-visions. Knowing these African or Afro-diasporic philosophies will allow the student body to know what we were denied, to know what made us believe that that knowledge was not relevant to our lives. From this learning process, in the absence of doubt, new realizations will emerge, new projects that will broaden Afro-diasporic knowledge from separate categories for analysis into distinct universal truths.

In a final reflection on the work of Paulo Freire and Ernesto "Che" Guevara, Paul McLaren (2001) writes: "As Che and Freire both knew, it is impossible to celebrate life under conditions that do not obtain for all . . . As long as others suffer, celebration is empty. But when collective struggle triumphs, that is—and continues to be—a cause for joy" (103). This quote relates intimately to the mission of the leaders whose life trajectories and visions have been expressed in this chapter. Their ongoing struggle for justice, for the recognition and implementation of rights and resources for Afro-descendant communities, and for national recognition and respect for the voices, bodies, and histories that form the life force of collectives stem from a vehement opposition to all forms of oppression, and any other structure that produces inequality and denigrates humanity. Their participation in the school for leaders is an investment in the very same kind of collective action that Che and Freire dreamed of, and their commitment to social change, to the eradication of inequality, to younger generations, and to liberation through education is admirable.

In an effort to address inequalities among Afro-descendants, the collaborators of the school have noted the importance of integrating discussions about gender and gender disparities into the school curriculum in order to create awareness about these imbalances. There is a noted absence of black female leaders, even among those represented in this chapter, which is not for lack of their participation or interest in activism. Just as African Americans in the United States have made space among Malcolm X and Martin Luther King Jr. for Assata Shakur, Fanny Lou Hamer, and Betty Shabazz, who have contributed and made advances for Afro-descendants in their country, so too must Afro-Latin Americans acknowledge and recognize the sacrifices of Gregória Jímenez and other Afro-descendant women, including Sueli Carneiro, Shirley Campbell, and Dorotea Wilson, whose voices, messages, and work are powerful and deserving of appreciation.

As preparations for the leadership school continue, and as Afro-descendants continue to press for recognition, for the rights they are entitled to as human beings, as ethnic and racial minorities, and as citizens of their respective countries, the trails that these leaders have blazed will help future generations to further advance their shared cause.

NOTES

1. Bilbao is referring to the 2001 World Conference Against Racism, Racial Discrimination, Xenophobia and Related Intolerance that was held in Durban, South Africa. This summit was an important moment for Afro-descendants as they were able to network and gain recognition that would later result in the attribution of key rights to their communities.

REFERENCES

Afrolatinos.tv. (2011). Leonardo Reales. Http://www.afrolatinos.tv/index.php?creator.display/1134/Leonardo-Reales#lang1pag.

Andrews, G. R. (2004). *Afro-Latin America, 1800–2000*. Oxford: Oxford University Press.

Bravo, L. (2010). El Cimarrón Contemporáneo, Juan de Dios Mosquera, quiere llegar al Congreso. *El Tiempo*, March 1. Http://www.eltiempo.com/blogs/afrocolombianidad/2010/03/el-cimarron-contemporaneo-juan.php.

CADIC. (2013). Http://www.cadic.org.bo/#.

Centro de Desarrollo Étnico (CEDET). (2011). Http://www.cedet.net/index.html.

Centro de Desarrollo Étnico (CEDET). (2008). *La población afroperuana y los derechos humanos: Diagnóstico sobre el Plan nacional de derechos humanos en localidades con presencia afroperuana*. Breña, Lima: Centro de Desarrollo Étnico.

CODAE. (2010a). Quienes somos. Http://www.codae.gob.ec/index.php?option=com_content&view=article&id=135&Itemid=112.

CODAE. (2010b). Perfil del secretario ejecutivo. Http://www.codae.gob.ec/index.php?option=com_content&view=article&id=137:perfil-del-secretario-ejecutivo&catid=34.

CODAE. (2010c). Los derechos ciudadanos de los afroecuatorianos en la Nueva Constitución del Ecuador. Http://issuu.com/codae.siet/docs/name438954.

EFLADH. (2012). Http://escuelalideresafro.blogspot.com.

Freire, P. (1968/1985). *Pedagogy of the oppressed*. Translated by M. B. Ramos. New York: Continuum, 1993.

Gilroy, P. (1993). *The Black Atlantic*. Cambridge, MA: Harvard University Press.

González, M. L. (2006). Más allá de los promedios: Afrodescendientes en América Latina. Http://siteresources.worldbank.org/INTLACAFROLATINSINSPA/Resources/Honduras_Final.pdf.

Gordillo, G., & Hirsch, S. (2003). Indigenous struggles and contested identities in Argentina. *Journal of Latin American Anthropology* 8 (3): 4–30.

INEC. (2012). *Las cifras del pueblo afroecuatoriano: Una mirada desde el Censo de Población y Vivienda 2010*.

McLaren, P. (2001). Che Guevara, Paulo, and the politics of hope: Reclaiming critical pedagogy. *Cultural Studies—Critical Methodologies* 1 (1): 108–131.

Ministry of Culture (Ministerio de la Cultura). (2009). Población Afrocolombiana. Http://www.mincultura.gov.co/?idcategoria=26030.

Minority Rights Group. (1995). *No longer invisible: Afro-Latin Americans today*. London: Minority Rights Publications.

Moraña, M., Dussel, E., & Jáurequi, C. A. (2008). *Coloniality at large*. Durham, NC: Duke University Press.

Morrison, J. (2007). Race and poverty in Latin America: Addressing the development needs of African descendants. *UN Chronicle*. Http://www.un. org/Pubs/chronicle/2007/issue3/0307p44. html.

ODECO. 2013. Http://odecohn.blogspot.com.

PNUD. 2012. *Visibilidad estadística: Datos sobre población afrodescendiente en censos y encuestas de hogares de América Latina*. Ciudad de Panamá: G. Cruces, C. García Domench, F. Pinto.

Reiter, B., & Simmons, K. E. (Eds.). (2012). *Afrodescendants, identity, and the struggle for development in the Americas*. East Lansing: Michigan State University Press.

Telles, E. E. (2007). Race and ethnicity and Latin America's United Nations millennium development goals. *Latin American and Caribbean Ethnic Studies* 2 (2): 185–200.

Whitten, N. E., & Torres, A. (1998). *Blackness in Latin America and the Caribbean: Social dynamics and cultural transformations*. Bloomington: Indiana University Press.

PART TWO

Negotiating Racialized and Gendered Positionalities

El Muntu en América (Our People in America)

Manuel Zapata Olivella

Translation by Jonathan Tittler

I

Muntu encadenado
mírate dentro de ti mismo
y verás libres
los ríos
las plantas
el polvo
y la semilla que llevas en tu seno.

    No eres prisionero
    pez, caza, noche
    que andas.

Muntu fuego,
tus dedos arden
cenizas encendidas
prendes las selvas
acosas las fieras
atizas el amor
carbonero de la vida.

    No eres prisionero
    flecha, ceniza, selva
    que andas.

Muntu agua,

I

Enchained people,
Look within yourselves
And you will see free
The rivers
The plants
The dust
And the seed you bear within your womb.

    You are no prisoner
    Fish, hunting, night
    That moves.

People fire,
Your fingers burn
Lit ashes
You kindle jungles
You hunt wild beasts
You incite love
Coal merchant of life.

    You are no prisoner
    Arrow, ash, jungle
    That moves.

People water,

fuente de los días
estanque de la noche
anegas la semilla
respiras en la nube
sin tu gota cópula
el vientre estéril
no germinaría.

    No eres prisionero
    día, nube, gota
    que andas.

Muntu planta,
los árboles del bosque
son tus huesos
horcones de la casa
nudo de las cañas
tizón de los fogones
humo de la leña
árbol sobre el río
polvo en las orillas
sembrador del fruto
dormido en la semilla.

    No eres prisionero
    árbol, leña, casa
    que andas.

II

Muntu semilla
fecundas la tierra
espiga en el suelo
sueño del árbol.
Junto al nido
sombra de los huevos
alimento de los pájaros
palabra leche
en la boca de los niños.

Fount of days
Pool of night
You inundate the seed
You breathe on the cloud
Without your copulating drop
The sterile belly
Would not germinate.

    You are no prisoner
    Day, cloud, drop
    That moves.

People plant,
The trees of the forest
Are your bones
Pitchforks of the house
Knot of sugarcane
Ember of woodstoves
Smoke of firewood
Tree over the river
Dust on the banks
Planter of fruit
Asleep in the seed.

    You are no prisoner
    Tree, firewood, home
    That moves.

II

People seed,
You fertilize the earth
Seedling in the soil
Dream of the tree.
Next to the nest
Shadow of eggs
Food of birds
Word of milk
In the mouths of children.

No eres prisionero
familia, palabra, nido
que andas.

Muntu río,
recorres las orillas
noticia de los remos
agua en el desierto
lluvia en agosto
naces en las nubes
y mueres en las manos
que mojan los labios.

No eres prisionero
lluvia, remo, río
que andas.

Muntu noche,
vela del insomnio
capturas la luna
en la red de tus sueños.
Chispa, astro,
en la noche de tu piel
tus ojos incendian
la oscuridad.

No eres prisionero
árbol, leña, casa
que andas.

III

Muntu pájaro
tus alas viento
recorren los espacios
relámpago desnudo
en los altos montes
en las ciénagas
en las cárceles
construyes tu nido.

You are no prisoner
Family, word, nest
That moves.

People river,
You traverse the banks
News of the oars
Water in the desert
Rain in August
You are born in the clouds
And you die in hands
That moisten lips.

You are no prisoner
Rain, oar, river
That moves.

People night,
Candle of insomnia
You catch the moon
In the net of your dreams.
Spark, star,
In the night of your skin
Your eyes inflame
The darkness.

You are no prisoner
Tree, firewood, house
That moves.

III

People bird,
Your wind wings
Travel through space
Naked lightning bolt
On high peaks
In swamps
In jails
You build your nest.

No eres prisionero
alas, viento, cárcel
que andas.

Muntu elefante
tus lomos gigantes
los pequeños ojos
esconden tu potencia.
Las ceibas abuelas
los leones
las serpientes
las zebras
las hormigas
te abren paso
en lo profundo de la selva.

No eres prisionero
ceiba, león, hormiga
que andas.

IV

Muntu pez,
en el fondo de los mares
en la corriente de los ríos
manatí de los pantanos
ballena en los océanos
cocodrilo de los trópicos
hipopótamo en la ciénaga
burlas las tormentas
conoces las bahías
las islas
los perdidos litorales
la foca dormida entre los hielos.
Tu reino agua
es más extenso
que tu pequeño hueco
en la bodega.

You are no prisoner
Wings, wind, jail
That moves.

People elephant,
Your giant flanks
Your small eyes
Hide your power.
The ancient ceibas
Lions
Serpents
Zebras
Ants
Open the path for you
In the depths of the jungle.

You are no prisoner
Ceiba, lion, ant
That moves.

IV

People fish,
At the bottom of the seas
In the current of the rivers
Sea cow of the wetlands
Whale in the oceans
Crocodile of the tropics
Hippopotamus in the marsh
You dodge storms
You know the bays
The islands
The lost littorals
The seal sleeping among the ice floes.
Your water kingdom
Is larger
Than your little hole
In the wine cave.

No eres prisionero
islas, hielo, manatí
que andas.

Muntu red
tu mano hábil
tejedora
flecha y arco
rueda y carro
palabra escrita
canto
danza
son tus trampas
ojos que atrapan
olfato que adivina
dedos que palpan
lengua que habla
distintos sabores.
Tu mano extendida
sin cadenas ni paredes,
Muntu pescador
los cuatro horizontes
serán prisioneros de tu red.

No eres prisionero
familia, palabra, nido
que andas.

You are no prisoner
Islands, ice, sea cow
That moves.

People net,
Your able hand
Weaving
Bow and arrow
Wheel and cart
Written word
Song
Dance
Are your traps
Eyes that snare
Sniff that surmises
Fingers that palpate
Tongue that speaks
Different flavors.
Your extended hand
Without chains or walls,
People fishermen
The four horizons
Will be prisoners in your net.

You are no prisoner
Family, word, nest
That moves.

Activism as History Making: The Collective and the Personal in Collaborative Research with the Process of Black Communities in Colombia

Arturo Escobar

It is not us who will save culture, it is culture that will save us.

—PCN activist, Tumaco, 1998

In January 1993, I went to Colombia for a year of field research on a project then titled "Afro-Colombian Responses to Modernization and Development." During that initial year, I was able to assemble a small research team to work in the southern Pacific Coast region of Colombia.[1] At that point this region was still customarily described as a poor and forgotten hot and humid forest crisscrossed by innumerable rivers and inhabited by black and indigenous groups—a *litoral recóndito*, as Sofonías Yacup, a local author and politician, put it in the 1930s. By then, the region was fully immersed in an ambitious strategy of development that had started in the mid-1980s. Armed with the tools given to us by the discursive critique of development of the 1980s, I set out to investigate ethnographically both the cultural and ecological impact of the various projects and the forms of resistance presented to them by the black groups of the river communities. Or so I thought, because what I discovered soon after my arrival was that the situation was far more complex than I had realized from a distance.

And indeed it has not ceased to grow in complexity, posing unprecedented challenges to research method, politics, and understanding. First, two or three months into the project it became clear to us that besides state-sponsored development and nascent capitalist enterprises (chiefly oil palm plantations and industrial shrimp farming at the time), albeit closely linked to them, there were two crucial factors in the struggle over the representation and fate of the region. The first was the concern with the region's biodiversity. The region is identified as one of the most important "biodiversity hot spots" in the world, and our arrival coincided with the beginning of a novel internationally funded conservation strategy of ambitious scope. As in other hot spots of the sort, the conservation of biodiversity had become the battle cry of the state, NGOs, academics, and local leaders alike. Closely related to this was a still small but highly committed and articulate social movement of black communities. Our initial conversations with activists of this movement, while not immediately trusting, were nevertheless auspicious. In mid-June of that year (1993), our small research team held the first day-long workshop with a group of these activists plus a handful of black intellectuals from the Pacific Coast close to the movement. Our explicit intent was to discuss concrete ways of articulating our project with the interests and agenda of the movement. From this meeting on, the group of activists known as Proceso de Comunidades Negras (Process of Black Communities, PCN) became our closest interlocutor.[2]

On January 3, 1994, we concluded our first year of research with an intense and productive day-long interview with about ten PCN leaders on issues ranging from ethnicity, environment, and cultural difference to gender, strategy, and movement heterogeneity. This meeting was held in the predominantly black city of Buenaventura on the Pacific Coast. Based on a set of questions that we had circulated in advance, the conversation was intended as a reflection on the organizing process to that date. The discussions centered on achievements and needs, the scope of the movement, the relations with the state and other black sectors of society, interethnic and gender relations, and so forth. Inevitably, the debate kept going back to persistent issues such as ethnicity and difference, environment and the need for their own vision of development, and the heterogeneity of the black experience. The result of this first year of work, plus five additional months of field research in 1994, was a collective volume, *Pacífico, desarrollo o diversidad? Estado, capital y movimientos sociales en el Pacífico colombiano*, published in Bogotá in 1996, with contributions from academics and intellectuals and activists from the region (Escobar & Pedrosa 1996), including chapters by members of the research team and the January 3, 1994, conversation. My relation to PCN remains close to this day. Indeed, my publications owe as much to this group's knowledge and acute political sensibility as they do to scholarly fields. In this way, my most recent book can be seen as an ethnography of the practices, strategies, and visions of this particular group of activists, including their own knowledge production (Escobar 2008). In fact, it is infused with PCN conceptualizations. Since 1994, the movement has grown, waned, and resurfaced. It has crafted a strong identity and seen that identity ebb; has risen to national prominence and then scaled down due to unfavorable conditions. By 2013 (the time of this writing) a core group of activists remained and a cadre of younger ones had joined the network, still focused on some of the key issues that moved them to organize from the beginning—difference, territorial autonomy, and identity—and some new ones, from economic and social rights to racism and reparations. In this chapter, I want to reflect on the beginnings of this movement, how it emerged out of a favorable political opportunity structure, and forged an identity based on the notion of ethnic and cultural difference, which would be constantly developed, refined, questioned, and reaffirmed throughout the organizing process. In particular I want to reflect on the meanings of the personal and the collective in these movement-building processes and how this activism can be seen as History-making with a capital H.

Building Organization and Identity

In 1991 Colombia adopted a new constitution that for the first time referred to the country's black populations as an ethnic minority. Transitory Article 55 (AT 55) paved the way for a legislation that was passed in 1993 and came to be known as Ley 70. This law granted collective land rights to those "black communities" that were living in the rural areas of the Pacific lowland regions along the myriad of river basins according to their traditional lifestyles. It was against this legal backdrop that the social movement of black communities in Colombia began to mobilize. In its initial years (1991–1994), and in the context of AT 55 and the struggle over the formulation of Ley 70, PCN gave preeminence to the social control of the territory and natural resources as a precondition for the survival, re-creation, and strengthening of culture. This emphasis was reflected in the geography of the movement's practices as much as in its organizational strategy. There was an initial focus on river communities, where activists geared their efforts towards advancing a pedagogical process with the communities on the meaning of the new constitution; reflecting on the fundamental concepts of territory, development, traditional production practices, and use of natural resources; and strengthening the organizational capacity of the communities. This sustained effort served to lay down the basis, during the 1991–93 period, for the elaboration of Ley 70, on the one hand, and to firm up a series of politico-organizational principles, on the other. It also helped PCN activists to recognize the various tendencies, trajectories, and styles of work found among the array of black organizations involved with Ley 70.

The first Asamblea Nacional de Comunidades Negras (National Conference of Black Communities) took place in July 1992 in Tumaco, with representatives from all over the Pacific, the Caribbean, and the Norte del Cauca regions. Its principal conclusions were geared towards laying down a framework for the regulation of AT 55. At the Second National Conference of May 1993, delegates revised and approved the text for the law negotiated by government and black-community representatives in the ambit of the High Commission created for this purpose. The collective elaboration of the proposal for Ley 70 was a decisive space for the development of the movement. This process was advanced at two levels, one centered on the daily practices of the communities, the other on a political reflection by the activists. The first level—under the rubric of what was referred to as "the logic of the river" (see also Oslender 2002)—sought a broad participation of local people in the articulation of their rights, aspirations, and dreams. The second level, although having the river settlements as referent, sought to raise the question of black people as an ethnic group, beyond what could be granted by the law. This level saw the development of a conceptualization of the notions of territory, development, and the social relations of black communities with the rest of Colombian society. This conceptualization took place in a dialogical process with a host of actors, including traditional black politicians linked to the liberal party, who attempted to manipulate the process to their own electoral advantage, and of course the state. Government officials realized that the demands of the organizations went well beyond the desire for integration and racial equality, as it had been maintained until then by other sectors of the black community. Besides, black organizations mounted a strategy of persuasion and consciousness-raising among the delegates to the High Commission appointed by the government for the regulation of AT 55. The entire process constituted a veritable social construction of protest that culminated with the approval by the Senate of the version of the law (Ley 70) negotiated with the communities.

The Third National Conference was convened in September 1993 in the also predominantly black town of Puerto Tejada, south of Cali, in the Norte del Cauca region. With the attendance of more than three hundred delegates, the conference debated the politico-organizational situation of the black communities. At the time of the conference, black sectors linked to the traditional political parties, eager to capitalize on the unprecedented legal mechanisms on behalf of the black communities, began to adopt a discourse of blackness that usually did not go beyond the question of skin color. Recognizing the existence of these sectors and the diversity of the social movement of black communities, the conference proposed a self-definition and characterization "as a sector of the social movement of black communities composed of people and organizations with diverse experiences and goals, but united around a set of principles, criteria and objectives that set us apart from other sectors of the movement. In the same vein, we represent a proposal to the entire black community of the country, and aspire to construct a unified movement of black communities able to encompass their rights and aspirations."[3] The objective of the organizing process was stated as "the consolidation of a social movement of black communities for the reconstruction and affirmation of cultural identity," leading to an autonomous organizing strategy "for the achievement of cultural, social, economic, political and territorial rights and for the defense of natural resources and the environment." One of the central features of the conference was the adoption of a set of politico-organizational principles that, in the activists' view, encompassed the practice, lifeworld, and desires of the black communities. These principles concerned the key issues of identity, territory, autonomy, and development:

1. *The reaffirmation of identity* (the right to be black). In the first place, we conceive of being black from the perspective of our cultural logic and lifeworld [*cosmovisión*] in all of its social, economic, and political dimensions. This logic counters the logic of domination that intends to exploit and subject our people . . . Secondly, our cultural affirmation entails an inner struggle with our consciousness; the affirmation of our being is not easy, since we are taught in many ways and through multiple media that we are all equal. This is the great lie of the logic of domination.

     This first principle clearly identifies culture and identity as organizing axes. As we shall see, despite its seemingly essentialist tone, it also partakes of a conception of identity as constructed.

2. *The right to the territory* (as the space for being). As a vital space, the territory is a necessary condition for the re-creation and development of our cultural vision. We cannot be if we do not have a space for living in accordance with what we think and desire as a form of life. It follows that we see the territory as a habitat and space where black people develop their being in harmony with nature.

3. *Autonomy* (the right to the exercise of being/identity). We understand autonomy in relation to the dominant society, other ethnic groups, and political parties. It arises out of our cultural logic. Thus understood, we are autonomous internally in the political realm, and aspire to social and economic autonomy.

4. *Construction of an autonomous perspective of the future.* We intend to construct an autonomous vision of economic and social development based on our culture and traditional forms of production and social organization. The dominant society has systematically imposed on us a vision of development that responds to its own interests and worldview. We have the right to make known to others the vision of our world, as we want to construct it.

5. *Declaration of solidarity.* We are part of the struggle for rights of black people throughout the world. From our own particularity, the social movement of black communities shall contribute to the efforts of those who struggle for alternative life projects.[4]

This declaration of principles constituted a rupture with the political and developmentalist formulations of the Left, past black urban organizations, and traditional political sectors. The differences existed around four main issues: (1) the perception of history and identity; (2) the views and demands concerning natural resources, territory, and development; (3) the types of political representation and participation of the communities; and (4) the conception of organizational strategy and modes of construction of the movement. With this strategy, the PCN sought to become a source of power for the black communities vis-à-vis the state and other social actors, and to contribute to the search for more just and viable societal options for the country as a whole. From then on, the PCN strategy and its successive transformations were to depend on the activists' assessment of the cultural *and* organizational reality of the communities, on the one hand, and of the balance of forces—from the local to the international levels—between the communities, the social movement, and other social sectors, economic groups, and centers of power, on the other.[5] While the principles are continuously refined and debated, their basic orientation and structure has remained the same.

Finally, what has been the main organizational strategy of the movement? At a formal level, PCN's organizational structure is simple: (1) A set of regional *palenques*, corresponding broadly to each of the main regions in the southern Pacific Coast (Valle, Cauca, Nariño), plus the Norte del Cauca and Atlantic Coast regions; these *palenques* gather together the existing ethno-territorial organizations within the region; (2) a national coordinating committee; (3) technical teams at national and, in some cases, regional levels. Originally designating the autonomous territories of maroon or freed slaves in colonial times, today's *palenques* are spaces for discussion, decision making, and policy orientation in each of the regions with important black presence. They operate in conjunction with the Asamblea Nacional de Comunidades Negras, ANCN (National Conference of Black Communities) and together constitute the Consejo Nacional de Palenques. Regional *palenques* are composed of two representatives from each of the region's organizations. The National Coordinating Committee is in charge of coordinating actions, implementing the decisions of the ANCN, and representing the PCN in national and international forums; it is also intended as a space to discuss the various tendencies within the movement, and to generate consensus on important matters. The committee also coordinates the technical teams and identifies the *palenque* representatives to special projects or commissions at the national and international levels.[6]

It would be a mistake, however, to see this "structure" as a rigid set of norms independent of the day-to-day practices of the activists. There is agreement among social movement theorists about the need to avoid the dichotomy that has prevailed between structure-oriented explanations and agency-focused ones. In the newer models (e.g., Scheller 2001, Peltonen 2006), agency and structure are inseparable and mutually constitutive; even when formalized, as in PCN's case, structures are not ready-made, waiting to be filled in by activists. The structure itself is made of movement and enacted in practice. The structure, if anything, is the result of patterned movement over time. PCN activists have their own awareness of this fact in the way in which they view the organizing principles. As one activist put it, "The principles have been the motor of our collective identity. We no longer construct in a vacuum—one is no longer just any black person. The principles confer coherence between discourse and practice, between organization and the everyday. *Everything we do is done out of the principles*; it amounts to creating structures and strategies out of a political project and not out of a pre-fabricated scheme" (emphasis added).[7] The five principles then link structure and agency in everyday practice. PCN activists have generally been successful at developing their approaches and strategies—from the very small to the important ones—from the perspective of these principles.[8]

This also has to do with the reproduction over time of the collectivity called PCN. PCN is the product of an intense set of practices developed around local contentious struggles (some of which we have seen in some detail, especially in the environmental arena). These practices involve a permanent degree of communication among activists at various levels: horizontally, at the national, regional, and local levels; vertically, across levels. The communication is particularly intense at the national and regional levels. At the national level, there is a high degree of face-to-face and electronic communication among the National Coordinating Committee members and with some of the main members of the technical teams. This group forms a tight collective with individuals in constant contact, with active—not infrequently heated—debates on ongoing and concrete issues, decisions, and so forth. The consensus on decisions is arrived at often only after the disagreements have been discussed substantially. For some outside observers, this intense level of debate and communications hinders effective action. Be that as it may, it is this practice that has enabled a core group of activists to remain steadfast in their resolve and committed to the collective identity of PCN and what it represents. Communications are weaker at the local level. While national- and some regional-level activists have internalized the principles as a political vision, this has been much more difficult to accomplish at the local level. In some regions, this has led to the dismantling of local organizations and, coupled with the armed conflict, to the decimation of the regional *palenques*. At the national level, as activists put it, "we construct on the basis of the collective, not from the individual. Our aim is not to be 'me' but to be 'us.'"[9]

There is a tight connection between culture and identity in the understanding of the activists. As one of the most well-known Tumaco activists put it, "It is not us who will save culture, it is culture that will save us." This does not mean, however, that for the activists, culture is a static variable; on the contrary, "culture is a process of construction that is constantly being enriched and fed back into the situation" (Organización de Comunidades Negras 1996, 262). There are, of course, tensions in this conception. The collective identity construction by PCN bears similarities to the construction of Caribbean and Afro-British identities analyzed by Stuart Hall. For Hall (1990), ethnic-identity construction entails cultural and political negotiations characterized by a certain doubleness: on the one hand, identity is thought of as rooted in shared cultural practices, a collective self of sorts; this conception of identity involves an imaginative rediscovery of culture that lends coherence to the experience of fragmentation, dispersal, and oppression. On the other hand, identity is seen in terms of the differences created by history; this aspect of identity construction emphasizes becoming rather than being, positioning rather than essence, and discontinuity as well as continuities at the cultural level. For the activists, the defense of certain cultural practices of the river communities is a strategic question to the extent that they are seen as embodying not only resistance to capitalism and modernity, but elements for alternative world constructions. Although often couched in culturalist language, this defense is not essentializing to the extent that it responds to an interpretation of the challenges faced by the communities and the possibilities presented by a cautious opening towards forms of modernity such as biodiversity conservation and alternative development. Identity is thus seen in both ways: as anchored in "traditional" practices and forms of knowledge, and as an always changing project of cultural and political construction. In this way, the movement builds upon the submerged networks of cultural practices and meanings of the river communities and their active construction of lifeworlds, although it sees such practices in their transformative capacity. To the fixed, static, and conventional notion of identity implicit in the 1991 Constitution, the movement thus opposes a more fluid notion of identity as political construction (see Grueso, Rosero & Escobar 1998 for further elaboration).

The Productivity of Identity Constructions: In, Against, and Beyond the State?

The 1990s saw the appearance of a variety of organized black sectors with different, and at times conflicting, agendas, seeking to profit from the space created for black people's rights.[10] Over the years, the conflicts and contradictions among all of these groups impinged upon important issues such as the composition and work of the High Commission, the formulation of the National Development Plan for Black Communities, the negotiation of environmental conflicts, electoral representation, and so forth. Notwithstanding, PCN's concrete achievements have by no means been negligible. Some of them have already been mentioned, such as the central role played in the formulation of Ley 70, and in other areas of environmental conflict and cultural policy. PCN also made significant contributions over the years to the creation of community organizations in a number of rivers in the southern Pacific Coast, to the configuration of community councils and the titling process, and to the funding of specific projects. In recent years, PCN has been at the forefront, along with the Association of Displaced Afro-Colombians, AFRODES, in the organizing against displacement, the free-trade agreement with the United States, various human-rights causes, and key policy issues, such as the debates and legislation on prior consultation and prior, free, and informed consent, as well as on rural development and the Victims' Law; they have done so nationally and transnationally, becoming again highly visible (say, in their work with the U.S. Congress Black Caucus in Washington, DC).

Let us try to assess these engagements from the perspective of their contributions to identity. First, the history and agency approach shows the extent to which activists take the current histori-cal conditions as resources for collective self-authoring. It is certainly the case that by using the tools of modernity, the activists also further entangle themselves in the worlds from which they seek liberation. In doing so, however, they attempt to redraw the existing hierarchy of power and privilege and to maintain alive the heteroglossic potential of all world-making practice. In the process of struggling with modernist discourses, activists' discourses distance themselves, even if in minor ways, from the authority of the dominant norms, and in so doing produce differentiated voices. In other words, to take the notion of dialogism seriously, one has to bracket the ultimate one-directionality that characterizes state- and capital-centric perspectives, and that makes the idea of genuine difference impossible.

Indeed, from the very beginning, PCN activists demonstrated a high degree of awareness of the limits of negotiating with the state. Most of the engagement with the state by activists was influenced by two factors: the need to "buy time" (that is, to lessen or slow down the cultural and ecological dam-age of the Pacific Coast), and organizational strengthening. There are high costs in the involvement with the state in terms of time and energy. This is why each situation involves a conscious decision. As activists put it, "It is not only through direct confrontation that fissures in the structures of power can be created; we can, and should, work within the structures of the State. Here lie possibilities to heighten contradictions and create trouble, at the risk of being out of a job every six months and of the movement having to take care of the problem of daily sustenance for family and children" (Organización de Comunidades Negras 1996, 264). Influenced by older idioms of the Left (the analysis of the contradictions), this principle nevertheless reveals a political strategy of working in and against the state, but also despite and beyond the state. The state does not capture completely the time and imagination of the activists. If in the late 1990s PCN decided to pull back from relations with the state, after 2004 (second Uribe administration) it decided again that this was a space they could not afford to abandon, in light of the counteroffensive by the state on many vital fronts, particularly a series of deleterious legal reforms on forests, water, rural development, and the TLC or free-trade agreements.

To sum up. In this section I have attempted to use the framework of "history-in-person" to interpret the experience of the collectivity called PCN. This collectivity constituted its identity through dialogical processes of various kinds, some of which involve interpersonal relationships at the interior of the group, other encounters with a host of actors (from state actors and experts to armed actors) in local contentious practice concerning the control of local territories, the defense of particular cultural practices, and the struggle for the right to difference. These local conflicts are related to broader struggles concerning the destruction of the humid forest, racism, development, neoliberal capitalism, and so-called free trade agreements. As a collective identity constructed around a particular figured world—the social movement of black communities—this collectivity constitutes a community of practice that makes possible the production of discourses, performances, and activities. In so doing, and despite ups and downs, they have achieved some durability. In the period 1993–2000, this figured world was able to construct a relatively stable audience, including other sectors of the movement, environmentalists, NGOs, and state programs. In this way, it can be said that the collective identity called PCN is the outcome of an intense participation in communities and activities organized by figured worlds—their own and those of others.

Activism as History-Making: The Personal and the Collective

The emphasis on *lo colectivo* does not mean that *lo personal* (the personal) is completely neglected. The question of "the personal project" has begun to be raised within PCN only recently, and with the general understanding that even if the personal is important, it cannot be construed at the expense of the collective. The starting point is that the personal also has historical and political dimensions—it is, in short, history-in-person all the way down. I believe this notion is useful for thinking about the personal dimension of activism in the context of a strong collective identity such as PCN's. It also allows us to underscore a certain ethics of activism.

In the personal narratives of activists, the personal dimension of collective action starts with their early experience of difference, discrimination, and the sense of injustice. Many of the PCN activists were born in small river towns of the southern Pacific Coast, or in the port cities of Tumaco and Buenaventura, where they spent the formative years of childhood and adolescence, sometimes in their grandparents' homes. At this level, the memories are generally of happy times, pleasant remembrances of life by the river or by the sea, under attentive parental or grandparents' care, enveloped in local culture (food, the drum beat of music and dance, the carefreeness of childhood in river and forest, and so forth). Perhaps the most common memory of the first encounter with difference is that of traveling to the Andean cities and finding themselves being black, with various degrees and forms of discrimination thrown at them. In the larger towns of the Pacific Coast, the formative experience of difference often had to do with the difficult relationships with the *paisas*, although in a few instances it was related to nearby minority groups of *indígenas*. A few were moved to activism by family history (e.g., parents who were union activists, or dedicated mothers who were school teachers), and a few others by involvement since their late teens or early twenties with the leftist parties of the 1970s and 1980s, or through the reading of Marxism. In many of these cases, the progressive Church (what is called the *Pastoral Afro-Americana*, a Liberation Theology–inspired movement focused on the rights of black people, chiefly in the Pacific Coast) played an important role. Most PCN activists, however, came to activism through their own encounter with injustice and difference; this was usually, but not necessarily, of racial character. With the emergence of black identity as a social fact in the 1980s in the cities (especially with the Movimiento Nacional Cimarrón) and throughout the Pacific Coast in the 1990s, many of them turned to ethnic activism as their main form of political engagement.

One activist's recollection of her first awareness of being black is illustrative. Growing up in a river community that was predominantly inhabited by blacks, she says that

> to be black was not a determinant fact; it wasn't something that conditioned me negatively from the outside, it did not mean anything different from being a person. I belonged to a community with whom I shared a way of life, beyond racial conditioning. It was when I traveled to Popayán—a "white" Andean city—when I first learned the meaning of blackness for Colombian society. The racial discrimination I experienced there greatly shaped my perception of being black, changing my process of identity formation which until then was something quite positive and largely unconscious. (Hurtado 1996, 332)

Years later, attending university in Bogotá, she began to make sense of this situation, first by participating in the Movimiento Nacional Cimarrón and, after 1990, in the social movement of black communities:

> The encounter with ethnicity involves a re-encounter with oneself, by countering the de-humanization that arises from society's denial of difference based on skin color. The constitutive elements of the Afro-Colombian person are reinforced by affirming her humanity through the fact of difference . . . Identity is constructed and mobilized through a series of encounters and mis-encounters, it's learned and unlearned, since we are not finished beings but in constant change in relation to others."[11]

For another activist, about thirty years old, who returned to her native rural town in the Tumaco area after living for many years in Cali, the urge to do something for those around her was present from an early age. "Some say," she recounts, "that my desire to work on behalf of the community was present since I was a child." In high school, she was already known for having "revolutionary ideas." For her, however, these ideas "were just an expression of the need to be equal to others; we live under deplorable conditions, and we have the right to be better off." Experiences in Cali and Tumaco with progressive priests and nuns were important in giving shape to her work as cultural activist and entrepreneur on behalf of her communities. Her conviction, however, was rooted in the community itself. In the early 1990s, she said, "we worked for Ley 70 from a perspective called 'pastoral,' but I always said that we also need to work from the community's own vision." Passionate about injustice ("when I hear mention of a *palmicultora* I feel as if my blood is boiling in my veins, and I feel as if I were myself in the plantation, and I would not want any of my people to be there"), by the early 1990s "culture" had already become the focus of her political work. One of her first actions was to start a dance group with young girls and boys "to counter the acculturation introduced by the media." It was her conviction that "if it is true that it is important to be part of other cultures, if we lose ours everything is gone, we would be nothing; the Pacific is recognized for its cultural manifestations, for its way to work the land, its chants and dances; this is what enables us to keep on living. If it ceases to exist we will be nothing." Indeed, while working with AT 55, she learned that those who lost their lands realized that "with the land they lost their lives." In her activism, she seeks to combine cultural work with concrete projects to improve people's living conditions. Together, and despite tremendous challenges, both aspects gave her an unshakable courage and commitment. "Today," she said in 1993, "I feel as strong as a rock." In retrospect, we can see that for this particular activist, as for the previous one, the personal dimension was important from the outset. As she put it, "the important thing was to be able to recognize myself, to know who I was as a person; this brought me closer to the people . . . If today they [the local politicians] think I am crazy, this gives me greater strength to work for the people."[12] These meaningful personal experiences can be of many kinds, from the happier to the most painful.

For another woman activist in her early forties who was taken away from the river when she was twelve years old to make a living in the city, to return to her river almost twenty years later, the memories of, and identification with, life along the river (fishing collectively, sharing of food, planting and harvesting, etc.) are particularly strong. After years of working as a domestic in Cali and enduring abuse ("you try to serve your bosses as best as you can, but they always treat you badly, and this makes you feel bad"), she made the decision to return to the river and work for PCN as a grassroots activist. For her, the fight for rights is important because "it seems that everything is denied to us, including the opportunity to study, because we are black." That is how, she explains, "I became PCN." Today, this woman is one of the most effective local leaders and organizers along one of the rivers of the Buenaventura rural area.

That memories of life on the river can be important in giving shape to activism is also illustrated by the experience of one of the most prominent PCN activists, who spent her first years as a child on a river of the Buenaventura area. The following account is from one of her more important memories:

> My mother, who was a rural teacher, was always organizing activities in the community, such as projects around the school; any important celebration became a big community affair. I remember with special fondness a great *minga* (community work project) to prepare a plot of land to plant trees and food crops, in which children and adults participated. On that day there was a huge community meal [*olla comunitaria*] and the main dish was *mico tití* [a local monkey]. The hunters had brought this meat from the *monte* especially for the *minga*. I did not eat on that day because I saw part of the monkey in the pot. I can say that I learned in this community the value of collective work, the great satisfaction of solidarity. I have the inclination towards working with people ever since.

For this activist, the river was also the site of cultural practices that she would find later on to be profoundly different from those in the cities (e.g., the *chigualo* or ritual on the death of a child). These differences were to become more and more central with the growth of ethnic consciousness. As a young college student, her influences came from her father (a worker's organizer in the docks of Buenaventura), and from her own work as a young woman with poor black people in this city, under the influence of the teachings of Gerardo Valencia Cano, the so-called "red bishop" of Buenaventura and one of the main advocates of Liberation Theology in Colombia, who died in an unexplained helicopter crash in the late 1960s. The language of this period spoke of the betterment of conditions for poor black people. One could say that in this language and practice there was an ethnic consciousness *in statu nascendi.* This consciousness would blossom fully once the language of ethnic identity became available.

This consciousness and these experiences ground powerful visions of the struggle and the future. PCN activists have a conviction that their struggle goes well beyond the issue of rights for black people. The ultimate goal is to contribute to the search for more just and viable societal options for the country as a whole. This was clearly stated early on:

> Anthropologically speaking there are multiple groups among the black people, but politically speaking we are an ethnic group. We struggle for the right to have a different vision, one that constitutes a possibility and an alternative to today's enormous crisis of societal models. This does not mean that there cannot be other groups within the black movement. We cannot conceive of a movement only for the black community, nor do we overlook the fact that the great problems faced by Colombia and Latin America are not only the product of the *mestizo* mind; there are black people who have adapted to this system and contribute to our oppression. Our discourse does not focus only on the ethnic question. There are problems in common with other people, and we know we have to work towards the construction of a project that encompasses many sectors, black and non-black, who share similar problems. (OCN 1996, 255–256)

This orientation has been present in the many facets of the movement's work—for instance, in the persistence of the vision of the Pacific as a region-territory of ethnic groups; in their alternative frameworks of development and sustainability that envision a Pacific that retains much of its cultural and ecological aliveness and diversity; and in the PCN's contribution to the broader project of self-definition for the black groups of Latin America. This latter issue, under development in recent years, is based on the idea of a model of solidarity with people and nature, as a contribution to society as a whole and towards the recuperation of more dignified ways of existence for all living beings on the planet.

It is fitting to quote the vision of the future of the Pacific stated by one of the activists:

> I imagine a Pacific that preserves its landscape and its people; a Pacific with all its trees, all its rivers, all its animals and birds, all its mangroves. I imagine a Pacific where people live well according to their cultural vision, where money serves to facilitate exchange and does not become life's goal. I imagine a Pacific where music and happiness accompany all activities in individual and collective life. I imagine a Pacific

where black and indigenous peoples are able to contribute their cultural values to the construction of societal options based on the respect of the other's difference.[13]

The important point is not whether the memories are idealized, nor whether the visions of the future are romantic. The point is to understand how memories and visions come to be integral elements of a sustained and coherent political practice. Perhaps these activists are dreamers, but they anchor their dreams with great intelligence in a caring and courageous political practice. They sing songs of freedom, of emancipation from the mental slavery that has seemingly become commonplace in the age of the total market—the market as the ultimate arbiter and framework of life. And, as the well-known song says, they are not the only dreamers. Many others today have come to believe that another world is indeed possible. In this, as some philosophers would have it, they are just retrieving their history-making skills, out of their place-based (not place-bound) commitments.

Activism and History-Making

Activism can also be seen in this light. The notion of the retrieval of history-making skills has been developed by a handful of phenomenology-oriented scholars and has great promise for understanding activism. Phenomenology enables a view of identity as an expression of the profound historicity of one's encounter with the world. According to this view, we are constituted on the basis of concrete encounters with the world in our everyday coping, and knowledge is built from small domains and tasks that make up micro-identities and micro-worlds; this is a different way of looking at history-in-person, one that brings to the fore the embedded and embodied character of all human action. Varela (1999) builds his argument by bringing together new trends in cognitive science, his own phenomenological theory of cognition as embodied enaction, and the traditions of Taoism, Confucianism, and Buddhism. His goal is to articulate a theory of "ethical know-how" (an embedded understanding of action) as opposed to the Cartesian "know-what" (abstract, rational judgment) that has become prevalent in modern worlds.

PCN activists could be seen as having ethical expertise (know-how) of the sort Varela describes. To be sure, this expertise is coupled with rational judgment (know-what) all the way through, but what defines PCN the most is a continuous engagement with the everyday reality of Afro-Colombian groups, grounded in the last instance (although with layers of mediation, as we saw) in the experience of the Pacific as a place. Activists are skilled at responding to the needs of their own collectivity and those of others. This process involves *ethical expertise* more than, or at least as much as, rational deliberation. This ethical expertise is cultivated throughout the activists' lives. For those whom PCN activists call "traditional authorities" (*autoridades tradicionales*—roughly, local wise people who always know what to do because they are profoundly rooted in the community), embedded ethical know-how predominates. As the narrative of an elder leader of the Yurumanguí River demonstrates, these "natural leaders" do not even see themselves as contributing anything to the process as individuals, because they do not see themselves as "individuals" contributing to something separate ("the community"), and because they only do what they know is good to do. For the more cosmopolitan PCN activists, political practice is already a combination of both types of ethics. Commenting on Confucian and Buddhist traditions, Varela suggests that although everybody has ethical know-how of a certain type because of the basic fact of being part of a collectivity, true expertise at virtuous action comes after a long process of cultivation. This involves a pragmatic and progressive learning process that goes well beyond the intellectual process and results in non-dual action that refuses to separate subject and object. This non-dual action becomes well grounded "in a substrate both at rest and at peace" (Varela 1999, 34). This explains what many outsiders describe as the steadfastness and peace that seem to characterize many activists, even those who face horrendous conditions, including many of those in PCN.

In contrast to the detached view of people and things instilled by modern science, the phenomenological perspective highlights the retrieval of history-making skills, which implies building on a contextualized, embodied, and situated notion of human practice (Spinosa, Flores & Dreyfus 1997). In this argument, we live at our best when engaged in acts of history-making, meaning by this the ability to engage in the ontological act of disclosing new ways of being, of transforming the ways in which we understand and deal with ourselves and the world. This happens, for instance, when activists identify and hold on to a disharmony in ways that transform the background of understanding in which people live (say, about nature, racism, sexism, homophobia, or what have you). There is also a connection to place in this argument, to the extent that the life of skillful disclosing, which makes the world look genuinely different, is only possible through a life of intense engagement with a place and a collectivity. Skillful disclosing requires the immersion in particular problems and places, with the real risk-taking that such rootedness entails. Only under these circumstances can the kind of *interpretive speaking* worthy of attention to a community be exercised. Place-based activists, intellectuals, and common people do not act as detached contributors to public debate (as in the talk-show model of the public sphere, or as in attempts to explain problems in terms of abstract principles), but are able to articulate the concerns of their constituencies in direct ways. Identities are thus the result of engagement with cultural worlds; they arise not out of detached deliberation, but out of involved experimentation. This is the role of disclosure properly speaking, which requires sensitivity to problematic practices that might have become habitual, or to marginal or occluded practices that could be fostered or retrieved. In sum, historical identities are neither rigid or essential nor fully contingent. They are grounded in a familiar style of practices, and it is out of this contextual grounding that they change.[14]

The partially embedded and place-based character of activism is a feature of social movements that often goes unacknowledged (Harcourt & Escobar 2005). It should be evident that in places such as the Colombian Pacific Coast region, the place dimension of movements is of paramount importance. Movements are situated in place and space, and this situatedness is an important component of their practice. "Involved experimentation" in cultural worlds is often as important, if not more so, than explicitly articulated strategies in some instances.

Coda

I would like to address very briefly the critiques by academics of the approach presented in this chapter and of the book *Territories of Difference* as a whole. Indeed, maintaining an active and close relationship with PCN for two decades now has been far easier for me than satisfying the demands of some fellow academics for "good scholarship." While most reviews of this particular book have been largely positive, some have been harshly critical. Critical reviewers have remarked, for instance, about my "lack of distance" in relation to PCN, the difficulty readers find in distinguishing PCN's from my own views, my apparent unwillingness to analyze critically PCN's conceptualization, the scant information I present about other sectors of the Afro-Colombian movement, and insufficient ethnographic evidence for some of my claims. All of these comments, in turn, converge in the most common critical charges, namely, "lack of critical distance" and "romanticism." In my mind, these critiques cannot be settled on the basis of better or worse scholarship; rather, they refer to contrasting understandings of (a) the place of ethnography in anthropological research; (b) epistemological and ontological assumptions regarding the nature of "theory" and the role of "reflexivity"; (c) the relation between theory, the academy, and politics.

While I cannot provide an appropriate answer to these various critiques here, I would like to make a few points regarding the two most common charges I just mentioned, particularly my alleged lack of distance and reflexivity vis-à-vis PCN. First, to paraphrase Law (2004), there is not an "out there" out there that is not enacted through particular practices (including method). "Critical distance" is made possible by historically intensified practices, including ethnography and the use of logocentric language. We need to see critical distance as an artifact of our practices.[15] Second, if we adopt a relational and nondualist view, the relation to our subjects changes significantly. The idea of a social movement as object of study disappears entirely; issues such as "idealization of activists," "keeping a distance," and "romanticizing" the movement all take on a different meaning, given that the relation between theory, politics, also becomes very different. Let me offer the following counternarrative in lieu of a full explanation. To the charge of romanticism leveled against those who speak about the need for alternatives *to* development, I often say that the true romantics are the world bankers, IMFers, and developers of all kinds that still insist, after six decades of failure, that yet one more round of "development," no matter how qualified, will bring about significant improvements, or the alleged radical Marxist whose analyses of globalization and development continue to be fixated on capital as the master narrative of their views—almost to the point of becoming a mirror image of the liberal postures. Now I would add that "romantic" is s/he who believes that our knowledge can be assessed on the basis of how dis/connected we can be from our subjects; s/he who believes that "distancing" ensures more adequate knowledge; s/he who operates within a naturalized view of knowledge in which politics can take the form of "not taking sides," truth corresponds to empirical evidence, and the real exists independently of our actions. By contrast, those who place as much trust in popular or activist knowledges as in academic knowledge, or who seek to validate their knowledge in relation to the subjects' knowledge more than with reference to any academic canon, could be seen as more politically realistic. A politics of the possible, in any case, should be seen as valid as a politics of the objectivist real (Gibson-Graham 2006; Osterweil, 2013). These different epistemological and ontological readings should at least be part of how we assess collaborative works with social movements.[16]

NOTES

1. The research team included Alvaro Pedrosa, professor of popular education at Universidad del Valle in Cali, who by then had been working in the Pacific for some years on popular education and

communication programs; Betty Ruth Lozano, an Afro-Colombian sociologist from Cali who had recently graduated from the same university, and who went on to develop the first approach to the intersection of race (blackness), gender, and development for the Pacific; Jesus Alberto Grueso, Afro-Colombian anthropologist from the town of Timbiquí, on the river by the same name in the Southern Pacific; and, for part of the project, Jaime Rivas, by then a young recent graduate from the communications program at Universidad del Valle—Jaime was from Tumaco and had moved to Cali to attend the university. It was very important for me to include Afro-Colombian women and men in the team, and I was lucky to put together such a fine team shortly after my arrival for the first full year of fieldwork in January 1993.

2. This first meeting was held at a conference center near Cali; besides our team and seven PCN activists, the meeting included the Guapi expert in oral traditions Alfredo Vanín and the anthropologist Michael Taussig.

3. This and the succeeding quotations in this section are from the proceedings of the Puerto Tejada conference of September 1993.

4. This declaration of principles has remained the same throughout the years, with minor adjustments. However, the principles have been progressively spelled out and operationalized, and the emphasis has shifted among them throughout time. In recent years, the fifth principle has taken on salience, as the PCN adopts more actively a diasporic position in light of the need for internationalizing solidarity to face the conflict.

5. From these early years, conventional black politics started to capitalize on the newly open political and public spaces—getting public jobs for their constituencies, bureaucratic representation, the use of public funds to ensure reelection and political survival, etc. This affected the meaning of the demands raised by the ethno-territorial organizations, which nevertheless have remained an important interlocutor ever since. It was the ethno-territorial sector of the movement that trained the majority of activists capable of carrying out a critical dialogue with the state, and of endowing some river communities with a tool kit for the defense of their rights within the framework of Ley 70 and Ley 121 of 1991 (this latter ratified Agreement 169 of the International Labor Organization concerning indigenous and tribal communities). Today, it is the same organizations that are organizing nationally and internationally against displacement and the free-trade agreement with the United States, among other causes. These accomplishments became key ingredients of the political practice of many grassroots organizations.

6. This structure worked relatively well until 2000, when some of the *palenques* started to fall apart as a result of the armed conflict. The *palenque* of Tumaco was decimated by paramilitary action, causing most members to leave the region. By 2007, the Palenque el Congal from Buenaventura remained quite active, and there were attempts to reconstitute some of the other organizations in the southern Pacific hurt by displacement.

7. Conversation with Julia Cogollo, of the Palenque el Congal (Buenaventura) at the Cali PCN office, June 2002.

8. The trends briefly referred to here that seek to problematize the binary between structure and agency are largely based on theories of complexity, self-organization, and nonlinearity. Similar attempts from the perspective of more established sociological and anthropological theories have been those by Tarrow (1994), Melucci (1989), and Alvarez, Dagnino & Escobar (1998). An early attempt at applying a framework of self-organization to social movements is found in Escobar 1992.

9. Conversation with Julia Cogollo, Alfonso Cassiani, and Libia Grueso, Cali, June 2002.

10. In the mid- to late-1990s these included, besides the Process of Black Communities, the Working Group of Chocó Organizations, Afro-Colombian Social Movement, Cimarrón National Movement, National Afro-Colombian Home, Afro-Colombian Social Alliance, Afro-South, Afro-Antioquia, Malcom, Cali Black Community Council, Vanguard 21 of May, Raizales, and Federation of Organizations of the Cauca Coast. Some of the avatars of black movement organizing in Colombia, with attention to urban movements in particular, are discussed by Wade (1995).

11. The last two quotes come from an interview-article by Mary Lucía Hurtado, who belonged to PCN in the early 1990s, and published in Escobar and Pedrosa (1996). See Hurtado (1996), 332–333. Hurtado's explanation is clearly influenced by black-consciousness writings, especially Fanon.

12. This particular account is based on six hours of taped interviews in 1994. Part of the interview was written up as a narrative and can be found in Escobar and Pedrosa (1996), 265–282: "Relato de Mercedes Balanta," a pseudonym. This courageous and creative activist remained an important actor in local activism until 2003 when she was forced to move to Bogotá, where she continues to work as a black cultural activist.

13. Response to interview with Libia Grueso, October 2002.

14. This perspective is presented as a critique of Cartesian modernity, and advocates for the historical viability of an alternative modernity based on connections to place and relatively stable, albeit deeply historical, identities. It is impossible to do justice to this complex argument in these few lines. The argument is based on, and inspired largely by, Heidegger's philosophy and the phenomenological biology of Maturana and Varela.

15. The consequences of academic practices (including those from critical scholarship) are beginning to be discussed in novel ways, as in those works emphasizing epistemic decolonization in Latin America, and attempts focused on decolonizing methodologies, such as Smith (1999).

16. I deal with these dimensions of the critiques at length in a forthcoming article in *Social Analysis*.

REFERENCES

Alvarez, S., Dagnino, E., & Escobar, A. (Eds.). (1998). *Cultures of politics, politics of cultures: Re-visioning Latin American social movements*. Oxford: Westview Press.

Escobar, A. (1992). Culture, economics, and politics in Latin American social movements theory and research. In A. Escobar & S. Alvarez (Eds.), *The making of social movements in Latin America: Identity, strategy, and democracy*, 62–85. Oxford: Westview Press.

Escobar, A. (2008). *Territories of difference: Place, movements, life, redes*. Durham, NC: Duke University Press.

Escobar, A., & Pedrosa, A. (Eds.). (1996). *Pacífico: ¿desarrollo o diversidad? Estado, capital y movimientos sociales en el Pacífico colombiano*. Bogotá, Colombia: ICANH/CEREC.

Gibson-Graham, J. K. (2006). *A postcapitalist politics*. Minneapolis: University of Minnesota Press.

Grueso, L., Rosero, C., & Escobar, A. (1998). The process of black community organizing in the southern Pacific coast region of Colombia. In S. Alvarez, E. Dagnino & A. Escobar (Eds.), *Cultures of politics, politics of cultures: Re-visioning Latin American social movements*, 196–219. Oxford: Westview Press.

Hall, S. (1990). Cultural identity and diaspora. In J. Rutherford (Ed.), *Identity, community, culture, difference*, 392–403. London: Lawrence & Wishart.

Harcourt, W., & Escobar, A. (Eds.). (2005). *Women and the politics of place*. Bloomfield, CT: Kumarian Press.

Hurtado, M. L. (1996). La construcción de una nación multiétnica y pluricultural. In A. Escobar and A.

Pedrosa (Eds.), *Pacífico, desarrollo o diversidad? Estado, capital y movimientos sociales en el Pacífico colombiano*, 329–352. Bogotá, Colombia: ICANH/CEREC.

Law, J. (2004). *After method: Mess in social science research*. London: Routledge.

Melucci, A. (1989). *Nomads of the present: Social movements and individual needs in contemporary society*. London: Hutchinson Radius.

Organización de Comunidades Negras (OCN). (1996). Movimiento negro, identidad y territorio: Entrevista con la Organización de Comunidades Negras de Buenaventura. In A. Escobar & A. Pedrosa (Eds.), *Pacífico: ¿desarrollo o diversidad? Estado, capital y movimientos sociales en el Pacífico colombiano*, 245–265. Bogotá, Colombia: ICANH/CEREC.

Oslender, U. (2002). The logic of the river: A spatial approach to ethnic-territorial mobilization in the Colombian Pacific region. *Journal of Latin American Anthropology* 7 (2): 86–117.

Osterweil, M. (2013). Rethinking public anthropology through epistemic politics and theoretical practice. *Cultural Anthropology* 28 (4) (November): 598–620.

Peltonen, L. (2006). Fluids on the move: An analogical account of environmental mobilization. In Y. Haila & C. Dyke (Eds.), *How nature speaks: The dynamics of the human ecological condition*, 150–176. Durham, NC: Duke University Press.

Scheller, M. (2001). *The mechanisms of mobility and liquidity: Re-thinking the movement in social movements*. Paper presented at the "Are Social Movements Reviving?" Conference, organized by the International Sociological Association Research Committee on Social Movements, Social Change and Collective Action, and the British Sociological Association Study Group on Protest and Social Movements, Manchester, England. November 3–5.

Smith, L. T. (1999). *Decolonizing methodologies: Research and indigenous peoples*. London: Zed Books.

Spinosa, C., Flores, F., & Dreyfus, H. (1997). *Disclosing new worlds*. Cambridge, MA: MIT Press.

Tarrow, S. (1994). *Power in movement: Social movements, collective action, and politics*. Cambridge: Cambridge University Press.

Varela, F. (1999). *Ethical know-how: Action, wisdom, and cognition*. Stanford, CA: Stanford University Press.

Wade, P. (1995). The cultural politics of blackness in Colombia. *American Ethnologist* 22 (2): 341–357.

Out of Bounds: Negotiating Researcher Positionality in Brazil

Elizabeth Hordge-Freeman

The transnational dialogues between black researchers from the United States and Brazil have been documented by a number of scholars (Hellwig 1992; Yelvington 2006). While the historical import of these dialogues have been discussed at length, only rarely does the analysis of these dialogues focus on dilemmas in the field that are related to how researchers practice activism and research (see Twine & Warren 2000 for an exception). This is, indeed, unfortunate as black scholars find themselves in a truly unique position to provide insight into these negotiations. Their positionality allows them to, at times, slip seamlessly through social spaces and, in other moments, stumble awkwardly through an unpredictable "web of interlocking social categories," on "multiple levels," and simultaneously (Caldwell 2007, xv). Gilliam writes of her experience in Brazil: "We were white to the degree that we spoke English and refused to speak Portuguese properly, since it reinforced our status as foreigners. We were black to the degree that we seemed Brazilian. This bifurcation of the subject position was to become more complex in Bahia" (Gilliam & Gilliam 1999, 72). While this statement is persuasive, I argue that positionality is characterized by multilevel fragmentation rather than a dual or bifurcated negotiation. Along these same lines, black researchers in Brazil are perhaps best framed as being positioned "out of bounds." Rather than moving in and out of boundaries strategically, or unpredictably, they are never completely in or out. They hover in the uncertainty of constantly shifting positions, but they also exert agency in guiding these transitions. Researchers benefit greatly from a more candid discussion of these shifts because they have significant implications for how researchers can maximize their contribution to the very communities that they hope to empower.

This chapter provides concrete examples of how I navigated fundamental dilemmas when conducting research in Brazil. My research approach was one that was deliberately both feminist and activist, which I found to be more flexible and dynamic. Instead of distantly observing, this approach anticipates empathy and action with research participants. I draw heavily on black feminist theory to argue that it is beneficial and necessary for scholar-activists to reject the false dichotomy of insider/outsider status, in exchange for discussing complex negotiations of identity, power, and positionality. I refer to myself as an "outsider-within," both because of my resistance to normative approaches to qualitative research and my ambiguous position within the Afro-Brazilian community (Collins 1991).[1] Though I instinctively aligned myself with a black feminist orientation, I argue it was not always clear what this orientation meant in complicated situations in the field. Below, I will focus on several thematic areas through which I illustrate how I managed my subjectivity and the demands of research, and struggled to dismantle interactional styles that reinforced privilege and unequal power dynamics, while also promoting the goals of scholar-activism.

Reconciling the Researcher Gaze and Activist Deeds

While the bulk of my research is based on my time in Salvador, Bahia, Brazil, my first visit to Brazil was when I spent six weeks in a language program in Rio de Janeiro. It was here that I had first-hand exposure to race relations in Brazil. As a black, female PhD student in sociology, I had diligently read seminal works on Brazil by both U.S. and Brazilian scholars, and trained with interdisciplinary mentors in history and anthropology. I benefited from the works of a growing cadre of black female scholars from the United States (among whom I perhaps presumptively situated myself) who had written about race, gender, and subjectivity in the field. I stood on the shoulders of giants and had planned to use their works to develop my intellectual trajectory and navigate my positionality in Brazil. On the van ride from Rio's airport to my apartment, I took notes furiously, noting how the dilapidated favelas were juxtaposed against both the beauty of Rio's beaches and the upscale community in which I would reside. These observations were consistent with how researchers have discussed the spatial topography of racial inequality in Brazil and other countries (McCallum 2005). On a narrow street in Copacabana, the airport van came to a halt, and directly outside of the van window I noticed a very dark-skinned woman unambiguously identifiable as black (*preta*) sitting on the edge of a sidewalk. Near the corner, she sat on a dusty, dull blue blanket with sundry knickknacks including dishes, plastic bottles, newspapers, and a tattered pillow. Next to her sat a young girl who could not have been over four years old. The tiny brown-skinned girl wore her hair parted down the middle in two matted puffs with stray afro-textured hair peeking out across her hairline. In the girl's hand was a worn baby doll with dirt spots on her face and patches that hinted at the doll's original blond hair.

This image of an apparently homeless black mother and daughter living on a blanket on a sidewalk was provocative and deeply disturbing. It represented Brazil's stark social inequality, and the face of racial inequality and poverty in Brazil. As I fumbled through my bag to find my camera, I did not take my eyes off of the young girl, hoping to beat the change of the traffic light. As I brought the camera up to my face, suddenly and unexpectedly, the little girl pulled the tattered blanket over her head to cover her face. I was paralyzed, or rather, mortified. Frozen with embarrassment, I lowered the camera, feeling as though I had betrayed her . . . with my imposing gaze. I would later describe this encounter to interested colleagues—explaining that the young girl and I were locked in a gaze. But, after reviewing my field notes later on, I realized that though my eyes were fixed on her, her eyes darted around uncomfortably, only coming back to meet mine to see if I was still looking. This fleeting moment in Rio left an indelible impression on me and raised questions about my privilege, my positionality, and the tension between being a researcher and an activist.

In this first encounter in Rio, I was using what has been referred to as the "white ethnographic gaze"—observing, inspecting, evaluating, and making conclusions without even consulting these two Afro-Brazilians (Zuberi & Bonilla-Silva 2008, 180). I had naively presumed that privilege and exploitation were mainly issues for white researchers to work out, and had not anticipated the degree to which I would also feel ambivalent about the researcher gaze and the activist posture. As a black North American, I felt solidarity with Afro-Brazilians, but as Few, Stephens, and Rouse-Arnett (2003) suggest, "Sharing certain identities is not enough to presume an insider status. Idiosyncrasies are embedded in our identities that inevitably create moments of intimacy and distance between the informant and researcher" (207). My sincere investment in documenting racial disparity by taking a photo did not inevitably translate to activism, and at worst could even be considered exploitative and dehumanizing. Few et al. (2003) note: "Good qualitative feminist research must not only be able to assist the researcher in gathering accurate and useful data, but, more importantly, the researcher must ensure that the informant is central in the research process" (207). Despite the fact that a significant portion of my own academic experience had been spent embracing the importance of "decolonizing methodologies," de-normalizing epistemological approaches, and resisting expectations to produce a particular narrative of race and inequality, I still found myself in a position where, in practice, I was poised to do quite the opposite (Smith 1999, 3).

In retrospect, my propensity to so easily slip into the more problematic researcher gaze reflected my inculcation in the norms of sociology and a particular social-science tradition that includes the casual dismissal and manipulation of marginalized communities (Ladner 1973, Smith 1999 Zuberi & Bonilla-Silva 2008). This made me potentially complicit in reproducing inequality; as researchers have argued, "White rule, or the theoretical, methodological, epistemological, and practice domination of Whites . . . can happen without Whites at the helm" (Hordge-Freeman, Mayorga & Bonilla-Silva 2011, 96). Not only had this moment uncomfortably revealed my privilege, but it clarified the extent to which I would need to closely monitor my gaze and more consciously reevaluate how my socialization in the academy influenced how I interacted with marginalized communities (Zuberi & Bonilla-Silva 2008; Collins 1991). When the van drove away to deliver me to my nice apartment in Copacabana, I was left feeling ambivalent: what I knew about who I was, my research, and what I was doing in Brazil were now fragmented ideas that needed to be reconfigured and reassessed.

When U.S. Researchers Come Knocking

One of the first examples of how I navigated my status as "out of bounds" is reflected in my interactions with established faculty in Brazil. Social-science researchers, intentionally or not, often neglect to describe the complications of gaining entrée into the communities that they research, particularly in international contexts. From my experience, the Institutional Review Board (IRB) offers significant latitude in terms of dealing with international populations, which puts the researcher at an unfair advantage. But, if one were to assess how qualitative researchers discuss how they identify and enter into their community of study, this process is written about as though it occurs spontaneously and with little fanfare. This was certainly not my experience in Bahia, Brazil. I arrived in Bahia wanting to develop relationships with race scholars and become incorporated into important academic circles. My efforts to develop relationships with renowned scholars depended on my access and mobilization of various forms of capital, including my identification as a U.S. researcher and institutional affili-ation. Some of these initial contacts were exceedingly helpful, particularly those with Dr. Antonio Alberto and Gildete Lopes, who are both researchers at the Federal University of Bahia (UFBA) and are also close friends of Dr. Sherman James, who served on my dissertation committee. But outside of them, I often felt that female faculty interacted with me tentatively, while some male Brazilians were uncomfortably eager to help me find my way. I anticipated that my nationality and gender would provide advantages, and while they often did, there were moments when they did quite the opposite.

Researchers at prominent universities who had initially agreed to assist me in my research were unresponsive, dismissive, or simply too busy to meet. I struggled during my first weeks to make inroads and often felt frustrated by the lack of support that I was offered. But my disappointment was rooted in my expectation that when I knocked, other researchers would answer. But, why should they? As my Brazilian colleagues and friends would soon reveal, it was likely that some of these scholars felt that assisting me would be undermining their own efforts to develop a name for themselves in their respective fields. In some ways, they were correct that the work of U.S. research-ers (produced in English) often received more visibility and was viewed as more legitimate than theirs. It was obvious that I had much to gain from associations with them, but it was less clear that an affiliation with me was a worthwhile investment. Researchers idealistically speak about intel-lectual exchanges, but some Brazilian researchers, familiar with the unidirectional way that these interactions can and often do unfold, were perhaps rightfully resistant. And so, the privilege that nationality offered me, which compelled people on the streets to rush to my aid the moment they heard English, had much less currency among well-known faculty. In fact, academic and intellectual events occurred all over Salvador, but my attendance did not necessarily translate into developing meaningful relationships with the faculty at the helm of power. In contrast, at conferences around Brazil, Brazilian graduate and undergraduate students *were* eager to engage me in conversations about racism and social movements in the United States. Idealizing the civil rights movement in the United States, they were unduly attentive to my responses to questions and, at times, interacted with me in a way that reinforced the very "power asymmetry" that I had hoped to diffuse (Alcalde 2007, 143).

My difficulties in developing relationships with faculty is one issue, but the very fact that I so highly prioritized developing ties with university faculty represented my internalization of a hierarchy of legitimate knowledge that undervalues the importance of community groups with alternative knowledges (Smith 1999). More interestingly, these institutions, though they had international reputations, had a different local reputation. Most of the brief meetings that I managed to organize with major scholars ended in disappointment. On one occasion one of the more renowned scholars of race asked me, "Why study race, when class is so much more important?" The paradox that a race researcher in Bahia did not want to critically discuss race was disconcerting. After months of being in Salvador, I began to expand my network of potential allies and collaborators, and only when I did so was I able to develop relationships that would form the basis of my research.

My relationship with activist-scholars whose knowledge was based on their close interaction with Afro-Brazilian communities was pivotal to helping me frame my project in ways that would resonate with the community. The ultimate selection of my research site evolved from a relationship that developed organically with an Afro-Brazilian woman in my apartment building in Salvador. My informal relationships and not the more formal institutional connections were the ones that were fundamental to my research trajectory. But, after only a few weeks in the field, I realized that my formal doctoral training had not prepared me to reconcile the multilayered positionalities that I occupied. How do I conduct research and negotiate friendships? Where does the research end and the friendships begin? Can a researcher be an activist, and what does that even mean? Recognizing that I was in a privileged position vis-à-vis my informants, how do I negotiate the unequal power relations that are inescapable? Social scientists provide some suggestions about this process, but what did their suggestions mean in Brazil, particularly for me?

Almost universally, I was read as black, as one respondent affirmed directly by brushing her finger over her forearm and stating, "você é como a gente" (you are like us). Another respondent would later question my blackness, stating directly, "You are not black, I am black," but the latter was exceptional. Certainly, being mistaken as Afro-Brazilian had its moments of convenience, yet at other times it was devastating. I enjoyed the conveniences of standing at a bus stop and being ignored by peddlers targeting gullible tourists. At the same time, my ability to blend in with other Afro-Brazilians meant that I would be ignored while standing in lines, and I had to avoid police batons that targeted black crowds during Carnaval. But, for all the ways in which I appeared to be an insider, I was simultaneously an outsider, and vice versa. There was an assumption that as a black female researcher from the United States, my blackness and sense of shared experience would open most doors and make me feel at home. This grossly underestimated the extent to which my subjectivity was negotiated in complex and contradictory ways.

Among Afro-Brazilians, I was often embraced and given "partial insider status." Paradoxically, white Brazilians who positioned me on their level and "superior" to Brazilian blacks embraced me. A white Brazilian associate refused to group my husband and me with Afro-Brazilians, stating, "You all are not like our blacks." I was privy to a number of similar comments and other "intimate secrets of white society" in Brazil (Collins 1991, 35). Exposure to anti-black sentiments and racism angered me, but I learned to "suppress a sense of outrage while in the field . . . and take advantage of [my] rage" in order to make key inferences about racial discourse and white habitus in Brazil (Erikson 1984, 61).

Flipping the Script, Redefining Roles, and Promoting Liberation

Beyond the difficulties of developing ties with faculty and negotiating my multiple positionalities in Brazil, there are important ways that the researcher's gaze and activism collided during the data-collection process. I arrived in Salvador, Bahia, Brazil, to research the complicated ways in which Afro-Brazilian families negotiate racial hierarchies. One of the major challenges was making decisions about when I would remain in my researcher role and when I would take on a more activist approach. While I had the expressed goal of engaging in feminist and activist research, putting this approach into practice was considerably more difficult than I had anticipated.

The tension between the researcher and activist role became salient as I spent time in my research site located in the Lower City of Salvador and listened to family members, neighbors, and children mercilessly tease a young Afro-Brazilian girl to the point of tears because of her "cabelo duro" (hard hair). Though I have written about interactions like these previously, I have seldom discussed how I responded to the mistreatment of children (Hordge-Freeman 2013). Refusing to simply document instances of her humiliation by family and friends, but cognizant of my role as researcher, I adopted the role of hair braider in the community. I offered to braid or twist the hair of young Afro-Brazilian girls who wanted a new hairstyle. In this role, I provided a service to the community that was desired, and created a place for young girls to be exposed to counter-discourses about blackness and beauty. At one point, as I styled a young black girl's hair, I complimented her on how healthy and thick her hair was, and she turned and looked up at me quizzically, reminding me that people in the neighborhood said that she had "hard hair." These moments of affirmation would certainly not erase the constant messages that reproduce racial hierarchies, but they did expose her and other young girls to alternative readings of her racialized and gendered body. As hair braider I created a safe space for young girls, and simultaneously created an opportunity to engage in sustained conversations about race, gender, and beauty. The women and girls who I interviewed were not merely internalizing and reproducing prepackaged aesthetic norms, but rather the conversations illustrated how they "weave 'between and among' oppositional ideologies of femininity and anti-racism to find self valorization and liberation from hegemonic power structures" (Sandoval 1991, 270–271).

Subjectivity is defined as "the quality of an investigator that affects the results of observational investigation, which have the capacity to filter, skew, shape, block, transform, construe and misconstrue what transpires from the outset of a research project" (Peshkin 1988). Rather than perceiving an obstacle to be avoided at all costs, Peshkin recognizes that "subjectivity can be seen as virtuous for it is the basis of researchers' making a distinctive contribution, one that results from the unique configuration of their personal qualities joined to the data they have collected" (14). I relied on this interpretation of subjectivity to guide my interviews, interactions, and presentation of self in Brazil. While there were elements of my subjectivity that I "tamed," throughout my time in Brazil, I embraced and manipulated my subjectivity in ways that led to theoretical insights. The extent of my subjectivity expanded beyond my role as hair braider, as there were intentional ways that I manipulated my own personal appearance both as a form of research and activism. Realizing how much racialization processes and notions of beauty are framed in terms of hair, I begin to manipulate my own hair in response to racialized comments about "cabelo bom" and "cabelo ruim" (good and bad hair). Every several days, I changed my natural afro-textured hair using hair styles ranging from intricate braid and twist patterns to a natural afro style. Both young girls and women became curious about my hair designs and started to request them for themselves or ask to learn how to do them. Contrary to the argument that social scientists are not "necessarily conscious of [subjectivity]," I was manipulating my subjectivity and destabilizing the status quo in ways that had implications for both my research and activism (Peshkin 1988, 17).

In other situations, my negotiation of research and activism was much more complicated, with far more consequential results. Though I was studying biological Afro-Brazilian families, on several occasions, I met women who had been informally adopted into families as children. Luana, like so many of these informally adopted women, had remained bound to her adoptive families, even continuing to live with them past the age of forty years old. After knowing Luana for several weeks, she eventually confided that she had been horribly abused in her family. Her revelations alarmed me, as did her tearfully emotional narratives. As I asked her more questions about her life, she confessed that she had never discussed her abuse with anyone and welcomed our conversation as a space to further describe her mistreatment. After our discussion, she resolutely stated that she was going to leave the house and find a home for herself because she was tired of being "explorada como se fosse escrava" (exploited as though I were a slave).

I felt deeply conflicted and anxious about what seemed to be an important and life-altering decision. Horrified by her life history, yet concerned about whether or not she would be able to support herself outside of her adoptive family, I was uncertain about how to respond. What role had our conversation played in her decision to leave her home? I had been intentionally cautious about not making any suggestions one way or the other, but obviously our conversation was a turning point. Were my questions part of the reason why she had decided to leave? What responsibility did I bear for her well-being? I wanted to support her decision to leave because it was an assertion of her independence, but I also knew this decision would profoundly change the dynamics of the only family that she had known. This significant life decision needed to be made by Luana. Eventually, I would be returning to the United States, whereas she would have to live with the consequences of this transformative decision. Instead of responding with emphatic enthusiasm, I responded that I understood why she would want to move, but I also asked her practical questions about how she planned to support herself. Did she know how much it would take to live on her own? Would she be able find a job that could sustain her? She answered each question slowly yet deliberately, and within one month of our conversation she had moved out into her own house. I was frightened for Luana, uncertain about whether she would be able to find a home, concerned about how her adoptive family would respond, and nervous about the long-term impact of this decision. Liberation is a goal of feminist and activist research, but this was a gray area.

The Dilemmas of Intimacy and Researcher Responsibility

Over the course of several months, Luana and I had developed a very close relationship. But, our growing relationship posed what researchers refer to as "dilemmas of intimacy" (Taylor 2011). After her move, Luana struggled to pay her bills in the home. At times, she asked to borrow money, and our relationship started to become more complicated. I did not want to reproduce the patronage relationship that she enjoyed with middle-class white Brazilians on whom she depended. At the same time, my refusal to allow her to borrow money was like a violation of a practice that occurs throughout Brazil among status unequals. In her job as a cook, Luana sold meals to men who were working at a local factory. To distance myself from the patronage role but also help Luana, I purchased and overpaid for meals from her that she used to support herself.

While this was a short-term solution, a larger issue was that Luana enjoyed reinforcing the "power asymmetry" that was part of our relationship. She relished in introducing me as her American friend and considered our friendship the basis of her bragging rights. While she often framed me as an "outsider" or foreigner, she simultaneously cultivated the idea that I was an "insider." She often referred to me as her "filhota" (diminutive form of daughter), introduced me to others as her *filhota*, and took pride in caring for me as though she was my mother. This was not the type of relationship that I had envisioned we would have. Luana was accustomed to interacting with others as a mother, but I wanted to be her friend because it seemed right. But, this was not a comfortable role for her. On Mother's Day, I was busy writing up my field notes in my apartment and did not plan to spend time in the community. When I stopped by the next day, Luana would not even look at me. She was furious that I had failed to call her on Mother's Day, that I did not spend Mother's Day with her at home, and that I had not given her a gift on the special day. I was stunned by her anger and sadness. Similar to how Beoku-Betts (1994) describes her experiences, "my negotiated status as insider implied a kin-like expectation . . . and conformity with expected behavior and traditions in the communities I studied"; my relationship with Luana was based on me being simultaneously a foreigner and a family member, which meant that I was held to standards that I had to learn and negotiate (418).

Initially, I felt Luana's insistence on treating me as if I were her daughter was problematic. What I did not realize was that though we had different visions about our relationship, we were both interested in maximizing our relationship and minimizing "power asymmetry." Luana was accustomed to functioning in the capacity of mother and caregiver in her adoptive family and took pride in being able to do it well. When I would ask that she not cook, she refused and explained that she enjoyed cooking for me because I appreciated it. I accepted her explanation, but did not feel comfortable with the arrangement. As a black, female North American, I was welcomed into her life, but in return she capitalized on the status that our friendship offered and used our relationship to perform a type of motherhood that she could not fully express in her adopted family. Navigating the boundaries of our relationship, which fell somewhere between friendship and family, was an ongoing process that involved me negotiating what I felt comfortable with as a researcher, and being open to allowing Luana to set the terms of our relationship. What I did not expect is that the interactional style that made Luana feel empowered would make me feel uncomfortable.

Apart from the intimacy that I developed with my formal respondents, after spending over a year in Brazil, the friendships that I created outside my research became much stronger. I soon learned that friendships were also laden with expectations for assistance and support. This was the case with Matheus, who as an ally and friend served as a sounding board to help me understand some of the more complicated cultural and racial dynamics in Salvador, Bahia. When I received a phone call from his business partner and wife in the middle of the night, I knew that something had gone terribly wrong and that they would be asking for some type of assistance. They were calling because Matheus, who is Afro-Brazilian, had been beaten, arrested, and thrown in jail, as a result of racial profiling and police brutality.

As he explained, during a visit to Itaparíca Beach with his brothers and cousins, they were accosted by police officers who claimed that the group fit the description of several men who had robbed and assaulted a couple on the island earlier that day. According to Matheus, he explained to the officers that they had just recently arrived at the island and there was no way that they were involved with the robbery or assault. The police continued to harass the group of young men, and Matheus stated that he was a student studying law and from what he understood, the police had no just cause to accuse them. Matheus's "arrogance" angered police officers, who not only brutally beat him and his friends, but also forced them into the police vehicle, accusing them of assault, and later planted drugs on them once they arrived at the police station.

It was that same evening that I received a phone call from Matheus's wife begging that I help her explain the situation to Matheus's American business partner, who she hoped could help him get out of jail. Through numerous Skype conference calls, with me translating back and forth between the two, I helped them find a lawyer who could plead Matheus's case and arrange bail. The process extended over three weeks, during which Matheus's wife and I met with representatives from the

Public Ministries to file a report against the police officers who attacked her husband. The situation took several months to resolve, and in the process I spoke with two administrators at the jail, two lawyers, and a civil rights group in Salvador, and was asked to write a letter of support for Matheus. Part of the reason why I was central to this process is because of the assumption about how my Americanness would potentially help his situation. By illustrating that Matheus was well-connected with two Americans in Salvador, he and his wife hoped that my phone call might compel officers to refrain from beating him and ultimately release him. On the other hand, the phone call could also lead to the officers requesting a bribe in exchange for Matheus's release. In the end, both of these occurred. They stopped beating Matheus, but coerced a confession and requested a hefty bribe for his release and expungement of his record. Matheus and his wife's initial phone call to me reflected the expectation that our friendship meant that he could rely on me to use my privilege to help in this vulnerable situation. Researchers can benefit from their positionality in the field, and instead of ignoring this reality, there are ways that this needs to be problematized and, in some cases, mobilized.

Conclusion—Rewriting the Rules

In conclusion, as a black, female U.S. researcher in Brazil, my experiences provide important insights about how race, gender, nationality, status, and "gradations of endogeny" are negotiated in the field (Nelson 1996). The struggles that I faced from the inception of my project to the very end revolved around me being an "outsider-within," both in terms of my position within the field of sociology and my ambiguous role in the Brazilian context. My experiences illustrate that I did not have everything worked out before arriving in Brazil. In fact, I struggled to implement a feminist and activist research approach while avoiding the methodological and epistemological traps of mainstream sociology. This was further complicated by the difficulty of managing my multiple positionalities and obligations, which were both complex and contradictory. My engagement in efforts to embrace rather than tame my subjectivity, in addition to the ways I handled dilemmas of intimacy, power asymmetries, and my privileged position illustrate the extent to which being an outsider-within is negotiated. This chapter is entitled "Out of Bounds," which in sports refers to being outside the playing boundaries of the field. Game play can be chaotic, and going out of bounds can happen often—and sometimes players go "out of bounds" intentionally if it can be an advantage. This aptly describes the position that I found myself in while I was in Brazil, and it is consistent with how other African descendants have analyzed their positionality. Taming subjectivity may be promoted in mainstream sociology as a way to achieve (the illusion) of objectivity, but there are ways in which developing and manipulating this subjectivity can provide tremendous insight into the very phenomenon that we study.

During my time in Salvador, I became involved as a research collaborator in a unique interdisciplinary project on Violence in Feira de Santana. One of the first of its kind, this group was organized by Dr. Edna Araújo at the State University of Feira de Santana (UEFS) and composed of scholars who worked in middle schools to empower young people to address violence in schools through technology. Having the opportunity to work in a research group like this one helped to root me in a research community that was grounded in community organizing, and encouraged me to also seek ways to ensure that my research and presence had a positive impact on the community that I studied. After several months of research, the principal of the school was pleased to report that levels of violence in the schools had decreased. I also spent time teaching English for free at a community center, as a way to give back to the community that had invested their time and shown me their hospitality.

Activist or emancipatory scholarship should at its core intentionally foster relationships with non-mainstream institutions in order to create a space of alternative knowledges to be heard and represented in research (Smith 2003). Fortunately, though admittedly through circumstances beyond my control, I became much more integrated into Afro-Brazilian communities by redefining my notions of who was an expert on race, and seeking out individuals and groups outside the realm of the conventional power structure. Activism and research do not always involve elaborately planned protests and institutional transformation. To the contrary, researchers should reframe what activism means for them and work to foster ruptures in the status quo, consciousness-raising, and empowerment that reflect their own capabilities. Fieldwork is necessarily messy and rife with contradiction. The only element that we can control is our commitment to the communities that we research, and our willingness to put their humanity and well-being before all else.

NOTES

1. Throughout the text, "black" and "Afro-Brazilian" are used as racial terms. When referencing Brazilians of African descent, I use the term Afro-Brazilians in order to be consistent with how activists in Brazil have defined themselves. When referring to researchers of African descent from the United States, I use the racial term "black," which is more commonly used than "Afro-descendant."

REFERENCES

Alcalde, M. (2007). Going home: A feminist anthropologist's reflections on dilemmas of power and positionality in the field. *Meridians* 7 (2): 143–162.

Beoku-Betts, J. (1994). When black is not enough: Doing field research among Gullah women. *NWSA Journal* 6 (3): 413–433.

Caldwell, K. L. (2007). *Negras in Brazil: Re-envisioning black women, citizenship, and the politics of identity.* New Brunswick, NJ: Rutgers University Press.

Collins, P. (1991). Learning from the outsider within: The sociological significance of black feminist thought. In M. Fonow & J. Cook (Eds.), *Beyond methodology: Feminist research as lived research*, 35–39. Bloomington: Indiana University Press.

Csordas, T. J. (1994). *Embodiment and experience: The existential ground of culture and self.* Cambridge: Cambridge University Press.

Erikson, F. (1984). What makes school ethnography "ethnographic"? *Anthropology and Education Quarterly* 15: 51–66.

Few, A., Stephens, D., & Rouse-Arnett, M. (2003). Sister-to-sister talk: Transcending boundaries and challenges in qualitative research with black women. *Family Relations* 52 (3) (June): 205–215.

Gilliam, A., & Gilliam, O. (1999). Odyssey: Negotiating the subjectivity of mulata identity in Brazil. *Latin American Perspectives* 26 (3): 60–84.

Griffin, A. (1998). Insider/outsider: Epistemological privilege and mothering work. *Human Studies* 21 (4) (October): 361–376.

Hellwig, D. (1992). *African-American reflections on Brazil's racial paradise.* Philadelphia: Temple University Press.

Hordge-Freeman, E. (2013). What's love got to do with it: Racial features, stigma and socialization in Afro-Brazilian families. *Ethnic & Racial Studies* 36 (10): 1507–1523.

Hordge-Freeman, E., Mayorga, S., & Bonilla-Silva, E. (2011). Exposing whiteness because we are free: Emancipation methodological practice in identifying and challenging racial practices in sociology departments. In John Stanfield (Ed.), *Rethinking race and ethnicity in research methods,* 95–122. Walnut Creek, CA: Left Coast Press.

Krieger, S. (1985). Beyond subjectivity: The use of the self in social science. *Qualitative Sociology* 8 (4): 309–324.

Ladner, Joyce A. 1973. *The death of white sociology.* New York: Random House.

McCallum, C. (2005). Racialized bodies, naturalized classes: Moving through the city of Salvador da Bahia. *American Ethnologist* 32 (1): 100–117.

Merton, R. K. (1972). Insiders and outsiders: A chapter in the sociology of knowledge. *American Journal of Sociology* 78 (1) (July): 9–47.

Nelson, L. (1996). "Hands in the chit'lins": Notes on native anthropological research among African American women. In G. Etter-Lewis & M. Foster (Eds.), Unrelated kin: Race and gender in women's personal narratives (183–199). New York: Routledge.

Peshkin, A. (1988). In search of subjectivity: One's own. *Educational Researcher* 17 (7) (October): 17–21.

Sandoval, C. (1991). U.S. third world feminism: The theory and method of oppositional consciousness in the postmodern world. *Genders* 10: 1–24.

Smith, L. (1999). *Decolonizing methodologies: Research and indigenous peoples.* New York: St. Martin's Press.

Taylor, J. (2011). The intimate insider: Negotiating the ethics of friendship when doing insider research, *Qualitative Research* 11: 3–22.

Twine, F. W., & Warren, H. (2000). *Racing research, researching race: Methodological dilemmas in critical race studies.* New York: New York University Press.

Van Wolputte, S. (2004). Hang on to your self: Of bodies, embodiment, and selves. *Annual Review of Anthropology* 33 (October): 251–269.

Yelvington, K. (Ed.). (2006). *Afro-Atlantic dialogues: Anthropology in the diaspora.* Santa Fe, NM: School of American Research Press.

Zinn, M. B. (1979). Field research in minority communities: Ethical, methodological, and political observations by an insider. *Social Problems* 27: 209–219.

Zuberi, T. (2001). *Thicker than blood: How racial statistics lie.* Minneapolis: University of Minnesota Press.

Zuberi, T., & Bonilla-Silva, E. (2008). *White logic, white methods: Racism and methodology.* Lanham, MD: Rowman & Littlefield.

Between Soapboxes and Shadows: Activism, Theory, and the Politics of Life and Death in Salvador, Bahia, Brazil

Christen A. Smith

On June 16, 2009, over one hundred civil, military, and special operations police officers invaded Canabrava, a peripheral neighborhood located in the northern part of the city of Salvador, Bahia, Brazil. Five young men from the community were summarily executed. Three of the young men, Edmilson Ferreira dos Anjos (22), Rogério Ferreira (24), and Manoel Ferreira (23) were brothers. According to their sister, the police invaded their house, pulled their mother out, and shot the boys while they were watching TV on the couch and sleeping in a bedroom (Rebouças & Lima 2009; Lima 2007). The raid was allegedly executed in response to the murder of civil police officer José Carlos Gonçalves Teixeira, who was investigating drug trafficking in the neighborhood. The five young men who were killed were deemed suspects in the crime. Distraught with grief, the mother of the three, who identified herself to journalists as Maria da Conceição, denied that her boys had had any involvement with drug trafficking or homicide. That same week three different suspects in Teixeira's murder were taken into police custody.

A few months after the Canabrava massacre, black organizations Quilombo X, the campaign React or Die! (Reaja ou Será Mort@), and ASFAP (Association of Friends and Family of Prisoners in Bahia) held the First People's Gathering for Life and a Better Model for Public Safety (I ENPOSP) in August 2009. I ENPOSP was a grassroots effort to create a national public forum for victims of police violence, their families, and families of prisoners to debate racism, sexism, homophobia, and the genocidal effects of the public safety system in Brazil. I was invited to the meeting to serve as an international observer by Quilombo X and ASFAP (Association of Friends and Family of Prisoners in Bahia), two organizations with which I have collaborated since 2005 and 2006. Among the participants at the gathering were mothers from the neighborhood of Canabrava who had organized following the massacre in 2009. The mothers quietly participated in the opening day's events. However, when it was time for them to get up on stage, denounce the crimes that they had experienced, and share their experiences, they instead chose to stay seated in the dark shade of the plaza's trees at dusk and watch, for fear of retaliation from the police, lodged in that liminal space between soapboxes and shadows.

This essay critically examines black organizers' efforts to address and denounce the genocidal effects of state violence on the black community in Salvador through community collaboration and transnational and trans-local dialogue. What do these efforts tell us about the very real life questions of survival we must address when attempting to marry practice with theory and scholarship? Since 2001, I have been collaborating with black organizers in Bahia around issues of racism and violence. One of the primary focuses of these collaborations has been the question of police violence—a real-life, everyday racialized experience with the state that fundamentally shapes the black experience in Salvador. Through an ethnographic reflection on my experiences with the parents of victims of state violence at the First People's Gathering for Life and a Better Model for Public Safety in August 2009, I reflect on the fundamental role that the ontological question of the human plays in our ability to marry the theoretical and the practical in our activist research. Literary theorist Sylvia Wynter (Scott 2000), in her philosophical discussion of the meaning of the human and its importance to our political projects, notes a need to "reimagine the human in the terms of a new history whose narrative will enable us to co-identify ourselves with the other" (198). Wynter's suggestion pushes us to consider the human beyond the definition of human rights, in reflective terms, paying attention to the epistemes that frame our experience of being. In defining the human, she moves us away from "a bioeconomic concept of the human that defines humanity based on the attainment of the ethno-class criterion of the global middle classes" (180–182). These criteria, she argues, are based on white supremacist, colonialist, heterosexist, patriarchal structures that define black people and indigenous people as subhuman. Faye Harrison's analysis of the struggle for rights and dignity in the African Diaspora engages Wynter's work in order to frame "the debate over persistent black dehumanization and struggles for *re*humanization" (Harrison 2012, 9). Harrison's observations also follow the work of João Costa Vargas, who argues that we must use the concept of a "genocidal continuum" in order to analyze the global black condition (Vargas 2008, 10). This framework engages directly with the question of the human, particularly interrogating the extent to which dehumanization and premature death define the lives of black people throughout the African Diaspora. However, this question of the human is a complex one. Frank Wilderson, following the intellectual genealogy of Franz Fanon (1965), suggests that to be black in the world necessarily means being located outside of the Human in the space of the Slave (Wilderson 2010). This thesis locates anti-blackness and violence as a global organizational logic, and confronts the notion of the human as one that emerges from a humanism that is and always was intended to refer to the white body, not the black body. Wilderson's premise is a provocative one that both challenges and engages Wynter's work. The (il)logics of anti-black violence in Brazil push us to consider the possibility that black people are epistemologically removed from the human in the nation. However, I disagree with Wilderson when he argues that this reality necessarily means that black subjectivity is impossible. As Faye Harrison writes, "African-descended activists in the United States, both indigenized and immigrant, as well as those struggling throughout the Diaspora, have long struggled over what it means to be human, to enjoy human dignity, and to have racially subjugated people's claims to citizenship seriously acknowledged and respected" (Harrison 2012, 9). Redressing wrongs to the black human necessitates an acknowledgment of black sentience, black suffering, black presence, and black transcendence.[1] The assertion that black sentience, suffering, and transcendence exist allows us to consider subjectivity beyond the immediate political economy of our global circumstances. In this sense, black humanness (the coeval sentience of black existence) must be the governing logic of any activism and/or scholarship in, on, and about black spaces in order for this work to be politically effective. Without this basic premise, activism, scholarship, and the bridges we construct between the two are not in the service of the people we presume to work for.

Although black people seem to be everywhere in Brazil, black suffering is in many ways invisible. Ironically, the hypervisibility of the black body—as dynamic, lived, embodied presence—is often pushed to discursive margins of the social imaginary, rendering black suffering an epistemological impossibility in the social imagination. As a result, any politically engaged project to redress black suffering and black violence, from the academy or from the streets of protest, must be a project of perception. In order to redress the black human, black people must be perceived—literally marked as present, coeval, and real. The black body must be registered as a sentient political subject.

In many ways, the politics of visibility are the driving force behind most acts of protest and many social movements. As activists, we often take to the streets to be seen, heard, and perceived. However, the politics of visibility are complex in a space where visibility and erasure are closely tied together. State violence in Bahia renders black bodies (those of the assassinated and their family members) ghosts—shadows disintegrated into the unrecognizable. To make the claim that the black body is a ghost that literally sits in the shadows of the discursive margins of the social imaginary is admittedly a controversial one. Anyone who knows Brazil well, particularly Bahia, will note that black people— people of African descent classified as *pretos* (dark-skinned/black) and *pardos* (brown-skinned/ brown) by the national census—are everywhere. Indeed, according to the 2010 census, for the first time, people of African descent make up more than half of the national population, 50.7 percent (IBGE 2010). Those numbers are even higher in Bahia, where an estimated 85 percent of the population is of African descent. Black people are hypervisible across the nation, and with the gradual implementa-tion of racial quotas in the university system and beyond, black visibility in society is increasing exponentially. However, just as scholars like performance theorist Peggy Phalen have argued, increased visibility equates neither to power nor an epistemological acknowledgement of psychic presence (Phelan 1993). Her statement echoes the work of minority-studies scholar Paula Moya, who also claims, albeit from a different disciplinary perspective, that the increased visibility of "minori-ties" in mainstream U.S. culture does not equate to increased acceptance of these communities by mainstream society (Moya & Hames-Garcia 2000). In other words, even when marginalized groups are visible and in the limelight, this does not mean that society has accepted these groups as social citizens who belong, have power, or even truly exist as human beings. In the case of black organizers protesting against police violence and death-squad murders in Bahia, visibility is a dangerous game. On the one hand, this violence erases the black body, pushing the black community to need to be seen in order to survive. On the other hand, being seen often means becoming a target for more repression, abuse, and even death. In this essay, I consider the delicate politics of negotiating the space between invisibility and hypervisibility in the fight against genocide in Bahia. Specifically, I reflect on the experiences black mothers and fathers have with living and trying to fight back after the assassination of their children, and what this means for those of us who want to do all that we can to help them. The essay begins with a discussion of the participation of the mothers of Canabrava in I ENPOSP. It then moves into a discussion of the story of Ricardo, a young man killed by the police in January 2008, and his father's quest for justice. Finally, the essay ends by asking hard questions about the realistic risks and consequences of speaking up and speaking out, and what they imply for our journeys to bridge activism and scholarship.

The Mothers of Canabrava

I ENPOSP was a direct affront to the Brazilian government's First National Conference on Public Security, which was organized in 2009 in order to garner support for PRONASCI (National Citizenship and Security Plan—Plano Nacional de Segurança com Cidadania). Organizers and grassroots organizations initiated the event as a community response to state violence. It provided space for victims and their families to publicly share their experiences, thoughts, ideas, and critical reflections on racism, sexism, homophobia, policing, and prisons. Three hundred people participated in this unprecedented event, including organizers, scholars, and organizations from across Brazil and a few international guests. I ENPOSP held its opening rally downtown in Praça da Piedade, the plaza across the street from the Department of Public Safety of the State of Bahia (Secretaria de Segurança Pública do Estado da Bahia), where many of the rallies against police violence and racism have occurred over the years.[2] The event organizers rented a platform and microphones, setting up a temporary stage in the middle of the tall shade trees, statues, and the fountain of the square. The gathering began just before dark, the squeaking feedback of the mic announcing the start of the evening. The organizers rallied the crowd with speeches and singing. Representatives from various organizations spoke out passionately against the violence the state metes out to the majority black working-class population regularly and with impunity. The plaza was filled with organizers and protestors from various sectors, including mothers of victims of state violence who had traveled from Rio de Janeiro and São Paulo for the meeting. As the evening progressed, the mothers from Rio de Janeiro and São Paulo climbed the large black stage to speak out about their experiences with violence and death at the hands of the police. Many of the women who spoke were those whose children had been killed by the police in the Baixada Fluminense region of Rio de Janeiro in 2005 and beyond. That year, twenty-nine people were killed by a group of men, believed to be military police officers, who drove through the Baixada Fluminense between 8:30 pm and 11:00 pm, shooting randomly at passers-by (Amnesty International 2005). Others were from the group Movimento Mães de Maio,[3] an organization of mothers whose children were killed by the police in São Paulo in 2006, when the military police retaliated against the peripheral community in response to the revolts of the PCC (Primeiro Comando da Capital) and killed 493 people.[4] The women shared their stories of pain, heartache, and anger in the wake of the assassinations of their children. Emboldened by their loss, they stuck fists in the air and screamed for justice. However, as the women from other states climbed the stairs one by one to give their testimonials, other black mothers sat in the shadows, watching silently but not daring to show their faces or speak. These women sitting under the darkness of the trees were the mothers of those killed in the police massacre in Canabrava in June 2009, just weeks before I ENPOSP.

The mothers of Canabrava were caught in a liminal space between life and death at the rally that day. In my role as international observer, I was naively cheery when I met them. At the time, I had no idea who they were. They were introduced to me as mothers, and understanding the very delicate emotions of the event, I did not talk with them about why they were present or what they had experienced. It was enough to just recognize them as mothers. When I encountered them, however,

I immediately noted a stark difference between their demeanor and the demeanor of the mothers from out of town. The mothers from Canabrava were deeply quiet, whereas the mothers from Rio and São Paulo (with more distance between their loss and the rally) were upbeat and excited to have a platform to speak. Their deep sadness was punctuated by a sense of fear. As the day went on and the sky darkened, the mothers from Salvador remained in the shadows, whispering among themselves. After many speeches, songs, and greetings, the event's coordinators called the mothers from Salvador to the stage (generically) to talk about their experiences. However, the contingent from Canabrava remained silent. Several U.S. visitors began to ask me when the women from Bahia would speak. Knowing that something was wrong, but not quite sure what was going on, I spoke with the coordinators, who quickly brushed off my questions so that no one would perceive that anything was wrong. I read their signal and proceeded to fudge through an explanation for our international guests that would draw attention away from what was going on. At that moment it became clear to me what was wrong. The magnitude of the rally, and its strategic location in front of the Department of Public Safety, had paralyzed the mothers into silence. Afraid of (further) retaliation by the police, whose headquarters was just steps away, the mothers from Canabrava refused to speak because they were afraid of the consequence if they did. Their refusal to speak, carefully hidden by the event's organizers, drew criticism from honored international guests who came to hear "the mothers not political organizers." This criticism made me uneasy. I struggled to negotiate the embarrassment of an apparent failed political moment in which the privileged voices of experience seemed not to want to speak. As someone who strives to promote black feminist politics, I was well aware that the reality of silent black mothers in the shadows made the event, and the collaborators with whom I had been working for so long, look politically void. But there was something that I was completely missing in my selfish embarrassment, and that was the real-life consequences of political manifestation for the mothers present that day. Although having black mothers speak about their own experiences with police violence was critical to my black feminist theoretical politics, the realities of the lives of the black women who sat in the shadows begged a different response—a recognition of their ontological presence, their epistemological reality, and consequently, an acknowledgment that their experiences, feelings, and choices had to be honored above all else. Speaking up and speaking out is an important political marker of authenticity for organizers of social movements, but those politics leave the community in a precarious position. The following section looks at the story of one father whose experience in search of justice for his murdered son personifies the fear that the mothers of Canabrava felt that day.

Living between Life and Death

In January 2008, military police officers killed four black youth between the ages of sixteen and twenty-one in twelve days. None of these boys were suspected of a crime. The officers either justified their actions by claiming that the young men were resisting arrest, or made no justification at all. A few days before I ENPOSP began, I would come to see the repercussions of this massacre in painful relief. I attended one of the last pre-conference planning meetings for I ENPOSP in downtown Salvador shortly after I arrived in the city. The room was dimly lit by a single iridescent light bulb hanging from the middle of the ceiling, which bounced golden light around the white walls of the space. The organizers of the gathering and community leaders met there that night to discuss the logistics for the upcoming weekend. After the meeting was over, we all hung around chatting for a bit. I was waiting to get a ride home, so I struck up a conversation. There was another gentleman, with caramel brown skin and salt and pepper hair, probably in his late forties, who was also waiting. Stuck there together, we began to chat. I had no idea who he was, but we soon started to talk and get to know each other as we bided the time before our rides were ready to go home. He was carrying a black soft-side briefcase with an envelope full of papers. He pulled out a picture of a young brown-skinned adolescent in a circus pose smiling brightly. He explained to me that this was his son, Ricardo. The picture was carefully laid amid newspaper clippings, letters, and pieces of paper. As he showed me the picture, he began to recount the story of his son to me, and a conversation that began as casual banter quickly evolved into a deeply disturbing, winding tale of pain and loss. Ricardo was home visiting from the circus[5] when he was shot and killed by police officers while playing soccer with his friends. He had been out at the neighborhood field, where he had gone every day for the week he was home, when the police came. The boys ran, but Ricardo was shot in the back and died. Ricardo was one of the four young black men who were killed by military police in Salvador in January 2008. After his death, Mr. Lazaro, an experienced environmental activist and respected community member, joined friends, neighbors, and family members to organize protests in the streets of the neighborhood, holding placards and chanting for justice. And then things got worse, as if that were even possible. The family began to receive threats. They were put into a witness protection program. They were relocated to a motel in Santo Amaro, just outside the city of Salvador, but everyone in the town knew that they were staying there. It was no secret that this motel was the state's chosen relocation spot for the witness protection program. The family started to receive threats again—threats they strongly suspected came from the very police officers involved in their son's death. On top of that, the motel—a place couples regularly go to have sexual encounters with a little privacy—was no place for a family with young children. So they left. Not only did they lose a son and brother to the police shooting, they lost their whole lives. As Mr. Lazaro put it, "In hiding, you can't work, it's hard to be enrolled in school, you can't live." Eventually Mr. Lazaro and his family went back into witness protection. In 2013, while still under the auspices of the state, police officers killed Ricardo's brother, Enio.

According to an article published in the Bahian newspaper *Correio da Bahia*, on March 2, 2008, "[a] black [man], living in the periphery, unemployed, with an elementary school education, between the ages of 15–29, who easily speaks in slang, and generally has a tattoo on [his] body . . . [is] marked to die" (Reis 2008). The statistics for race, gender, and violent death generally parallel those for police aggression. Although there are few statistics on race and police violence in Bahia, examining what little we do know gives us a firm idea of the severity of the problem. Brazil has one of the worst problems of police brutality found anywhere in the world (e.g., Amnesty International 2005). Couple that with racial profiling, and you have the perfect storm for anti-black genocide.[6] Sociologist Ignácio Cano's work on police violence in São Paulo and Rio de Janeiro concludes that while *pretos*—men of African descent with dark skin—represent 3.89 percent of the general population, they make up 13.30 percent of those killed by the police (Cano 2000). This supports the previous findings of Michael Mitchell and James Wood, who found that *pretos* are 2.4 times more likely to be victims of police abuse than any other subset of the population throughout Brazil, even when controlling for socioeconomic factors (Mitchell & Wood 1999). Race and gender, regardless of class, determine a citizen's chances of falling victim to police brutality, everywhere in the nation, and the majority of the victims are poor, black, and living in the *periferia* (periphery).[7] There is a hegemonic racial epistemology that frames policing in Bahia, and that epistemology locates black people outside of the realm of the human.

Returning briefly to Vargas's concept of the genocidal continuum, genocide, in the context of Brazil, must be read as a complex matrix of physical, structural, and symbolic violence (Vargas 2008, 10). As Vargas states, "The notion of a genocidal continuum allows us to not only link these various genocidal phenomena [lynching, segregation, police brutality, the cultural environment] into a permanent, totalizing, and ubiquitous event . . . but also trace the resulting mass killing of Black people to quotidian acts and representations of discrimination, de-humanization, and ultimate exclusion" (10). Vargas's holistic approach to understanding genocide as a total social phenomenon follows the work of generations of black activism inside and outside of the academy in Brazil. In 1976, black Brazilian scholar and activist Abdias do Nascimento argued, "Brazil as a nation proclaims herself the only racial democracy in the world, and much of the world views and accepts her as such. But an examination of the historical development of my country reveals the true nature of her social, cultural, political and economic anatomy: it is essentially racist and *vitally threatening* [my emphasis] to Black people" (Nascimento 1989, 59). Abdias do Nascimento's assessment of Brazilian racism as genocide emerged out of his scholarly reflections and personal trajectory, but also out of the emerging dialogue over racism and black experiences with violence that was occurring in the black movement at this time. Since its inception in 1978, the Unified Black Movement (Movimento Negro Unificado) has defined the crisis of state violence in Brazil (exemplified by police brutality) as one of the fundamental threats to black life (Movimento Negro Unificado 1988). In the 1970s and 1980s, the MNU argued that black people's experiences in Brazil were part of a genocidal continuum. This theorization is also present today among black organizers. The React or Die!/React or Be Killed! Campaign's manifesto delineates the anti-black, genocidal politics of the Brazilian state as a complex system of violence that is not only symbolic, structural, and physical but also gendered, sexualized, and classed (React or Die! 2005). Denouncing the dehumanization of black people and blackness in Brazil has long been a battle cry of black Brazilian activists from the community to the academy.

The idea of the "death mark," mentioned above, draws us back to the question of the black human, state violence, and the politics of survival in contemporary Brazil. Somewhere between lagging rhetorics of racial democracy and racial inclusiveness professed by the state, and the stark reality of black youth dying at the hands of the police, there is a lived experience of anti-black violence that is visible, embodied, seen, heard, felt, but not spoken, that has tangible effects on people's lives, particularly in the city of Salvador. By using the term "anti-black violence," I frame police aggression with impunity as a manifestation of a politics of white supremacy intimately tied to racial democracy in Brazil. Steve Martinot and Jared Sexton (2003) argue that the spectacle of police violence conceals the banalization of white supremacy in the everyday. Martinot and Sexton carefully define what white supremacy truly is: not merely some exotic form of deviant behavior like the Ku Klux Klan and Nazism, but the mundane affair of racial oppression premised on white superiority that is embedded in the everyday. As scholars like Thomas Skidmore (1974) and Jerry Dávila (2003) have found, Brazil's social project has been intertwined with eugenics and whitening since the colonial/slavery period. Moreover, as João Costa Vargas and Michael Hanchard observe, the racial hegemony of Brazilian society follows the logic of white supremacy today, even if this logic is not widely discussed (Vargas 2008; Hanchard 1994; 1999). Vargas, Moon-Kie Jung, and Eduardo Bonilla-Silva (2011) take this critique even a step further in their more recent work to suggest that we must move away from a reliance on the nomenclature of white supremacy to describe the Brazilian state, and instead take up the term "anti-black" because it is clear that the state's genocidal practices are directed specifically at the black community (Jung, Vargas & Bonilla-Silva 2011). Despite claims to the contrary, Brazil is and has always been a nation shaped by the logics of white supremacy, and these logics cannot be separated from the question of anti-blackness.

There was a heavy sadness hanging in the air between Mr. Lazaro and me as he told me the story of Ricardo. As he spoke, my eyes began to fill with tears. I felt so overwhelmed by the apparent randomness and sadness of it all. As he recounted the details of his son's death and his family's odyssey, his voice took on the humming rhythm of desperation and repetition. Ricardo's murder was senseless. Despite my academic and activist knowledge of the deep-seated racism of extra-judicial police violence in Brazil, something made me desperately try to rationalize what had happened. (Had he been in the wrong place at the wrong time? Could it have been mistaken identity?) I wanted to distance myself. I could feel the warmth of Mr. Lazaro's pain and it made me uncomfortable, angry, and sad all at the same time, as if simply hearing his story brought its randomness dangerously too close, and I, or someone I loved, could be next—the reality-imperative of the Black Diaspora. I knew that there was nothing that Mr. Lazaro could have done to avoid his son's death. He raised his children well. He was guilty of two things only: being black and living on the edge of poverty. Yet, I also knew that this was no case of mistaken identity or happenstance. A young black man, Ricardo was not mistaken by the police as a criminal, he was assumed to be a criminal; scripted as expendable, his humanity[8] was dismissed precisely because he was a young black man living in a working-class neighborhood. The fact that he was shot and killed in the back (running away, not threatening) along with another young black man who was a known criminal was not a counterpoint. It was Ricardo's expendability, and not his guilt or non-guilt that made him a target. Like the unsuspecting yellow duck that sits next to the duck with the target on its back in carnival games, Ricardo was a necessary casualty of the sport. As I sat there listening to Mr. Lazaro tell his son's story, I was struck by his cadence. He had told this story so many times before, his words echoed. They killed his boy. This was not only a reiteration, it was a reverberation of the liminal space between life and death, the space where all families of victims of state violence reside in Brazil and beyond—the space of ghosts of the dead and the living.

Spiritual Terror

In some ways, police raids and death-squad assassinations (as police-related forms of violence) are spectacular displays of "spiritual terror" (Brown 2003) enacted to instill fear and maintain the race/gender/sexuality boundaries of the moral social order in the city of Salvador. Police raids and death-squad assassinations represent the use of spectacular terror as a form of social control. Vincent Brown, in his research on the plantocracy's use of spectacular terror as a form of social control over the enslaved in the colonial West Indies, argues that slavers who feared losing their "stock" to suicide turned to spiritual terror and fear as a strategy for maintaining social control over the enslaved. Dismembering and mutilating dead bodies and then putting them on spectacular display for the enslaved to witness became a widely practiced method for trying to instill fear in the enslaved and deter them from committing suicide or otherwise rebelling in order to escape the horrors of slavery. For decades, black activists in Brazil have claimed that there is a direct connection between contemporary policing practices and the legacy of slavery (e.g., Moura 1994, Movimento Negro Unificado 1988, Silva Jr. 1998). Criminal sociologist R. S. Rose corroborates these sentiments by mapping the historical genealogy of police death squads and urban police violence onto Portuguese practices of torture and repression during slavery (Rose 2005). The contemporary practice of spectacular killing and displaying the dead that both the police and death squads routinely employ in extrajudicial killing suggests that what happened during slavery in the colonial West Indies is happening in contemporary Brazil.

There is often a tension between the rhetoric and performance of activism versus the realities of survival. As we as protestors and researchers energetically organized conversations around police violence at I ENPOSP, the realities of the political consequences of police raids and extrajudicial killing for the families of those who were killed sometimes slipped to the edge of our consciousness and conversations. The Canabrava mothers' silence was a conditioned, conscious political response to the real threat of further terror in their communities and upon their families. As activist-researchers, we are often quick to want to privilege the voices of the victims of violence in order to personalize our fights against injustice. Romanticized notions of resistance often haunt our interpretations of grassroots activism. Within activist research, we frequently advocate fighting back as if it were a mere political choice, rather than a life-or-death reality. However, remembering these life-or-death stakes allows us to complicate our interpretations of resistance and activism, and recognize that our political projects should often take a back seat to immediate survival needs. In order to lay bare these stakes and de-romanticize the very real life and death decisions many people, like the mothers of Canabrava, make to speak or not speak, fight back or not fight back, we must deal with the real-life terrors and complexities of what it means to live with this violence in the everyday, and survive after it. The fear of the mothers of Canabrava became even more palpable to me when I began to revisit the death-squad assassination of mother and Movimento Sem Teto activist Aurina Santana, her partner, and her son in 2007.

In July 2007, a sensationalist photo of three black bodies laid across a floor, hands behind their heads, in a pool of blood, was prominently displayed in the pages of the Bahian state newspaper, *A Tarde*. The three, Aurina Rodrigues Santana (44), an activist in the Homeless Movement (Movimento Sem Teto) and mother of eleven; her son, Paulo Rogério Rodrigues Santana Braga (19); and her partner, Rodson da Silva Rodrigues (29), had been assassinated by a group of masked men that invaded their home in the community of Calabetão (Cirino 2007). According to Mrs. Santana's two young daughters, who witnessed the crime, the men forced the three to lie face down, execution style, in a back room and then shot them to death. They then ransacked the house and stole 300 *reais*. Oddly, three bags of marijuana and thirty rocks of crack were found by the bodies. Neighbors were quick to deny that these murders were drug-related, however. One neighbor had the following to say: "They planted the drugs in the house . . . What rival drug trafficker would invade a house and not take the drugs?" It was clear that drug traffickers had not killed Mrs. Santana. Two months prior to her murder, on May 22, 2007, Aurina Santana denounced police officers from the 48th

Independent Military Police Precinct of Sussuarana (48a Cipm–Sussuarana) to the Legislative Assembly's Commission on Human Rights (Comissão de Direitos Humanos da Assembleia Legislativa) for torturing her son, Paulo Rogério Rodrigues Santana Braga (19) and his sister (13) at home on the morning of May 21, 2007. The family reported the case to the Legislative Assembly's Commission on Human Rights (Comissão de Direitos Humanos da Assembleia Legislativa) and gave an interview with Bahia's state newspaper, *A Tarde*, detailing the torture, which lasted for over three hours that morning as neighbors witnessed in fear in the doors of their houses. Police officers had ransacked the house, beat and tortured the two young people, and told neighbors that if anyone reported the incident, they would come back to kill everyone (Lima 2007). Curiously, two months later, Mrs. Santana, her partner, and her son were shot and killed execution style in the middle of the night.

Mrs. Santana's murder, like the murder of Ricardo's brother and the living hell that Ricardo's family has been experiencing since his death, reminds us of the dangers that black parents face when they choose to protest state violence. The fear that the mothers from Canabrava felt that day in 2009 was very real and justified. Mr. Lazaro's life inside the zone of death makes this fear palpable. How can we begin to grapple with these life/death matrices of power without slipping into unrealistic readings of activism as a utopic space of political manifestation, without regard to the human experiences that go along with it? Understanding the need to privilege experience over theory, discourse, or even activist practice is one of the first steps. In order to address and redress racism and its violent effects, activism must reclaim the human experience of blackness—its everyday realities and relevance to the lives of black people—by recognizing its lived reality.

The violence that affected Canabrava in June 2009 did not stop at the five young men who were killed on June 16. The police continued to sweep the neighborhood that night after the boys were killed and for days to come. The swiftness of the police response (the police raid occurred just hours after officer José Carlos Gonçalves Teixeira was killed), the execution-style assassinations of the three brothers, and the fact that days after the raid, three other suspects in the murder of the police officer were apprehended, led many to wonder if the 100-man raid was really about capturing murder suspects, or revenge against the community and intimidation. The extrajudicial killing of the alleged suspects punctuated this suspicion. Why kill first and ask questions later? The circumstances of this violence and the way that these executions were carried out leads us to ponder the true motives behind this invasion and subsequent assassinations. If the five who were killed were innocent, what messages do their deaths broadcast? In order to address this question, we must consider the framing of this scene. As mentioned at the beginning of this chapter, the three brothers who were killed in their home were shot while watching TV and sleeping, after the police pulled their mother out of the house. Although this act of removal might be read as a gesture that the police made to shield the mother from witnessing her children's death, I believe that quite the opposite is true. Pulling the mother out of the house in actuality shifted the focus of the action from the boys to their mother, drawing her directly into the heart of the scene.

The association between death-squad murders and vigilantism hides the fact that off-duty and on-duty police officers follow the same script. They engage in similar acts, use similar procedures, and seek similar results. However, in both on-duty and off-duty police violence, the gratuitousness and sensationalism of the spectacle of death (the pictures of the body being carried off in the bloody sheet, the bodies laid across the ground in a pool of blood, the shoeless, dirty foot of a faceless victim) mask the routinization and banalization of police terror, its effect on families and communities, and its role as a mechanism for maintaining the social moral order. Haunting scenes of death-squad murders and police raids repeat themselves across the landscape of the city of Salvador. These scenes, through dismemberment, torture, spectacle, and performance, mark the bodies of the victims, the community, and produce the geopolitical landscape of race/gender/sexuality and violence in the city. This process of marking is both a disciplining and meaning-making process that inscribes the body and the landscape, imbuing it with racialized, gendered, and sexualized meaning. When death squads murder black youth and place their bodies back on display in plain view for their neighbors and family members to see, or military police invade peripheral homes, single out and kill young black men while they push their mothers to the side, the bodies of the dead become messages for the community. These symbolic acts create a complex, interwoven relationship between the black body, peripheral communities, and police violence.

Traditionally, death squads are read as vigilante groups who kill petty criminals for hire when contracted by local merchants, and police raids are widely accepted as excessive uses of force by the police in a necessary fight against crime (e.g., Cavallaro et al. 1997, Chevigny 1995, Pinheiro 1991, Huggins 1991, Espinheira 2004). According to this line of thinking, the spectacular display of the tortured, mutilated, and murdered bodies of the dead is intended to send a message of warning to potential criminals. At the heart of this approach is the assumption that police raids and death-squad assassinations are apolitical manifestations of justifiable social violence whose root cause is crime. However, I would like to challenge this approach and its assumptions, and argue that death-squad murders and police raids have little to nothing to do with the problem of crime and violence itself. Rather, these scenarios, and the haunting of possible retaliation from protest that follows them, are performed acts of violence enacted to maintain the race/gender/sexuality moral social order by keeping the black community silent and in its place. If this is indeed the case, what are the implications for our work as activist-scholars stuck between redressing the erasure of the black body and black humanity (black suffering and black sentience) in our organizing efforts by drawing attention to the lived experiences and stories of the survivors of this violence, and respecting survivors' real fear of losing their lives, the lives of their loved ones, and/or their sanity if they speak up and speak out?

Conclusions

It is tempting to read the murder of Aurina Rodrigues Santana as the state's successful use of spiritual terror. I am convinced that the recent memory of her death, the death of her partner and son, and her two little girls who lived to witness was not lost on the mothers of Canabrava as they sat in the shadows that day in Praça da Piedade. The combined threats of losing one's own life to torture, losing the life of your loved ones to torture, and the possibility of leaving your young children behind to fend for themselves are overwhelming. The direct connection between Mrs. Santana's denunciation of the police and her assassination sends a clear message: giving birth to revolution is an offense punishable by death. However, there are other readings we can offer for this story as well.

Ms. Santana knew that she was running the risk of being killed when she denounced her children's torture. She knew that this would invite the masked backlash under the cover of night of the very police officers who came to her home in uniform during the day to torture her children in front of their neighbors. Given this, I would like to suggest that we read her actions as purposeful. Aurina Santana was a mother whose speaking out challenged the life-and-death configuration of state violence as spiritual terror. By naming the state as torturer-murderer, despite the sure possibility of death, Ms. Santana defied the politics of spiritual terror by denouncing the state at the risk of certain death (in this case, hers, her partner's, and her son's), thus removing death from the arsenal of the possible weapons of control the state could use to quell her voice. Harnessing the power of death is a potent cosmic tool. As Vincent Brown notes, Caribbean slave owners used spectacular terror to "deter Africans from self destruction" (2003, 26). This strategy was grounded in the knowledge that Africans engaged in suicide because of their strong belief that in death they would be able to return to their homeland and be free. The mutilation and dismemberment of dead bodies literally truncated this fantasy, placing the marks of the terrors of slavery on the body as it extended into the afterlife. When Africans continued to kill themselves, slavers continued to invent more grotesque ways to violate the dead in the hope of deterrence. Putting the mutilated body on display as a message to the rest of the community played a key role in this performance. Brown notes that "slavers mutilated the body of the first 'Ibo' slave to die in a given shipment: they beheaded it, or sliced off its nose and pried out its eyes to prevent losses among other captives from the Bight of Biafra, who were widely reputed to be suicide-prone" (27). This practice extended beyond the Caribbean throughout the slaving culture of the Americas. When Zumbi, the warrior and leader of the *quilombo* kingdom of Palmares, was captured by the Portuguese in the sixteenth century, he was quartered and his head was put on display in the public square. Spiritual terror has been a crucial aspect of controlling black resistance throughout the Americas since slavery. The intent, however, has not merely been to intimidate, but, as Brown notes, "to give governing authority a sacred, even supernatural dimension" (27). He goes on to write, "Spectacular executions attached worldly authority to transcendent concerns and allowed the plantocracy's power to reach into the spiritual imaginations of slaves. As with the punishments for suicide, the punishments for rebellion were meant to inspire in the enslaved spiritual terror by visiting extraordinary torments on their bodies before and after death" (27). The connection between suicide and rebellion is an important one to note here, as is the calculated invocation of affect intended by these displays. Marking the territory of the plantation with dead, mutilated bodies, like the actions of death squads and police raids, was and is intended to inscribe the landscape with memory and social meaning.

The spiritual, religious practices of the enslaved were a direct challenge to the spiritual terror that the enslavers performed. While the plantocracy burned alive, beheaded, dismembered, and disfigured those who committed suicide and/or rebelled (which we should read in continuum), Africans also tried various methods to reclaim the dead, harnessing spirits, catching shadows, and stealing the ears and personal effects of dead slavers in order to control their ability to haunt after death. Spiritual warfare was a two-way street. The dead were an active presence on all sides, and harnessing the powers of death meant harnessing the powers of freedom and liberation for the enslaved.

Where does this configuration take us politically, and what does it mean to a discussion on bridging activism and scholarship? By removing the power to kill from the state, and redefining the terms of birth and death, black mothers and fathers, by speaking out, reconceptualize resistance outside of the current political framework of spiritual terror. This reconfiguration—at once terrifying and potentially liberating—challenges the life/death power of state-sanctioned murder and shifts the control over life and death back to black people. Speaking up and speaking out means controlling how and when you die, even if there is no choice to live. For those of us who collaborate with survivors, acknowledging these stakes means acknowledging the black human as sentient, coeval, political, and transcendent.

We must acknowledge and honor the epistemes that frame our experience of being, at all points, in order to begin a discussion on the politics of protest, collaboration, dialogue, and activist scholarship. This requires, in the case of redressing the injustices suffered by black people in Brazil, acknowledging the power structures of spiritual terror, heterosexist white supremacy, and anti-blackness that deny that black people are the human, and recognizing the humanity and epistemology of the experience of being black in Brazil—an experience that is dynamic, complex, and at times contradictory. Transnational and trans-local conversations, activist interventions, and theoretical reflections cannot grapple with the actual life-or-death realities of the politics of protest (i.e., speaking up and speaking out) without first addressing the question of the human that sits at the heart of everyday survival in the spaces where we work. Within the context of traditional approaches to research on race and blackness in Bahia, blackness has become a hyper-folkloric, synchronic, cultural trope buried in faceless statistics or the overdetermined assumptions of the popular imagination that are completely dissociated from the human experience of black people. Consequently, the anti-black discourses associated with everyday experiences with violence, like police violence, get invisibilized in the minds of many who fail to identify blackness as a material, dynamic, lived reality within this national context. We cannot possibly begin to think about the possibilities for bridging practice with theory and politics without recognizing the life-and-death realities of those who are affected by the issues we seek to address. This requires, in this context, recognizing blackness as an ontological reality rather than reifying it as a faceless, nameless abstraction. In order for me as an activist-researcher to even approach the question of practice/theory/discourse/power, I must get comfortable with the complexities, contradictions, and unromantic realities of what it means to live as a black person within the context of violence that is the subject of my research, and this means confronting the realities of spiritual terror, and acknowledging the stakes of speaking up and speaking out.

NOTES

1. I use the term "transcendence" here to refer to both ancestrality and religious transcendence in African-based religious traditions like Candomblé in Brazil.
2. In 2005 black organizers rallied in Praça da Piedade to hold an all-night vigil protesting police violence against the black community. In March 2008 the MNU hosted a rally in the same location to protest the execution of rap artist Negro Blul, who was killed by a death squad in 2007.
3. Http://maesdemaio.blogspot.com/.
4. Http://www.petitiononline.com/maesmaio/petition.html.
5. Le cirque—they had been traveling around the country.
6. For a more in-depth look at the question of race and genocide in Brazil, see J. C. Vargas 2008.
7. Peripheral neighborhoods are the low-income neighborhoods located on the outskirts of Brazil's major

urban cities where the majority of black residents reside. I prefer the term "periphery" (which translates directly to *periferia* in Portuguese) rather than "favela" because of the latter's negative connotations.

8. In using the term "humanity" here, I invoke the work of Sylvia Wynter and her brilliant deconstruction of the traditional use of the acronym N.H.I. (No Humans Involved) by the Los Angeles Police Department in the 1990s and beyond. Wynter's open letter "No Humans Involved" unpacks the (il)logics behind officers' popular employment of the reference N.H.I. and its relationship to the "thingification" (to borrow from Aimé Césaire) and physical degradation of young, black, underemployed men (and women, although Wynter focuses on men exclusively) by the police and middle-class North American society.

REFERENCES

Amnesty International. (2005). *Brazil: 'They come in shooting': Policing socially excluded communities.* London: Amnesty International.

Brown, V. (2003). Spiritual terror in Jamaican slave society. *Slavery and Abolition* 24: 24–53.

Cano, I. (2000). Racial bias in lethal police action in Brazil. In *XXIV Encontro Anual da Associação Nacional de Pos Graduação e Pesquisa em Ciências (ANPOCS).* Brazil.

Cavallaro, J., Manuel, A., & Human Rights Watch/Americas. (1997). *Police brutality in urban Brazil.* New York: Human Rights Watch.

Chevigny, P. (1995). *Edge of the knife: Police violence in the Americas.* New York: New Press.

Cirino, H. (2007). Família é morta depois de denunciar policiais. *A Tarde*, August 15, 1, 4–5.

Danile Rebouças, George, & Lima, Samuel. (2009). MP Investiga Mortes em Canabrava. *A Tarde*, June 18.

Dávila, J. (2003). *Diploma of whiteness: Race and social policy in Brazil, 1917–1945.* Durham, NC: Duke University Press.

Espinheira, G. (Ed.). (2004). *Sociabilidade e violência: Criminalidade no cotidiano de vida dos moradores do Subúrbio Ferroviário de Salvador.* Salvador, Brazil: Ministério Publico da Bahia.

Fanon, F. (1965). *The wretched of the earth.* New York: Grove Press.

Hanchard, M. (1994). Orpheus *and power: The movimento negro of Rio de Janeiro and São Paulo, Brazil, 1945–1988.* Princeton, NJ: Princeton University Press.

Hanchard, M. (Ed.). (1999). *Racial politics in contemporary Brazil.* Durham, NC: Duke University Press.

Harrison, F. (2012). Building black diaspora networks and meshworks for knowledge, justice, peace, and human rights. In B. Reiter & K. E. Simmons, *Afro-Descendants, identity, and the struggle for development in the Americas.* East Lansing: Michigan State University Press.

Huggins, M. K. (Ed.). (1991). *Vigilantism and the state in modern Latin America: Essays on extralegal violence.* New York: Praeger.

Jung, M., Vargas, J., & Bonilla-Silva, E. (2011). *State of white supremacy: Racism, governance, and the United States.* Stanford, CA: Stanford University Press.

Lima, S. (2007). PMs acusados de invasão e tortura. *A Tarde*, May 22, 11.

Martinot, S., & Sexton, J. (2003). The avant-garde of white supremacy. *Social Identities* 9: 169–184.

Mitchell, M., & Wood, C. (1999). Ironies of citizenship: Skin color, police brutality, and the challenge to democracy in Brazil. *Social Forces, 77,* 1001–1020.

Moura, C. (1994). *Dialética radical do Brasil negro.* São Paulo, Brasil: Editora Anita.

Movimento Negro Unificado. (1988). 1978–1988, 10 anos de luta contra o racismo: Movimento Negro Unificado,

Salvador.

Moya, P. M. L., & Hames-Garcia, M. R. (2000). *Reclaiming identity: Realist theory and the predicament of postmodernism*. Berkeley: University of California Press.

Nascimento, A. (1989). *Brazil, mixture or massacre?: Essays in the genocide of a black people*. 2nd ed. Dover, MA: Majority Press.

Phelan, P. (1993). *Unmarked: The politics of performance*. New York: Routledge.

Pinheiro, P. S. (1991). Police and political crisis: The case of the military police. In M. K. Higgins (Ed.), *Vigilantism and the state in modern Latin America*. New York: Praeger.

React or Die! Campaign (Campanha Reaja ou Será Morto Reaja ou Será Morta) (2005). *Manifesto*. Salvador, Bahia.

Reis, Pablo. (2008). Jovens negros são vítimas preferenciais de grupos de extermínio. *Correio da Bahia*, March 2.

Reiter, B., & Simmons, K. E. (2012). *Afro-descendants, identity, and the struggle for development in the Americas*. East Lansing: Michigan State University Press.

Rose, R. S. (2005). *The unpast: Elite violence and social control in Brazil, 1954/2000*. Athens, OH: Ohio University Press.

Scott, D. (2000). The Re-enchantment of humanism: An interview with Sylvia Wynter. *small axe* 8: 119–207.

Silva Jr., H. (1998). A crônica da culpa anunciada. In D. D. D. Oliveira (Ed.), *A crônica da culpa anunciada*. Brasília-DF; Goiânia-GO; Brasília, Brazil: Editora UnB; Editora UFG; MNDH.

Skidmore, Thomas E. (1974). *Black into white: Race and nationality in Brazilian thought*. New York: Oxford University Press.

Vargas, J. C. (2008). *Never meant to survive: Black genocide and egalitarian utopias in the African diaspora*. Lanham, MD: Rowman and Littlefield.

Wilderson, F. B. (2010). *Red, white & black: Cinema and the structure of U.S. antagonisms*. Durham, NC: Duke University Press.

State Violence and the Ethnographic Encounter: Feminist Research and Racial Embodiment

Keisha-Khan Y. Perry

Voce é negro, jovem e trabalhador? Não venha pra Bahia: morre-se fácil. Are you black, young, and a worker? Don't come to Bahia: you die easily.

—Lutz Mulert Sousa Ribeiro, 2000

O Muro	**The Wall**
eu bato contra o muro	I beat against the wall
duro	hard
esfolo minhas mãos no muro	I scrape my hands on the wall
tento de longe o salto e pulo	I try to jump over it from far away
dou nas paredes do muro	I bang against the wall
duro	hard
não desisto de forçá-lo	I don't give up trying to force it
hei de encontrar um furo	I must find a way
por onde ultrapassá-lo	that I can get through it

—Oliveira Silveira 1997, my translation

O *muro* (The Wall), a poem by Afro-Brazilian poet Oliveira Silveira (1997), embodies various meanings for the black[1] majority of Brazil who oftentimes confront innumerable social and economic barriers to their survival and advancement. Silveira's poem also invokes W. E. B. Du Bois's 1903 statement in *The Souls of Black Folk* that "the problem of the twentieth century is the problem of the color line,—the relation of darker to the lighter races of men in Asia and Africa, in America and the islands of the sea" (9). In Brazilian society today, the *muro* may refer to the thick glass ceiling in the job market, the university entrance exams, the police barricades, the gated communities, or even the man-controlled metal detector at the bank. The wall is a metaphor for understanding the spatialized forms of gendered racial and class inequality that govern Brazilian cities. Finding a hole in the *muro*, or even attempting to climb over it, becomes a lifelong struggle for black people, and even more so for poor black women. Moreover, breaking down the *muro* is potentially dangerous and is likely to get them injured, or worse yet, killed.

•   •   •

To understand the dangers that symbolic as well as actual physical walls in Brazilian urban communities produce for local residents and activist researchers in these communities, I begin this article with a confession. I confess that on January 4, 2008, when the military and SWAT police forces descended upon Gamboa de Baixo, a black coastal community in the city center of Salvador, I ran at lightning speed into the bathroom of the home of neighborhood activist Ana Cristina. It is difficult to describe in great detail what the terror of a police invasion sounds or looks like—the state confinement of an entire neighborhood; the self-imprisonment of residents behind burglar bars, closed windows, and concrete walls; policemen and policewomen threatening to kill; men and women being pushed onto the ground on the narrow streets and inside their homes; women screaming to get their children out of the ocean; divers and fishermen and fisherwomen desperately trying to paddle or swim to shore; low flying helicopters; roof tiles cracking; doors being broken down; and the smell of fresh blood. It is as difficult to narrate the horror of rapid gunfire that alerted residents of the invasion in the first place, which as one woman said, confused her as to whether they were from *bandidos* (bandits) or *policiais* (police), until she found they were one and the same in their treatment of local residents. She and her dog had found cover underneath her bed.

That the police would report to the media that *traficantes*, or drug dealers, from below the Contorno Avenue in Gamboa de Baixo shot at them first, was not surprising. However, when the police stood on the walls of the Contorno Avenue and shot down directly onto their rooftops without discretion, the community was outraged. As residents of black communities in Salvador and throughout Brazilian cities retell in the aftermaths of violent police invasions, in Gamboa de Baixo "the police arrived firing, aiming to kill" (personal communication 2008). They gave no warning, and the entire community was considered criminal, myself included. But that local residents found the courage to call the news media to bear witness to what they considered to be the "absurdity" of unjust police work illustrates that collective fear of police torture and death exists side-by-side with black communities' unwillingness to accept routine forms of state violence. In other words, out of police violence emerge black peoples' agency and political will to survive, their determination to defy individual and collective death.

At one point during the police raid, Ana Cristina looked at me kneeling on the bathroom floor with my head in my hands, and said, "*coitada da* Keisha-Khan (poor Keisha-Khan)." I immediately felt embarrassed because I wondered if she could read my thoughts of my packing my bags and running back to Central Pennsylvania. My voice shaking, I looked at Ana Cristina and responded, "NO, *coitada de nós* (poor us)!" The police siege held residents of Gamboa de Baixo hostage between 10 am and 2 pm. When the police then reported to the media that their work in the neighborhood had not been completed, many expected the worst, including retaliation from local drug traffickers. Ana Cristina immediately replaced her kitchen door with a concrete wall, and delicately told me that if I wanted to leave her home and the neighborhood, she and the others would understand. But since no black neighborhood in Salvador was immune to violence, specifically police violence,[2] I asked her, where would I go? Who would protect me in another neighborhood in the city, above the Contorno Avenue? Would I sleep any better knowing that I had abandoned a community of women, friends more than they were research collaborators, who had nurtured me for over a decade and whose lives had let me make a career?

In this chapter, I focus on the example of police attacks on Gamboa de Baixo as a way to locate the confinement and silencing of the activist anthropologist within the overall context of state policing of black communities and black women-led grassroots movements in Salvador. Reflecting on my own ethnographic experience in the Gamboa de Baixo neighborhood, I explore the role of the Brazilian state in determining the sociopolitical positioning of the black woman anthropologist as a gendered and racial captive. Captivity, in this context, refers to state-imposed imprisonment, but also reveals how the marginality created during criminalization processes can operate as a form of black women's agency and grassroots militancy and can become the site of radical scholarship. What is evident, especially in the moments when police abuse is rampant and the state legitimizes its role as captor, is that the black woman activist anthropologist is not merely a witness to violence. A focus on state violence reveals the impact of collective racial subjection on black women's bodies, specifically women who are fighting for social justice and an end to criminal and police violence. I argue that black racial subjection and anti-black violence, evident in symbolic and physical walls in urban communities of Brazil, have a direct bearing on the ethnographer's pragmatic ability to be an activist, carry out social-science research, and produce anti-hegemonic knowledge.

Thus, activist research,[3] while urgent for black social movements, requires the anthropologist working in solidarity with social movement actors to negotiate "dangerous fields." As J. Christopher Kovats-Bernat (2002) points out in his essay "Negotiating Dangerous Fields: Pragmatic Strategies of Fieldwork amid Violence and Terror," anthropologists working in "dangerous fields"[4] are not uncommon, though little theorizing on how violence and terror impact anthropological knowledge, methodology, and ethics exists. What is at stake for the activist anthropologist who decides to work in a black community under siege by the state police, drug traffickers, and urban development agencies? Reading this dilemma with feminist eyes, I find it possible to confront the institutional practices of violence that destabilize and limit activist research, and to interrogate how class-based racism and sexism shape the knowledge gained and lost during the investigative process. Also, if we accept the basic premise of black feminist thought, that feminist discourses cannot be "separated from [their] activist roots" (Radford-Hill 2000), that feminist research methods must involve engagement, community-building, liberationist politics, and an overall commitment to social change, conceptualizing how to break down the wall that exists between *feminist anthropologists* and *grassroots feminists* becomes a real possibility.

Territory cuts at the heart of this difference. Fighting racism, sexism, and other inequalities at the local and global levels are common political goals, but feminist anthropologists work primarily within academic institutions, though their research on social movements involves sustained, intense collaboration on their part. Grassroots feminists are accountable to their political organizations, communities, and families first. Anthropologists work in the field—grassroots activists work at home. Yet, we must confront "dangerous fields" and develop techniques of survival at the same time. This essay emerges from my own personal and intellectual struggle to grapple with a simultaneous sense of political identification and distancing between the two types of activists that exist within me. As black feminist Canadian geographer Katherine McKittrick (2006) writes, "black matters are spatial matters" (xii), and "space and place give black lives meaning" (xiii). Black women's geographies, for Gamboa de Baixo residents, are "coupled with black humanity/personhood" (xiv), or rather, the material conditions and socio-spatial realities of the urban landscape structure black women's social consciousness and political praxis. As a Jamaican-born African American keeping with the trans-geographical aims of black feminist anthropology,[5] no matter how much I claim to feel at "home" while in Gamboa de Baixo and in Salvador, "belonging" means something vastly different for those who have dedicated their lives to the struggle for permanence and an improved quality of life. How we as feminists and activists differ, if we differ at all, warrants exploration here, considering the complexities of our identities, geographic locations, and institutional limitations.

I organize this chapter into three sections. In the first section, I outline the context of violence for my research in Salvador, Bahia, and the geographic space of black women's struggle in which my personal and professional life have become entangled. The second section explores the complexities of being an ethnographer acting in solidarity, and how collective racial, class, and gender subjection in relationship to residents in Gamboa de Baixo advances the activist tradition of black anthropology. I will conclude with a reflection on how to grapple with the dilemmas we face as black women ethnographers who understand their primary purpose as the search for global black political solidarity and community as part of our professional work.

Fortress Neighborhood: Spatializing Black Women's Grassroots Struggle

Ana Cristina's encouraging words that I could, without apology, leave Gamboa de Baixo during the January 2008 police attack shows that there is no attempt to pretend that she and I have the same constraints. As Diane Wolf (1996) asserts, "Although feminist researchers may attempt to equalize relationships while in the field through empathic and friendly methods, these methods do not transform the researchers' personality or locationality. The 'equality' is short-lived and illusory because the researcher goes home when she is finished, reflecting the privileged ability to leave" (35). Julia Sudbury and Margo Okazawa-Rey (2009) also emphasize, "We are conscious of the dangers of producing an idealized vision of collaborative or anti-oppressive research, recognizing that even research with emancipatory intentions is inevitably troubled with unequal power relations" (3). However, to begin to understand the spatial and other hierarchies that define disciplines such as anthropology (how Gamboa de Baixo activists and I occupy two different trenches), it is necessary to describe the context of the research site, the actual and symbolic walls that exist around and within the Gamboa de Baixo neighborhood. These walls constitute an important geopolitical component of urban policing, and subsequently determine how black women experience, theorize, and organize against violence at the community level.

There are two walled structures that define Gamboa de Baixo's geographic identity on the urban coast, and that have been the focus of modernist urban restructuring in Salvador in recent decades. On the western shores of Gamboa de Baixo lies the São Paulo da Gamboa Fort (built in 1722 and named a Brazilian heritage site in 1937). Historically, Salvador was known as a "fortress city" that was constructed in the mouth of the bay to function as a military and commercial port linked to other Portuguese transatlantic routes, marking the expansion of the Portuguese empire and the intensification of the transatlantic slave trade. Salvador was indeed, and continues to represent, the capital of Portuguese America. The city's significance in the Black Diaspora rests on the fact that it has the largest urban black population in the world outside of Lagos, Nigeria. The restoration of the São Paulo da Gamboa Fort is an effort to recuperate this colonial heritage (minus the memory of the terror and genocide of slavery and conquest), and to develop the coastal lands for maritime tourism. However, the community has resisted the displacement of local families, some living inside the ruins of the fort during and after the restoration process, maintaining its local identity as a "fortress neighborhood." In Gamboa de Baixo, the fort continues to be a place of leisure such as soccer games and film screenings, and political events such as health fairs and rallies. The fort is where I first met neighborhood activists in 1998.

To get to the fort, I had to first walk underneath the Contorno Avenue, a raised expressway. The construction of the Contorno Avenue by the technocratic and military government in the 1960s also shaped significantly the neighborhood's identity within the city and solidified socio-spatial hierarchies. The street segregated the Gamboa neighborhood; it literally created a wall between Gamboa de Baixo and the upper-class neighborhoods of Gamboa de Cima (Upper Gamboa), Banco dos Ingleses (English Bank), Campo Grande, and Vítoria. Gamboa de Baixo became a neighborhood "below the asphalt" street, and the physical descriptive also refers to the public representation of the black neighborhood as a separate urban underworld where immoral and illegal activities proliferate and which the modern Contorno Avenue obscures from public view. Many Bahians, with whom I have discussed my research, have claimed not to know where Gamboa de Baixo is located while simultaneously believing as *a matter of fact* that the neighborhood is violent, drug-ridden, and full of prostitutes—or is a place where *marginais* (criminals), both male and female, of the worst kind live. Gamboa de Baixo is undoubtedly known by those living inside and outside of it as a black neighborhood, *um bairro popular e periférico de pretos e pobres* (a popular and peripheral neighborhood of black and poor people). Thus, in the public imaginary, Gamboa de Baixo is both visible and invisible, in plain view and out of view, a socio-spatial divide created by the construction of the street that continues to be a wall above the predominantly black neighborhood.

Though I had to traverse the white middle- and upper-class neighborhoods to arrive in Gamboa de Baixo, the moment I walked below the asphalt street, it was clear to me that I had entered a black world, a place where I may have been a "stranger" to many, but where I knew I belonged racially. I did not arrive as a researcher, but as a recent college graduate eagerly looking for volunteer work in a black organization, and the opportunity to make friends. When I found out that the neighborhood activists were mostly black women in my age group, I easily attached myself to them. My commitment to women-centered political movements and the issues of housing and land rights had already guided me to work with the homeless in Washington, DC, and Buenos Aires while an undergraduate student. I also believed that, as a single woman in a small fishing community defined by heteronormative behaviors, always being in the company of women rather than with their male relatives or husbands provided little excuse for local women who led social and political networks to mistrust me or to lose focus on my commitment to the neighborhood movement. In Gamboa de Baixo, I was simply doing women's work—*politics*.[6]

With certain plans of returning to a rapidly gentrifying Newark, New Jersey, to live with my mother and brother after graduation, my decision to move to Brazil was serendipitous. A year earlier in 1997, Georgetown University hosted a reception for participants of the Brazilian Studies Association conference being held in Washington, DC. Having just returned from year-long study in Argentina and brief language study in Brazil, I was convinced by my Portuguese professor to attend the reception in order to meet the Brazilian ambassador, practice my Portuguese, and eat an assortment of gourmet Brazilian food. It was during this reception that I met Bahian historian Elizete da Silva, one of a handful of black scholars participating in the conference. We immediately gravitated towards each other, both expressing curiosity about being two of few blacks, and she listened patiently to my Spanish-infused Portuguese as I described my nostalgic desire to return to Salvador, where I felt reminded of Jamaica, Washington, DC, and even Newark. I was taken aback when she invited me to stay with her family if I were to ever return to Bahia, and she was equally surprised when I accepted. I worked seven days a week for several months after graduation to save money before Elizete and her husband João Rocha, a labor historian and activist, met me at the airport in Salvador in October 1998. I stayed with her then for a few weeks until I moved closer to the center of the city, where I ran into Leo Ornelas, a well-known photographer and founding member of the UNEGRO (Union for Black Equality) black movement organization, in a local park. I had recognized him from a black movement meeting I had attended, and when he asked me what I wanted to do in Salvador, he introduced me to his wife, Ana Cristina, a leader of the Gamboa de Baixo neighborhood association.

By the time I integrated myself into the Gamboa de Baixo neighborhood association, they had been engaged in a fierce struggle for land and housing rights and neighborhood improvement for almost two decades, beginning with the Women's Association of the 1980s. Until the early 1990s, the neighborhood "below the asphalt" had been forgotten, abandoned by city officials, and lacked basic infrastructural services such as potable water, electricity, and sewer systems that had become standard elements of urban development throughout the city. When the municipal government proposed to forcibly remove the local black population in the mid-1990s, the neighborhood became hypervisible both spatially and politically. Developers utilized the underdevelopment and supposed marginality and "collective pathology" of the area as justifications for a mass moral, social, and physical "cleanup" and "renewal," a strategy used to remove poor black residents from the Historic Center and Agua Suja neighborhoods previously. Thus, the state criminalization and policing of the neighborhood increased during the same period, and fighting for permanence became enmeshed with the struggle against the barbarity of police abuse.

Thinking about the walls of the São Paulo da Gamboa Fort and the Contorno Avenue, as well as the increased criminalization of the area "below the asphalt" allows us to understand how local residents interpret the new wall that now divides the 37-story Odebrecht-owned luxury condominium O Morada dos Cardeais (the House of the Cardinals), built in 2005, and Gamboa de Baixo. Odebrecht[7] extended the height of a wall constructed by the Archdiocese of Bahia, the previous landowners, that existed on the eastern perimeter of Gamboa de Baixo. Today, the wall remains a constant reminder of that lack of collective land entitlement, a crucial exclusion from property rights that marks Brazilian citizenship. Whereas historically, since the slavery period, blacks constituted the majority of the coastal population (coastal lands were considered undesirable), recent urban-development policies privilege the verticalization of the coast. In an attempt to restructure, the city of Salvador threatens to expel poor black coastal communities from lands along the Bay of All Saints, while encouraging self-segregation among Bahia's white elite behind physical walls surrounding coastal condominiums.[8]

Security guards discourage any type of physical contact with the piers—an extension of the luxury apartment communities that require protection—by using buoys to demarcate their territories *even within the public waters*. As Angela—a professional diver who has been a board member of the Gamboa de Baixo neighborhood and fishermen and fisherwomen's associations—recounted to me, "They think that we are pirates, that we will jump out of the water to rob them, and then row our boats back home" (personal communication 2003). Angela motions the act of frantically rowing as she tells me of the frequency of violent encounters between these security guards and Gamboa de Baixo fishermen and women, which expresses what she considers to be the "ridiculous" yet systemic criminal assumptions about black men and women. She also tells the story of how a yacht almost killed her and another female diver when reckless boaters ignored them in the water. As many residents have affirmed, they feel increasingly displaced from the land and waters of the bay by the white elite, who act as if they are the only ones who are entitled to it. In fact, many Gamboa de Baixo residents express that they believe that this increased policing in their neighborhood is directly related to residential shifts in the coastal landscape. The public police serve to protect not Gamboa de Baixo residents, but the elite who live around them. Angela's view resembles what Brazilian anthropologist Teresa Caldeira (2000) describes of poor urban residents in São Paulo:

> Rich people are perceived as being outside the law and society; their social position assures that they will not be punished. Perception of this additional inequality, which perverts classifications and social contracts, is at the center of the total pessimism many residents of São Paulo feel about creating a more just society in Brazil. Since it is difficult to impose order through existing institutions, which are unable to control evil and therefore unable to build a better society, people feel that they are constantly exposed to the natural forces of evil and to the abuse of those who place themselves outside of the law. To protect themselves, they have to rely on their own means of isolation, control, separation, and distancing. In order to feel safe, that is, they have to build walls. (101)

As black women in Gamboa de Baixo like Ana Cristina and Angela fight to stake their claim to the land below the asphalt and around the historic fort, another type of wall has emerged as a popular feature of neighborhood housing design. In recent years, the number of homes in the Gamboa de Baixo neighborhood that have enclosed their verandas and door fronts with *grades* (metal bars), or have built walls around their homes, has increased significantly. For some local residents, the walls and the *grades* protect them from both internal and external terror, specifically from the drug traffickers and the police, who many residents believe contribute to the everyday increase in violent crime and a generalized culture of fear. One longtime resident born in Gamboa de Baixo, Simone, who is currently completing construction on a large two-story house, decided to build high concrete walls around the perimeter of her property. Simone's concerns about the possibility of theft, the use of her backyard as an escape route for police fugitives, and police gunfire are very real. The need for the wall as a barrier became even more crucial when during the January 2008 attack, the police fired into the unfinished concrete walls of the house's interior, barely missing the construction workers on the site. "Imagine if the house had been finished and we had been living inside?" Simone has asked me. For Simone and other Gamboa de Baixo residents, the wall is a design feature that is a matter of life or death.

How Gamboa de Baixo residents perceive fear and how they are also building "fortresses" and other mechanisms of security around themselves alerts us that fortresses are not limited to the colonial past, to modernist urban designs, or to elite residential communities. In fact, poor people in cities worry just as much about violent crime as do rich people. The earlier safety of a small, everybody-knows-your-name, seaside fishing community has changed significantly for temporary residents like myself, and more so for those who have known the coastal lands all their lives. The focus on walls and *grades* within the Gamboa de Baixo neighborhood illustrates the fear that poor black people experience, but also shows that in this instance, residents demonstrate the unwillingness to translate that fear into what development agents have argued is the "inevitable" removal of its residents from that area of the city. As one state developer *shamelessly* affirmed during a meeting with Gamboa de Baixo activists: "Gamboa is the face of Bahia," but "it is not an area for blacks and poor people to live." Though with limited resources, in some cases as domestic workers, Gamboa de Baixo residents continue to build homes and the security mechanisms necessary to protect them in order to remain on the urban land where they have claimed property rights. In other words, they build the walls and the *grades* as a way to enact *self-containment* as a practice of *self-inclusion* on the coastal lands rather than exclusion from it; they do not envision living anywhere else. In cities such as Salvador, black women who head households and lead social networks are the main ones making decisions about housing design, which increasingly includes physical forms of protection. Later on in this chapter, I will revisit this relationship between self-containment and self-inclusion as methods of protection and survival for both activists and researchers.

The report by Amnesty International, "Picking Up the Pieces: Women's Experiences of Urban Violence in Brazil" (2008) supports black women's fear of violence in Gamboa de Baixo. Amnesty International reported that "the reality for women in Brazil's slums is catastrophic. They are the hidden victims of the criminal and police violence that has engulfed their communities for decades" (*A Tarde*, April 17, 2008). Scholar activists such as Vilma Reis (2005) have written extensively about the trauma of black women who lose their children to police violence in black neighborhoods throughout the city of Salvador. One such example in Gamboa de Baixo is the death of forty-seven-year-old Iraci Isabel da Silva (known as Dona Iraci) during a police attack in September 2002 that occurred just a few days after I arrived in Salvador to begin my dissertation research. Dona Iraci was a board member of the neighborhood association; I had conducted my first ever ethnographic interview with her, and she had been like a mother to me during my visits to Gamboa de Baixo. During the police raid, she confronted the police about their beating her ten-year-old grandson as he was playing at the front door. The policeman screamed at her, and when she screamed back, he threatened her with physical violence. She fell ill during this violent confrontation with the police and was taken to the hospital, where she died from a heart attack.

I deliberately argue against those who would label the death of Dona Iraci an unfortunate case of a woman's poor health condition, and who minimize the intentional trauma inflicted upon her black body when she questioned the routine police violence in her neighborhood. Her death encourages us to think differently about how black women suffer from police abuse. As Gamboa de Baixo activist Rita asserts, "mulher também toma porrada (women get beat too)." While young black men experience police abuse at a higher level than women in Salvador's poorest neighborhoods, women and children are not exempt from police violence. As the Amnesty International report also states, "Women who fight for justice on behalf of their sons or husbands end up on the frontline, facing further threats and harassment from the police." The police's capacity to dehumanize Dona Iraci and the black residents of Gamboa de Baixo stems from established understandings of them as gendered as well as racialized "others" undeserving of respect, dignity, and other benefits of full citizenship in Brazil. Black women experience a tremendous amount of stress. The women residents of the Gamboa de Baixo neighborhood, whom I have known for almost a decade and with whom I have developed profound friendships, lose sleep over the violence, become ill, lose their hair, and in the case of Dona Iraci, die because of the violence they experience. Their lives have been disrupted. They are no longer *tranquila* (calm), and many have become *nervosa* (literally meaning nervous, but more in the sense of being anxious or having a nervous breakdown). The January 2008 attack I witnessed does not fully illustrate the impact of the various forms of neighborhood violence local women, particularly activists, have felt *na pele*, in the skin: police terror, intracommunity violence, the threat of forced removal and demolition of their homes, as well as what they consider to be other infringements on their rights as human beings and Brazilian citizens—inadequate access to potable water and basic sanitation, dignified housing, education, and employment. To quote Abdias do Nascimento (1989), "Marginalization of the black community accompanied the abolition of slavery, while miserable living conditions made the black man [and I would add black woman] a 'declassified' citizen" (46).

Constrained, limited, and trapped by the generalized criminalization and political impotence, Gamboa de Baixo's black women activists ask, "How are we supposed to fight the *homens* [men, referring to the police] when we also have to fight the *meninos* [boys, referring to the drug dealers] and vice versa?" The Amnesty International report that "poor communities remain trapped between the criminal gangs which dominated the areas in which they lived and the violent and discriminatory methods used by the police" reflects this general frustration experienced by black communities throughout Brazil. This political impotence is further expressed in a letter we wrote six years ago after the 2002 police invasion that led to the death of activist Dona Iraci:

> With a long struggle in search of citizenship, we, the people of Gamboa de Baixo have resisted against these acts of violence and many other acts of social and racial discrimination. We are black men and women who have had our history denied, we comprise the masses of unemployed workers, and even worse, we are the preferred targets of institutionalized violence, in other words, of the police. Our community lives terrorized, without security, without having anyone to run to in order to guarantee our rights. As if it were not enough that many of us have been victimized by the continued violence of the absence of public works, the abuses, physical and psychological torture are happening with greater frequency in our community. (Gamboa de Baixo neighborhood association "Open Letter," 2002)[9]

The collective writing of the open letter against police abuse is just one example of how Gamboa de Baixo residents have resisted. What the women of the neighborhood association describe as a broader preoccupation with anti-black racial violence is a complex understanding of the depth of everyday social and economic conditions that define their existence as a poor black neighborhood in the center of Salvador. Gamboa de Baixo, historically, has been a black community under siege, marginalized spatially as well as socially and economically. Resisting police violence in Gamboa de Baixo must be understood within the overall context of fighting for citizenship rights such as adequate housing, clean water, and land. As the local activists' letter boldly asserts, police attacks only skim the surface of the insidious war being waged against Salvador's poorest communities in the form of social and economic neglect on the part of the state. The technocratic military government's construction of the Contorno Avenue, the subsequent isolation and abandonment of the neighborhood, the threats of displacement during recent gentrification projects are related to the everyday victimization by the police. Race and gender overdetermine the police's relationship with the neighborhood and the enactment of "spatialized justice," which the Canadian scholar of aboriginal rights Sherene H. Razack (2002) defines as the "values that deem certain bodies and subjects in spaces as deserving of full personhood" (126). Yet, as a result of antiviolence struggle, Gamboa de Baixo remains intact as a community.

Black Feminist Anthropologists, Activists, and Political Silencing

After the January attacks, when residents expressed that they had lived in a scene "out of a war zone," they also made a comparison to the first of a Brazilian film series *Tropa da Elite* (Elite Squad) (2007). *Tropa da Elite* portrays the personal and professional experience of Brazil's most elite police squad in Rio de Janeiro (comparable to the ATF and SWAT teams in the United States), focusing on their violent encounters in Rio de Janeiro's supposedly "most violent" *favelas*. Some residents tried to lighten the seriousness of the elite squad's operations by joking that "*a tropa da elite* (the elite squad) was in Gamboa." However, as the film portrays, the elite police squads arrived in the neighborhood "shooting first, and asking later," using arbitrary policing techniques that endangered the lives of the noncriminal majority. As in the war against Rio de Janeiro's black communities, knowledge of police corruption and cruelty override the exaggerated representations of unnecessary barbarity among black poor residents that inevitably justify the actions of the elite squad, as also portrayed in the 2002 Oscar-nominated film *City of God*.

As Ana Cristina states, "I saw myself in the movie. They try to represent everyone as involved in criminal activity of some kind, even the social activists." The movie also portrays violence in black neighborhoods as a contagion—that even the most well-intentioned (and I would include the researchers here) become involved in drug use or other illicit activities. This resembles the general sentiment by residents of these neighborhoods that "all blacks continue being [represented as] a criminal or potential drug dealer, without justification or explanation" (*A Tarde*, June 9, 2008). Ana Cristina continues, "Though you find yourself questioning the destructive tactics of the elite squad, you find yourself saying '*eh isso mesmo*' [that's right!]." In an online news report of the Gamboa de Baixo invasion, one reader, Marcos, responded along these lines: "I want to congratulate here, our police and those who directly or indirectly contribute to these actions. We have to end at whatever cost, these actions on the part of these criminals that want to do with Bahia what they have been doing in Rio. That is not going to work here, because even with the horrible salary that our police receives, they still fight and protect our citizens" (iBahia.com, January 4, 2008). As Ana Cristina asserts, everyone below the walls of the Contorno Avenue is read as criminal, a prescriptive that includes black women activists, and anthropologists.

This belief that I am part of the collective racial and criminal subjection imposed on Gamboa de Baixo residents by the state may be better understood in the following narrative of a curious encounter with the police. The incident occurred in 2010 when neighborhood activists asked me to participate in a meeting with a representative of a nongovernmental organization that expressed interest in working with adolescent and young adult residents. The aim of the service project was to empower young people to pursue educational and economic opportunities in local fishing and maritime work as well as outside of the neighborhood. I arrived at the meeting after it had already started, in the neighborhood association building's main meeting room. Activists Ana Cristina, Lia, Marzinho, Adriano, Preta, and Lula were sitting in a circle with a young woman, with her curly hair tucked under a baseball hat, talking about the organization and its community-service intentions. She was accompanied by a social scientist from the local university who had participated previously in an annual meeting held in the neighborhood titled "Encontro das Águas" (The Meeting of the Waters), which discussed the politics of water distribution and environmental health in Bahia. Ana Cristina interrupted her to introduce me as a North American researcher who has been following, supporting, and documenting the neighborhood's movement over the years. The meeting continued with the NGO representative, and everyone listened to her idyllic methods of capturing young people's hearts and souls by grounding them in the arts, sports, fishing, and legitimate entrepreneurship, which inevitably would steer them away from the local proliferation of drug dealing, clandestine abortions, early motherhood, and perpetual urban poverty. The philanthropic organization would help to create a new generation of young people who might even become policemen rather than the men who ran away from them.

We sat and stared at her, annoyed by the uncomplicated repetition of the discourse of black urban pathology, unconvinced by the naiveté of a non-state-sponsored social intervention project, and suspicious of yet another service organization making unrealistic promises to local residents. "What did you say the name of your organization is?" "Who are its primary members?" "Where do you get your money from?" There was an onslaught of questions when the NGO representative paused and took a deep breath. She replied with an evasive description of an anonymous group of wealthy businessmen and professionals primarily from Bahia who were interested in the improvement of the neighborhood portrayed as violent in the media. "We know that there are good people here," she said. These philanthropists wanted to remain anonymous, since they wanted no attention to their wealth. I also listened attentively and with much curiosity as she and the Gamboa de Baixo residents spoke, and I did not raise my questions about the concern that in a Brazilian corporate culture heavily criticized by social scientists for its lack of social responsibility, anonymity seemed unlikely and lacking in credibility. As she fumbled to answer the activists' questions, I intervened and asked her, "Considering the vastness of the social service projects that are proposed to Gamboa de Baixo residents, you do understand why these questions about resource origins, intentions, and practical outcomes are important for us to know and for you to articulate to us?" She nodded affirmatively, provided a few concrete answers about her organization, and asked if it was possible to take a tour of the neighborhood.

Gamboa de Baixo activists took her on a tour, much like the tours on which they have taken many other visitors to the neighborhood. She asked questions and took pictures with her digital camera, and when she made a statement about having heard that there were different drug factions at war in the area, one of the activists looked at me with an expression of "oh boy, here we go again." Local activist Lia abruptly responded that she knew nothing of a drug war, and made up an excuse to end the tour when the visitor asked who the drug traffickers were. Though accompanied by a known social scientist, no one was buying her attempt to sound like an innocent schoolgirl turned NGO worker touring urban blight for the first time. I walked with Lia to her mother's house where, after we sat down, we blurted out at the same time, "That woman was strange." We both admitted that we thought that she was an undercover police officer, but were confused about the role of the Bahian social scientist, who had participated in several neighborhood events. Why would a service organization ask the names of drug traffickers? Why would she take pictures without asking? I added that during the police raids they usually have detailed maps and photographs that could only be drawn up and taken within the neighborhood. We were suspicious but had no proof, so I archived the event as yet another instance of the rampant condescension of NGO activists, oftentimes white, middle-class, and college educated with little experience in the black neighborhoods.

When I arrived at Ana Cristina's house later on that night, she received a phone call from another resident who told her that a local drug dealer had stated that the neighborhood activists had given a tour to an undercover officer earlier that day. The supposed NGO representative had worked under-cover years before in Gamboa de Baixo and had since worked in other neighborhoods in the city. "I knew it," Ana Cristina exclaimed on the phone. "Something was not right about her," I whispered in the background. Rumors had already been spreading that neighborhood activists had been seen collaborating with the police in a secret meeting in the association's building and had even given a tour and pertinent information on the local drug trade. I had become part of the conversation. "If you had suspicions that she was a policewoman, why didn't you say something or ask her a question that blew her cover?" In discussions on how to remedy the threat of danger that this situation posed for local activists, we all agreed that while local activists wanted state-sponsored social services aimed at the improvement of their neighborhood, they could not collaborate with the police to provide information that led to violent police raids. On the one hand, local activists wanted viable economic alternatives for young people that lured them away from illicit activities, but state-sponsored police work could not involve taking advantage of the desperation and vulnerability of neighborhood residents, nor could the state put the lives of local activists at risk.

The idea that my silence during the meeting may have somehow exacerbated or not prevented the problem troubled me. I explained to Ana Cristina that several things went through my mind as I sat through the meeting. If local activists and a well-respected social scientist with more knowledge of the Bahian political terrain had no suspicions, how could I? I am part of a generation of students who have read extensively information on how black organizations of the past and present in the United States have been infiltrated by undercover police agents. Had all this information made me paranoid, and was it unwarranted in the context of Salvador? If I raised information about this woman and the social scientist, willing to work for the greater good of Gamboa de Baixo, would that also mean that I should be put under the same kind of scrutiny? Also, would asking hard questions detract from what could possibly be a social good? Ana Cristina responded that perhaps if we *all* had been more critical during the meeting, we could have collectively unmasked the policewoman and prevented the messiness that it caused. I was no longer an outsider, and I could not merely sit back and observe. More importantly, my local knowledge and insights were just as important as theirs, and I had the responsibility of protecting them just as much as they had been protecting me over the years. In that meeting, the policewoman working for the state would not protect them if their lives were in danger as a result, nor would she protect mine.

As João H. Costa Vargas (2008) writes in a reflection on his own complex work as an activist ethnographer documenting black organizing against police abuse:

> Despite what is still taught in anthropological methods classes, no detached, fly-on-the-wall approach is possible. Such an approach in anthropology, considered an antidote to the influences of one's subjectivity on the research process, only obscures the fact that even those who try to be invisible are, at the very least, already influencing the social environment in which they choose to do their fieldwork and, more importantly, are already committing themselves to a very clear moral and political position—that of letting things remain as they are, of leaving the status quo untouched. (171)

Vargas's viewpoint rings true for my experiences in Gamboa de Baixo, and this became even clearer to me when a couple of weeks after our meeting with the undercover policewoman and social scientist, I saw her in uniform outside the entrance of a military police base in the city center. She was walking with her police colleagues, but her curly hair neatly tucked under her police hat caught my attention. I pretended to look past her, though she had already caught my eye and quickly adjusted her hat and looked to the ground. We both unsuccessfully tried to make ourselves invisible. My twisted hair, odd-shaped metal glasses, colorful handbag, and brown leather sandals were the same as when I had been introduced to her in the meeting in Gamboa de Baixo. Her striking light brown eyes had not changed, and I was internally perplexed at the sloppiness of Bahian police work, just as I was annoyed at my tendency to look into people's eyes where I thought I could usually see the truth. I felt my heart racing as I walked almost to a slow jog to get to Ana Cristina's house, where I immediately told her, "I saw the policewoman just now. She's the police. She had on a uniform. I saw her. And she saw me." I then tried to mask my fear with humor and exclaimed, "There will be no group of wealthy Bahians sponsoring the betterment of Gamboa de Baixo's black youth." The truth has been confirmed.

This above-mentioned example of my insertion into Gamboa de Baixo's everyday life shows the complexity of being an anthropologist and international activist working in solidarity away from home, and maintaining political and personal relationships simultaneously. To repeat Vargas (2008), there is no pretension that a "detached, fly-on-the-wall approach is possible" (171), nor is it possible to work in solidarity and be silent. An activist anthropologist of the Black Diaspora cannot sit in a meeting with state police officials and simply observe. My participation in this instance required that I not question who I am, how I had gotten to that meeting as a North American, nor my knowledge of violent police tactics from a black diasporic perspective. On the one hand, local activists understand that I can always leave Gamboa de Baixo and Bahia and return to my academic work, where I can avoid the violent police raids like the one I described at the beginning of this paper. On the other hand, while I am in Gamboa de Baixo and claiming to participate in solidarity within the grassroots movement, local activists are very critical of silence and inaction on my part.

Gina A. Ulysse (2007), a Haitian-born African American anthropologist, wrote along these lines on the impossibility of silence for black women researchers and the need to grapple with these practical issues we face while doing fieldwork:

In spite of Audre Lorde's warning that silence will not protect us (1984), our historical silences on certain subjects have allowed many to be taken seriously and, in some ways, have sheltered careers. Simultaneously, these survival strategies have also reified gendered ideals and reinforced the stereotype of the black superwoman. There is a political economy of reflexivity (Ulysse 2003). Indeed, who is reflexive, what they reflect on, where they reflect, and at what point do they begin to reflect are all subject to professional evaluation in the process of making careers. This monitoring of disciplinary ways not only upholds conventional forms, methods, and writings, but in the process also influences decisions about what types of work black anthropologists do or ought to do. (111)

The event challenged me to both grapple with my silence and give it attention in this essay. My experiences exemplify Ulysse's claim that we as black women ethnographers must dismantle the myth of black superwomanhood and admit to the dangers we face when subjected to the same kinds of racial and gendered subjection and violence as the black community members at the center of our research projects. In fact, the very process of making a career through engaged scholarship exposes us not only to the violence of oftentimes nontransparent academic evaluations, but more importantly to the violence against our bodies and minds doing the work that we need to do in order to survive academically. At the same time, as both Vargas and Ulysse have explained, the very methods that endanger our survival as black researchers are the methods necessary to carry out work in solidarity and advance the improvement of black communities. In this vein, as Robert Adam's recent reconceptualization of Audre Lorde's (1984) idea that "poetry is not a luxury" expresses, for most black anthropologists, ethnography—especially amid anti-black police violence—is not a luxury (personal communication 2010). In response to someone who had said that poetry is a luxury, Lorde wrote:

For women, then, poetry is not a luxury. It is a vital necessity of our existence. It forms the quality of the light within which we predicate our hopes and dreams toward survival and change, first made into language, then into idea, then into more tangible action. Poetry is the way we help give name to the nameless so it can be thought. The farthest horizons of our hopes and fears are cobbled by our poems, carved from the rock experiences of our daily lives. (1984, 37)

Ethnography is not a luxury, but rather a necessary and urgent form of political work that we have conceived of as being the driving force of our research questions, fieldwork engagement, analytical writing despite the violence.

Conclusion

My witnessing of violent police raids from within Gamboa de Baixo is not the anthropology that I tell people I do. Even after more than a decade, my family knows very little about the fieldwork process, and even less about how state and intracommunity violence might impact my ongoing research on black women's struggles for land and housing rights in Bahia. After research trips, I explain away any apparent fatigue and stress as jetlag. In my work, I have written very little about how trauma, death, and dying penetrate the everyday lives of women in Gamboa de Baixo, most of them activists of the neighborhood association, with whom I spend all of my time. I certainly do not write about my own trauma of witnessing police abuse, everyday forms of violence such as hunger and untreated curable diseases, lack of basic sanitation, and *the fear of my own death*. Yet, I cannot ignore my own vulnerability, the very real possibility of victimization and humiliation as an observer participant, and the moments I am conflicted about the *courage* of the black women's grassroots struggle I document and the power of my own political cowardice.

Why bother carrying out ethnographic research amid violence if you curl up on the floor and do nothing? How should I make sense of my ethnographic commitment to theorizing human rights in collaboration when I am held captive mentally and physically, and collective silence becomes the law? In the midst of a police raid when I feel my unwillingness to move, much less pick up a camera or a notebook, the dilemma of being an anthropological witness overwhelms me. I have had to piece together my own memory of the police raid with stories from local residents, bringing into question my credibility as a witness and the need to define the participant observer perspective. I ask myself the question that Ruth Behar (1996) asked more than a decade ago in her classic text *The Vulnerable Observer*: "Are there limits—of respect, piety, pathos—that should not be crossed, even to leave a record? But if you can't stop the horror, shouldn't you at least document it?" (2).

Similar to Vargas, who tells of his experiences in academia (2008, 172), when I present research on black women's political organizing at academic conferences in both the United States and Brazil, I am often asked about how my subjectivity as a U.S. black woman has impacted the "objectivity" of my "data" on anti-black violence. These questions ignore the centuries of racial inequality and black radicalism that had existed prior to my arrival in Bahia, and more importantly, assumed that my own experiences with violence and antiviolence politics have tainted the scientific legitimacy of my ethnographic conclusions. However, standing outside the collective experiences of black women in Brazil would have been impossible. The examples I cite in this chapter show that I am a part of local community politics as well as the global black experience and social justice movement.

However, my own actions during the January 2008 raid and the meeting with the undercover police officer provide examples of why I believe there are limitations to anthropological engagement. Is documenting enough? If you are confined, does that mean you really are equal, that sharing the suffering breaks down the wall? Black feminist anthropologist Asale Angel-Ajani (2004) asserts:

> One thing that I know for sure is that I cannot live with the fact that I peddle with the flesh of women's stories for academic consumption, making them pretty, because the realities of their lives are too difficult to bear. Through the incorporation of "theory" I have learned to water down difficult emotional moments so as not to appear sentimental. (134)

Surely, I too have devoted a lot of my ethnographic writing to describing the inspirational actions of black women community activists and the beauty of the coastal landscape that they have fought so hard to own. It may be purposeful that I fail to delve into the harsh realities of Gamboa de Baixo, the fractured political relationships, predatory fishing, the increased presence of crack and violent crime, and the gradual demise of traditional cordiality among neighbors. In a journal article that activist Ana Cristina and I coauthored, we theorized black women's liberatory discourses and practices as a result of their leadership and participation in the Gamboa de Baixo neighborhood movement; however, we made no mention of the very real death threats she and other activists suffered during the article's completion—how everyday survival took precedence over writing in collaboration; how focusing on the grassroots movements' successes provided moments of necessary distraction from psychological terror and forced political silence (Perry & Caminha 2008). I organized panels for the Latin American Studies Association conference and at my U.S. university that involved Ana Cristina as a way of bringing her social-activist perspective into academic discussions as coauthor and co-participant as a crucial way of building solidarity between *feminist anthropologists* in academe and *grassroots feminists* in Brazilian urban communities.

In April 2011, I brought Ana Cristina to the Brown campus to give a lecture alongside Libia Grueso, a longtime Afro-Colombia activist, in an event focused on bringing attention to mass land evictions and forging solidarity with these women-led movements in Latin America. They then participated in similar events with activist-scholar collaborators at the University of Massachusetts, Amherst and Smith College. Audience members asked about why there is no global outrage about the millions of blacks being displaced throughout the region, and if poor black communities such as Gamboa de Baixo should be concerned about development plans in preparation for the upcoming mega-sports such as the World Cup in 2014 and the Olympic Games in 2016. Others cautioned that these diasporic processes should not be geographically distanced from U.S. cities such as Providence and New York City. It was during these exchanges on New England college campuses with Ana Cristina that I realized that not only could I teach the violence, but it was her actual presence in my classroom speaking as an activist and scholar that gave the U.S. public greater insight into her gendered racial reality. The social movement classroom in Brazil necessarily had to become enmeshed with my classroom here, whose members formed the country's elite who would later make global policy decisions on development impacting the lives of black Brazilians. Now, in 2014, just months away from the World Cup, threats of land evictions in Salvador have indeed put the Gamboa de Baixo under siege by the police state and urban developers. The need for the feminist anthropologist and the grassroots feminists to work in solidarity (such as writing political manifestos in collaboration and translating my book that documents and critiques exclusionary practices in urban development) becomes even more urgent.

We are forced to recognize that our positionality as U.S.-based black researchers who return to the quiet confines of resourceful universities and suburban homes creates unequal "fields" of knowledge. As self-identified activist anthropologists, some of us provide detailed descriptions of the trenches in which we work and the social structures we hope our scholarship will transform, when it is clear that we are haunted by the geopolitics, the walls that limit our political commitments; when we are resentful of the competing academic demands and ever growing privileges that further distance us from the struggles that are the focus of our scholarship; and when we are deeply troubled by the violent realities that define the everyday conditions of our comrades abroad. As Vargas (2008) argues, we oftentimes benefit more in our academic careers from saying that we are "activist scholars" than we are hindered, and the political communities reap concrete benefits. In essence, we are terribly uncomfortable with the unequal relationships of power that not only make political connections possible but also limit them. This political uneasiness among social scientists compels us towards permanent relationships of engaged activist research and the theorization of the place of the university in social movements. As Angel-Ajani (2006) also suggests, by virtue of our position in the university, we are in danger of becoming part of the machine that reproduces racist ideas; but we can use our ability to produce critical thought to work towards liberation (77). As Allen Isaacman (2003) writes about African American scholarly commitment to social justice, "scholar-activists, by virtue of their critical engagement in the central issues of the day and their role in the production and dissemination of knowledge, have a unique opportunity to challenge the inherited orthodoxies in the academy and in the larger world in which we live" (29).

For that reason I recognize that activist research and collaboration are absolutely crucial to dismantling structural hierarchies inherent in the fieldwork process, a practice to which many of us have devoted much of our energy (Harrison 2007). At this intellectual moment when an increasing number of African American scholars are carrying out field research in Brazil amid an onslaught of gendered, racist critiques of "ethnocentrism," a discussion of engaged research emphasizes that solidarity among U.S. and Brazilian black women is not automatic. Solidarity requires hard work, oftentimes filtered by disappointment, heartbreak, and immense personal disclosure—more than what we are accustomed to, working in isolating academic environments. I would hardly consider myself "a stranger in the village," to borrow from Farah Griffin and Cheryl Fish's (1998) characterization of African American ethnographers such as Katherine Dunham, but I am reminded that fear, anxiety, and boundaries (or what I call "walls") deserve careful reading. The building of ethnographic relationships and the production of knowledge based on those relationships becomes a way for me as a Diaspora black woman researcher to understand how to belong politically to a social movement in Bahia; to be in place as an anthropologist, rather than *out of place*; to break down that wall; and to stay alive.

NOTES

This chapter is an updated version of the previously published journal article with the same title in *African and Black Diaspora Studies: An International Journal* 5 (1) (2012): 135–154.

1. As in the quote by Bahian scholar Lutz Mulert Sousa Ribeiro cited above, I use the term "black" in this text as the English translation of the term "negro." Bahians of African descent, especially poor people who constitute the masses living on the socioeconomic margins of Brazil, use "black" to identify themselves individually and collectively. The lexicon of "black" reflects not only a positive affirmation of blackness, but also a political mode of identification with black people throughout the African Diaspora.

2. According to a 2008 Human Rights Watch universal periodic report of Brazil, "police violence—including excessive use of force, extrajudicial executions, torture and other forms of ill-treatment—persists as one of Brazil's most intractable human rights problems."

3. I find Charles R. Hale's (2001) definition of activist research useful for this analysis. Hale characterizes activist research as including, though not limited to, three main objectives: (a) it helps us better to understand the root causes of inequality, oppression, violence, and related conditions of human suffering; (b) it is carried out, at each phase from conception through dissemination, in direct cooperation with an organized collective of people who themselves are subject to these conditions; (c) it is used, together with the people in question, to formulate strategies for transforming these conditions and to achieve the power necessary to make these strategies effective (13).

4. Kovats-Bernat (2002) defines "dangerous fields" as "those sites where social relationships and cultural

realities are critically modified by the pervasion of fear, threat of force, or (ir)regular application of violence and where customary approaches, methods, and ethics of anthropological fieldwork are at times insufficient, irrelevant, inapplicable" (208).

5. In the anthology *Black Feminist Anthropology: Theory, Politics, Praxis, and Poetics* (2001), editor Irma McClaurin explains that black feminist anthropological theory and praxis follow in the black intellectual tradition of conceptualizing the African Diaspora and processes of diasporic community building and survival (9). She writes, "This diasporic perspective is evident in the way that Black feminist anthropologists' ethnography is designed to look outward (at Africa, the Caribbean, Latin America, and Europe), a direction consistent with the aims of the conventional anthropological gaze, and simultaneously to look inward (at the United States), in keeping with the aims of a Black intellectual tradition" (9). In essence, black feminist anthropology has been profoundly impacted by African Diaspora studies and the theorization of the interrelationship between race, gender, and nation.

6. In a recently published book chapter, "Politics is *uma Coisinha de Mulher* (a Woman's Thing): Black Women's Leadership in Neighborhood Movements in Brazil," in *Latin American Social Movements in the Twenty-First Century: Resistance, Power, and Democracy* (Lanham, MD: Rowman & Littlefield Publishers, 2008), I explain how neighborhood politics in Gamboa de Baixo and other urban neighborhoods developed as women's political terrain. In Gamboa de Baixo, since the postmilitary dictatorship organization of the Women's Association of the early 1980s, politics has been considered "women's work."

7. Odebrecht is a major multinational real-estate developer known for its luxury construction projects in Brazil. It is known for its extensive airport renovations, such as in Atlanta prior to the 2002 Olympics and in Haiti after the recent devastating earthquake, and massive redevelopment projects in postwar Angola. The company has been celebrated for its role in redevelopment of the world's infrastructure more that it has been criticized. Oftentimes, this is because little attention has been given to the small communities or homeless populations that are displaced during redevelopment processes being carried out by Odebrecht and many other development firms.

8. As one newspaper article noted, 60.9 percent of household incomes of residents in closed condominiums are greater than 20 minimum salaries (20 times 300 reais; 1U$ = 1.7 reais) while 42 percent of residents in neighborhoods like Nordeste de Amaralina are classified as poor (*A Tarde*, March 15, 2007). Activists in Gamboa de Baixo argue that the poverty index in their neighborhood exceeds 50 percent.

9. The original quote from the "Carta Aberta (Open Letter)" in Portuguese: "*Com muita luta em busca da cidadania negada, nós, povo da Gamboa de Baixo temos resistido a estas e muitas outras demonstrações de discriminação social e racial. Somos negros e negras que temos nossa identidade negada, compomos uma grande massa de trabalhadores desempregados e ainda somos os alvos preferenciais da violência institucionalizada, ou seja, das polícias. Nossa comunidade sobrevive aterrorizada, sem segurança, sem ter a quem recorrer no que diz respeito à garantia dos nossos direitos. Como se já não bastasse os muitos de nós que foram vitimados pela continua violência da ausência de políticas públicas, os abusos e torturas físicas e psicológicas estão acontecendo com mais freqüência em nossa comunidade.*"

REFERENCES

Amnesty International. (2008). *Brazil: Picking up the pieces: Women's experiences of urban violence in Brazil.* London: Amnesty International.

Amnesty International. (2008). Brazil: Women's Lives Shattered by Public Security Crisis in Urban Shanty-
    towns. Amnesty International Media Centre, April 17. Http://www.amnesty.org/en/for-media/press-
    releases/brazil-women039s-lives-shattered-public-security-crisis-shanty-towns-200

Angel-Ajani, A. (2004). Expert witness: Notes toward revisiting the politics of listening. *Anthropology and
    Humanism* 29 (2): 133–144.

Behar, R. (1996). *The vulnerable observer: Anthropology that breaks your heart.* Boston: Beacon Press.

Caldeira, T. P. R. (2000). *City of walls: Crime, segregation, and citizenship in São Paulo.* Berkeley: University of
    California Press.

Du Bois, W. E. B. (1903). *The souls of black folk: Essays and sketches.* Chicago: A. C. McClurg & Co.

Griffin, F. J., & Fish, C. J. (1998). *A stranger in the village: Two centuries of African-American travel writing.*
    Boston: Beacon Press.

Hale, C. R. (2001). What is activist research? *Items (Social Science Research Council)* 2 (1–2): 13–15.

Harrison, F. V. (2007). Feminist methodology as a tool of ethnographic inquiry on globalization. In N.
    Gunewardena & A. E. Kingsolver (Eds.), *The gender of globalization: Women navigating cultural and
    economic marginalities,* 23–31. Santa Fe, NM: School of Advanced Research Press.

iBahia (2008). Vinte pessoas são presas na Gamboa em operação da polícia. iBahia.com. Http://ibahia.com.

Isaacman, A. (2003). Legacies of engagement: Scholarship informed by political commitment. *African Studies
    Review* 46 (1): 1–41.

Kovats-Bernat, J. C. (2002). Negotiating dangerous fields: Pragmatic strategies for fieldwork amid violence and
    terror. *American Anthropologist* 104 (1): 208–222.

Lorde, A. (1984). *Sister outsider: Essays and speeches.* Trumansburg, NY: Crossing Press.

McClaurin, I. (2001). *Black feminist anthropology: Theory, politics, praxis, and poetics.* New Brunswick, NJ:
    Rutgers University Press.

McKittrick, K. (2006). *Demonic grounds: Black women and the cartographies of struggle.* Minneapolis:
    University of Minnesota Press.

Nascimento, A. d. (1989). *Brazil, mixture or massacre?: Essays in the genocide of a black people.* 2nd ed. Dover,
    MA: Majority Press.

Oliveira, N., Ribeiro, L. M. S., & Zanetti, J. C. (2000). *A outra face da moeda: Violência na Bahia.* Salvador,
    Brazil: Comissão de Justiça e Paz da Arquidiocese de Salvador.

Perry, K. Y. (2008). Politics is *uma coisinha de mulher* (a woman's thing): Black women's leadership in neigh-
    borhood movements in Brazil. In R. Stahler-Sholk, H. E. Vanden & G. D. Kuecker (Eds.), *Latin American
    social movements in the twenty-first century: Resistance, power, and democracy,* 197–211. Lanham, MD:
    Rowman & Littlefield Publishers.

Perry, K. Y., & Caminha, A. C. d.S. (2008). "Daqui não saio, Daqui ninguém me tira": Poder e política das
    mulheres negras da Gamboa de Baixo, Salvador. *Gênero* 9 (1): 127–153.

Radford-Hill, S. (2000). *Further to fly: Black women and the politics of empowerment.* Minneapolis: University
    of Minnesota Press.

Razack, S. (2002). *Race, space, and the law: Unmapping a white settler society.* Toronto: Between the Lines.

Reis, V. (2005). *Atucaidos pelo Estado: As politicas de seguranca publica implementadas nos bairros populares
    de Salvador e suas representacoes, 1991–2001.* Master's thesis, Universidade Federal da Bahia, Salvador.

Silveira, O. (1997). O muro. *Revista Continente Sul-Sur.* Rio Grande do Sul, Brazil: Editora Estadual do Livro.

Sudbury, J., & Okazawa-Rey, M. (2009). *Activist scholarship: Antiracism, feminism, and social change.* Boulder,

CO: Paradigm Publishers.

Ulysse, G. A. (2007). *Downtown ladies: Informal commercial importers, a Haitian anthropologist, and self-making in Jamaica.* Chicago: University of Chicago Press.

Vargas, J. H. C. (2008). Activist scholarship: Limits and possibilities in times of black genocide. In C. R. Hale (Ed.), *Engaging contradictions: Theory, politics, and methods of activist scholarship,* 164–182. Berkeley: University of California Press.

Wolf, D. L. (1996). *Feminist dilemmas in fieldwork.* Boulder, CO: Westview Press.

The Challenges Resulting from Combining Scientific Production and Social-Political Activism in the Brazilian Academy

Fernando Conceição

Translated from Brazilian Portuguese by Bernd Reiter

When Barack Obama was elected to the presidency of the United States in 2008, the world celebrated. So did Brazil. A black man took command of the most powerful country of the world. Brazil is considered a developing country with a population of 180 million, half of which is black or mixed. To some 90 million Afro-Brazilians, the election of Barack Obama was very significant.

After the election, I published an article asking when my country would do the same. That is: when would Brazil elect a black person to the presidency—given that Brazil is the country with the largest black population in the world, after Nigeria.

In demographic terms, it was the nonblack vote that elected the Illinois senator to the presidency and reelected him in 2012. This can be obviously deduced from the fact that African Americans only make up 12 to 13 percent of the population of that country, thus constituting a minority. The Latino vote was important, but also not decisive for his 2008 victory.

It is thus plausible to affirm that the same white, Anglo-Saxon, Protestant elites, known as WASPs, who control the machines that move political power in that country, particularly the political party machines, assimilated the idea of having as leader a representative of the "race" deemed inferior not too long ago by the scientific racism that was so highly accepted in the Western world since the eighteenth century.

The United States and Brazil are two countries of more or less the same age. They are both located in the same territory, in continental terms. They are both part of the Americas, even if of opposing hemispheres. And, more importantly, they have similar experiences around slavery. But here, the similarities stop.

In Brazil, we never had a civil war or an Abraham Lincoln. We never had the Ku Klux Klan or Jim Crow laws, but slavery here was only abolished in 1888—without causing any political ruptures. Gilberto Freyre and Sergio Buarque de Holanda have described the Brazilian nature as tending towards conciliation and creating equilibriums out of contradictions.

What are the consequences? During the twentieth century, Brazil became the paradise of the hypocritically peaceful "racial" harmony. Different from its northern peer, Brazil to this day rejects the possibility of having African-descendants in elevated positions of power and command. Slavery, which between 1530 and 1851 brought some 4 million Africans to this country, was ended on the 13th of May 1888. Slave culture, however, is still with us.

As a result, resistance and the struggle against racism were a constant among those groups socially discriminated against.

Over the past thirty years, not only blacks, indigenous peoples, and Romanis—the groups that were historically discriminated against since the Portuguese colonial period (1500–1822)—but also other social sectors, such as women and homosexuals, have become the main actors to contribute, since the end of the military dictatorship (1964–1985), to broadening the rights of these social groups, thus making Brazil a democracy with more equality.

One of the fronts of this struggle is within the self-declared academia—that is, the institutionalized space for scientific knowledge production of higher education. Hence, if blacks were denied even the basic recognition of being human until 1888, it is no surprise that they have been excluded from the educational system—with only a few exceptions.

There also is the aggravating fact that the Portuguese colonizers vetoed any intellectual life in its American colonies until 1808, the year when the Portuguese crown moved its seat to Rio de Janeiro. It was only then that the press was made free and the first universities, of law and medicine, were created.

This is why the organization of the Brazilian university system started late, in the 1920s, in comparison to the United States or even Spanish Latin America. When it was finally created, it was set up as an exclusive space reserved to those who successfully claimed to be white. The majority were the sons of large landowners, industrialists, traders, and those active in the liberal professions—that is, the different socioeconomic facets of the bourgeoisie.

Overall, then, white elite Brazilians, different from those in the United States, have not accepted black and indigenous peoples among themselves, particularly not as peers and equals in the spheres of political power. This is so despite the much proclaimed "cordiality" towards others, and the fact that nonwhite Brazilians constitute a numerical majority in this country. Brazil, then, contrary to the widely propagandized image, is anything but a racial paradise, and white Brazilians are much more implicated in racist practices than they themselves like to admit. The question I seek to address in this essay thus is how structural and institutional racism affects black social activism.

•   •   •

To illustrate my reasoning, and without posing as a victim, I will examine my own experience as a person who has sought to combine political activism and academic life since the 1990s.

The academic space, understood as a reflection of broader society, also is a disputed terrain. Not only of egos, but also of ideas. Actually less of ideas than of egos, as we, the seasoned, well know. These disputes always have as their justification the advancement of science and knowledge. In the majority of cases, however, we fight over positions of power—whatever particular form of power that might be.

Due to being African-descendant, forged in the struggle for the right to housing for slum dwellers, and given that I was born and raised in a Brazilian slum (*favela*), the struggle against discrimination was always very present in my everyday activities. Coming from an extremely poor family and born to a single mother who took care of seven children after her husband had died, I already understood in my adolescence that education and political activism, but not political party activism, were the essential weapons to overcome misery.

So, always attending public schools and universities [i.e., free of charge, but with very competitive entrance requirements; translator's note], I graduated in journalism (1986), did a master's and a PhD in communication, and, since 2002, through a public competition [*concurso público*], I became a professor of the Federal University of Bahia (UFBA). It is where I still am, confronting what some consider structural racism.

Already during my graduate studies (1991–2000), which I did at the most important and recognized research university of Latin America, the University of São Paulo (USP), I confronted, together with some of my student colleagues, the power of an institution that stands out for its unwavering elitism and its vested conservatism.

After refounding the Black Consciousness Nucleus at USP (NCN) in 1992, we decided to open and enlarge the debate about the necessity for academia to create instruments that allow the access of poor black students. Our understanding was that if the Brazilian university was public, then it should reflect in all its human resources—professors, researchers, students, and staff—the same diversity of the broader Brazilian public, which ultimately finances its budget through taxes.

The public university, which in Brazil is the one offering the best quality education, could not and cannot be the almost exclusive domain of the mostly white bourgeoisie, as this segment is not the only one that maintains the institution. In 1993 NCN created a program of debates and a prep course for the USP access exams, which attracted the attention of a significant part of the community. It also attracted the eyes of the media and of the university administration, which reacted immediately, demanding through administrative and judicial channels that USP be disassociated from NCN.

Within the Brazilian NCN emerged, towards the end of 1993, the first debates and systematic studies about the implementation of compensatory affirmative action policies. From USP also emerged the seed of the Movement of Reparations for Afrodescendants (MPR), which reached national prominence on the 20th of November of that year, appearing on the front pages of the most important Brazilian newspapers, with its claim that the Brazilian society owes its black population. The claim was that the social debt should be paid by the state to every Afro-descendant. The amount was calculated at US $102,000 for each black individual.

During all of 1994, the MPR and the NCN organized a broad agenda of national mobilizations to disseminate the idea of reparations—evidently provoking a variety of public polemics and reactions. At the end of that year, we filed a federal lawsuit, demanding that the Brazilian state assume this debt, resulting from slavery and its consequences.

In 1996, we created the Pro-Quota Committee at USP, the first group of activists to demand the establishment of a quota system to secure a percentage of places for poor and black students in this aristocratic enclave. This group acted by organizing, among other things, monthly public demonstrations. It also opened the debate about this topic, inviting representatives of power and influence to participate. It elaborated a whole series of arguments, a great part of which were published in Brazilian journals and weeklies.

And, of equal importance, through its actions, it sought to persuade important leaders of the reluctant Brazilian Black Power Movement, who resisted the proposal, that the struggle for quotas and for reparations represented a new level in the debate about racism in Brazil.

What was the reaction of USP, as an institution, to these demands? On Easter Sunday of 1996, during an activity to divulge the struggle for quotas, which I carried out with another activist, I was arrested on the main university campus and taken to the police station, where I was threatened and detained for almost twelve hours for questioning.

The USP administration [*reitoria*] opened a criminal case against me, threatened to withdraw my matriculation as a doctoral student, and opened an internal investigation, demanding that I publicly recognize that I had committed an administrative crime.

To be sure, none of these processes went ahead, as other important sectors of society, inside and outside of the university, came out to defend me, demonstrating how ridiculous these accusations actually were. That way I could eventually finish my studies of communication sciences with a PhD.

Thus properly accredited, I looked for work in my native state, Bahia, which contains the largest black population in Brazil, in the same university where I graduated in journalism, the Federal University of Bahia (UFBA). This was an institution plainly following the pattern of all important Brazilian universities, dominated by the same socio-ideological white and bourgeois segment of society—i.e., conservative in the worst sense of the word.

Once hired, between 2001 and 2006, the academic department for which I worked knew how to take advantage of the accumulation of my academic production, my publications, and my activism, all of which I had placed at the service of the institution. Without aligning myself with any of the controlling castes, I reacted to them as much as I could. Starting in mid-year of 2006, after publishing an article that criticized the very common practice of using public goods for private ends, I lost institutional favor.

With this event, the hegemonic power structures of the academic hierarchy came to cut me off from even the remotest possibility of institutional growth. While I was elected to the post of department chair twice between 2002 and 2006, and I was called to participate in a series of committees, after 2006 none of these commitments could be recorded in my CV.

Worse, as a consequence of this article, following the pattern of USP, even without a concrete case, the leadership of the college opened an administrative case against me in July of 2007, demanding that I recant my opinions. When taken to an autonomous judicial court of the federal administration, I was not only considered unduly targeted by the university power holders. The whole process against me was reprehended, for inflicting "incurable damage" [*eivado de vícios insanáveis*]. An accusation of neglect to grant me the right of defense was made and deemed inconceivable, as according to the Federal Prosecution, the administrative leadership is not allowed to use the power of its institution to prosecute an employee because of his opinions and declarations. The university was informed that if the institution felt offended by my article, Brazilian law offered other ways of redress.

Despite this assessment from the federal judicial system, my department and university made several attempts to put me in academic limbo—among those to be taken out of academic courses, of the department's lab journal, and of other responsibilities and functions that I had previously performed. Of course this systematic institutional persecution cannot prevent me from keeping on producing, publishing, receiving research scholarships and different awards, as this happens outside of its realm, through external contracts. These are the articulations that have allowed me the kind of professional progress that every professor desires in his or her academic career.

In the following, I will provide some more illustrations that highlight the difficulties of seeking to bridge anti-racist social activism and academia under these conditions.

• • •

After returning from my first twelve-month postdoc, which I spent at the Free University of Berlin, Germany, I decided to apply for a project at the CNPq[1]—the most important institution supporting scientific research of my country.

Under the title *Media, Diversity, and Affirmative Action Policies in Brazil after the 1988 Constitution*, I proposed to verify if the Brazilian labor market had absorbed the graduates in the field of communication of those universities that had adopted, since 2012, quota systems. It was a never-before-conducted research project.

The Communication committee of the CNPq, composed of "peers,"[2] denied their support. In theory, negative replies to such requests is normal. In recent years, the average number of support hovered around 30 percent of all the proposals sent to this agency. Here is what the president of this organization has to say about this policy:

> It is a great competition and at the same time, it is difficult to evaluate each project profoundly. The committees end up applying a "science metrics." They calculate the number of publications on their computers, multiply those with the impact factor, relate those with the position of the author, and they give points for the number of students that he has already advised. With this formula, it gets a bit easier. To those . . . that did not receive funding, you reply that they received less points. With this, we achieve a certain objectivity, but it is not the best formula to achieve quality, because innovation and daring proposals are not given much emphasis.[3]

The problem for those that did not receive funding lies in finding out where they fell short. The problem for those who have the job of evaluating who gets the support is to decide whom to fund, given the scarcity of resources.

To better understand the context under which these decisions are made, some background seems necessary. Even if Brazil grew overall during the last decade, public and private investment in research and development grew more slowly.

According to official data from the Brazilian Ministry of Science and Technology, this ministry had a budget increase from 1.5 billion to 7.2 billion Reais between 2001 and 2010 ($63 million to $3 billion). However, this increase lagged behind the overall GDP growth of the country—even if Brazil's economic growth during those ten years experienced ups and downs (from 5.2 percent in 2008 it fell to –0.6 percent in 2009 and reached 7.5 percent in 2010). The average economic growth during these ten years was 3.6 percent (IBGE 2012). The expenditures in research and development during that same time remained timid. They went from 1.02 percent of the GDP in 2001 to 1.13 percent of the GDP in 2010, with the majority of funds coming from the public sector (Ministry of Science and Technology). In 2011, Brazil was the sixth biggest economy of the world.

Hence, with the exception of 2009, the growth rate of the Brazilian economy was robust. It almost doubled between 2000 and 2010. The same is, however, not true for the investment in research and development: it was 1.02 percent of the GDP in 2000 and reached 1.13 percent of the GDP in 2008, where it stagnated until 2011. The Action Plan for Science, Technology, and Innovation for National Development, launched in 2011 by president Dilma Rousseff, targets elevating the support to this area to 1.9 percent of the GDP. This is still meager when compared to 2006 data for other countries.

These preliminary data and information are necessary in order to situate the exact place of my proposed research, which is multidisciplinary, while at the same time solidly anchored in the analysis of the reproduction of institutional racism in Brazil, within the context of the research and development policies adopted in this country. In Brazil, the investment guidelines follow the global model, which gives priority to those areas called "hard sciences," i.e., the exact sciences, such as the different engineering sciences that are connected to a developmental model and ideologically allied to markets, commerce, goods, and services. Biology also falls under this model. In this market juncture, the social sciences, as well as the humanities and the arts, are left out in the cold, as they are not directly connected to the market logic that is being implemented in Brazil like an anathema.

It so happens that the enormous historical social inequalities that so shamefully expose Brazil to the world, considering that the country is economically rich while at the same time socially pornographic, would demand, particularly in this sui generis phase of political democracy that followed the military dictatorship of 1964, that special attention be paid to those scientific endeavors that promise to address these inequalities. This is even more urgent as we are confronting a situation where the society is still confronting symbolic racism, particularly in the area of mentalities, which hold us prey to an archaic past of slavery and of Eurocentric colonization.

The proposed research project, which was sent to the CNPq, was not the first I have sent to this institution during my academic career. It had all the ingredients to contribute to a better understanding of the current moment of Brazilian social, racial, as well as economic relations. It was strange indeed to read the arguments that led the committee to deny support this time around.

> The project has several relevant points. For example the familiarity with the theme of study, which the proponent not only knows well, but has lived and experienced. The authors referenced are all relevant and appropriately cited in the footnotes. Finally, the intention to bring the achieved results and data back to the involved groups strikes me as pertinent. However, I find the methodology of the different steps that guide the realization of this research project very incipient. The Chronogram (item 4) comes before the methodology (item 5) and the whole text is more taking position with regard to the study than a detailed description about how it will be conducted. Finally, I think that the curriculum of the candidate is not very significant to be a CNPq fellow. He confuses, for example, articles published in academic journals with news articles and he does not participate in events of this field. The topic seems to be treated, in terms of the bibliography, by the activist more so than by the researcher.

What most calls my attention in the argument denying support is the last phrase of the statement. Here, the project is condemned, even though it was at first deemed to have "several relevant points," due to the fact that the author is supposedly approaching the topic "as an activist more so [than] researcher." This is a false argument, for if it were true, the very Western founders of the social sciences, such as Durkheim, Weber, and Marx, would not be considered researchers.

The lack of government investment in the kind of research that responds to the necessity to

Investment in Science and Technology in Proportion to GDP/2006

COUNTRY	% GDP	% PRIVATE SECTOR	% GOVERNMENT
United States	2.68	63.7	31.0
United Kingdom	1.88	43.8	31.4
Sweden	3.95	65.0	23.5
Spain	1.07	48.0	41.0
Russia	1.15	31.4	60.6
Republic of China (Taiwan)	2.56	64.4	33.9
OECD*	2.26	61.9	30.2
South Korea	2.85	75.0	23.1
Japan	3.13	74.8	18.1
Italy	1.11	43.0	50.8
Germany	2.49	67.1	30.4
France	2.16	50.8	39.0
EU-25[†]	1.81	53.7	35.0
China	1.23	65.7	26.6
Canada	1.99	47.1	34.1

* OECD refers to the countries that are members of the Organisation for Economic Co-operation and Development.
† EU-25 refers to the countries that are members of the European Union as of 2006.

address and overcome historical inequalities that can be traced all the way back to colonial slavery of black and indigenous peoples is clearly evidenced by the eventual creation, in 2001, of the ABPN—the Brazilian Association of Black Researchers. As of December 2012, the ABPN had 1,852 registered researchers in all of Brazil. Forty-seven percent of those are concentrated in São Paulo, Rio de Janeiro, and Bahia.[4] In 2012, Brazil had a total of 2,416 institutions of higher education, 2,112 of which were private (INEP 2012). In 2009, the academic market employed 307,000 instructors, but at the time of the writing of this text, no specific data existed about the situation of black or African-descendant professors and researchers (INEP 2012). It is also worth noting that of all the ABPN-affiliated researchers, 43 percent worked in public institutions (ABPN, 2012).

It is important to remember that blacks and Native people were treated by the Brazilian university, since its institutionalization, as objects of research and as informants. For them, to be subjects of their own research projects is still a new phenomenon and only started to occur after the 100th birthday of the abolition of slavery.

Until March of 2013, the National Council of Technological and Scientific Development (Conselho Nacional de Desenvolvimento Científico e Tecnológico—CNPq) and the other government agencies dedicated to supporting research did not provide any information that would allow for a revealing of the ethnic-racial profile of those researchers receiving fellowships. This information would be relevant and complement the information about the rejection of my own research project by this institution.[5]

However, data the CNPq does provide allow for the drawing of some conclusions. During the five years of 2007 to 2011, the number of stipends actually given by this, the most important national institution to support research, never reached half of the number of applications. In 2007: 3,851 stipends were given versus 8,876 applications; in 2008: 3,237 versus 8,496; in 2009: 6,028 versus 11,976; in 2010: 4,553 versus 9,324; in 2011: 3,220 versus 9,110 applications.

We can only suspect that few resources are dedicated to those Afro-descendant researchers who have managed to enter the Brazilian university system after being selected through color-blind competitive national searches, thus based on their academic merit alone, and who dedicate themselves to researching racism. If we consider how many research projects on this topic are actually supported, the suspicion grows even larger.

If the concentration of resources dedicated to research into predetermined "hot areas" that are composed of the hard sciences must be criticized, the Eurocentric market vision of the political priorities of such research agencies as the CNPq should also be rejected. The same critique can most likely also be applied to twenty-three foundations that currently operate in the different states of the union.

The choices of the CNPq are a reflection of what happens within the structure of the Brazilian academic institutions today. The arguments of those denying support to projects like the one discussed above—undermining, under the protection of anonymity, any efforts that propose changes of the power structures and institutions of the country with reference to a lack of scientific merit and a contamination by social activism—are always the same, everywhere.

Both my particular case, as well as the more general design of funding priorities that favors technology over social justice and does not support those scientific endeavors that have an applied component, i.e., that clearly aim at targeting racism and thus achieving a more just society—both examples clearly testify to the shortcomings of Brazilian democracy. The country moves forward in the direction of democracy. To accept the alliance between the production of knowledge and the application of this knowledge for the construction of a society that accepts diversity as a guiding principle of democracy—this still remains an elusive challenge.

•   •   •

I finish by highlighting that the struggle I have been conducting since 2006 with the administrative structure of the Federal University of Bahia is neither exclusive nor particular. There are other individuals who throughout history have been suffocated and their performance maimed by the mediocrity that does not dare to out itself for what it actually is.

This also is a struggle whose end is in sight. On November 2012 I filed a federal lawsuit for moral damages against the Provost's office of UFBA and the three leaders that targeted me in 2007 with the administrative claim that kicked off the moral damage that is still affecting me today. The justice system has accepted my lawsuit and is treating them as perpetrators. If convicted, they will have to pay a fine in the amount of $300,000.

NOTES

1. The CNPq is the National Council for the Development of Science and Technology. In 2011, its current budget was R$ 1.8 billion (US$ 1.1 billion). It is the main research support agency of the Brazilian Ministry of Science and Technology.

2. Among the members of the committee during this time was a colleague from my own department, i.e.,

the Department of Communication (FACOM) of the Federal University of Bahia (UFBA). It is important to highlight that this same colleague put together, within less than a year of the occurrence, an internal department committee with the task to file an administrative complaint against me. The aim of the committee was to force me out of public service due to critiques I had made against the institution to the local media.

3. Glaucius Oliva, interview given to the newspaper *Estado de S. Paulo*, on January 23, 2011.

4. Cf. *Relatório de Perfil 2012/ABPN* at http://www.abpn.org.br/pesquisadeperfil/relatorio-de-perfil-2012.html.

5. This will change, as thanks to the struggle of organized black power, Law 12.288, known as the Statute of Racial Equality, was established in Brazil on July 20, 2010. This law will force state institutions to provide information on ethnic backgrounds.

REFERENCES

Brazilian Association of Black Researchers (ABPN). (2012). Associated profile report. Http://www.abpn.org.br.

IBGE (2012). Brasil em números/Brazil in figures. Vol. 20.

Instituto Nacional de Estudos e Pesquisas (INEP). (2012). Census of superior education. Http://portal.inep.gov.br/web/censo-da-educacao-superior/censo-da-educacao-superior.

Ministry of Science and Technology. National indicators for science, technology and innovation. Http://www.mct.gov.br/index.php/content/view/2068.html.

The Challenge of Doing Applied/Activist Anti-Racist Anthropology in Revolutionary Cuba

Gayle L. McGarrity

The present contribution to this critically important volume on activist anthropology traces my personal, academic, and professional development as an applied/activist anthropologist, as well as an advocate for social change—with a particular emphasis on furthering the transformation, and eventual elimination, of racist attitudes in the Hispanic Caribbean and Central and South America. I have focused here on my ethnographic research on, and analysis of, race relations in contemporary Cuba.

The often formidable challenge of charting one's own course, with only intermittent periods of participation within the walls of formal academia, is explored in this chapter. The frustrations of realizing—upon completion of my doctoral degree in anthropology from Berkeley, and having conducted tentative, preliminary forays into the sectors of the international job market that were of particular interest to me—that despite the encouraging claims of officials of organizations like the World Health Organization, UNICEF, and the Food and Agriculture Organization to be emphasizing the inclusion of anthropologists at every level of their organizations, positions for persons with my training and vision were actually severely limited.

Yet, in the two decades that have passed since that time, I have managed to put both my formal education, as well as my considerable body of experience—visiting and working in Central, North, and South America, as well as in the Caribbean region —to work, achieving tangible benefits for communities most at risk of sinking into dismal poverty, economic marginalization, and an acceptance of their societally ascribed lower status in their respective countries, because of their African and their indigenous ancestry. I have explored some examples of this in the body of the chapter, and so will focus here on the methodology I have used to achieve my goals.

I initiated systematic and pioneering ethnographic research upon my graduation from Stanford with a BA in anthropology. I have explored the cultural, social, political, and economic aspects of race relations in contemporary Cuba. I did have a genuine desire to learn about the Cuban approach to international public health when I opted to pursue a master's degree there from 1981 to 1982. As I had established close relations with Cuban medical staff in various countries—most importantly in

Nicaragua, where I would be doing my research on childhood malnutrition—I knew that the newly established Ministry of Health was modeled on the Cuban one. Therefore it seemed important to understand the Cuban system well, so as to facilitate my participation in the recently established Nicaraguan one.

I also saw the opportunity to actually live embedded in Cuban society—admittedly benefiting from the many advantages accorded all foreigners—as being useful for the theoretical development of the understanding of the delicate relations between ideology, class, and race in a "revolutionary" context. The study and practice of social anthropology was still prohibited in Cuba in 1981, so I depended mostly on participant-observation methodology and case studies, combined with the collection of qualitative data through informal, unstructured interviews in order to collect data that would illuminate the theoretical interest expressed above. My aim was to both experience and to understand as much as possible about the Cuban interpretation and implementation of what the ruling elites there claimed to be socialist ideology, and to examine how the latter impacted upon racist practices, traditions, and beliefs that were the norm throughout Hispanic Caribbean countries.

I came to the United States to pursue an undergraduate degree at Stanford University in 1970. I was seventeen and had just completed my secondary education at an international boarding school in Sussex, England. Although I had visited the United States on many occasions, I had never before lived there. When it came time to choose which universities I would apply to during my final year of high school, I disappointed my family by focusing on U.S., as opposed to European, universities. My decision was motivated by an intense desire to join in the wave of student activism that was sweeping U.S. society at the time. I particularly focused on Stanford, as I was drawn to the multicultural, liberal social environment of the San Francisco Bay Area. Along with students from Ghana, Argentina, Saudi Arabia, Nigeria, and Trinidad, I had been active at my boarding school in protesting against South African apartheid, and also organizing study groups on such topics as Pan-Africanism, Marxism-Leninism, and the fledgling international Black Power movement. While at school in Sussex, I had traveled extensively in both Western Europe and West Africa. I was eager to join in the Black Power movement in the United States as a university student.

However, upon entering the freshman class at Stanford, I encountered a series of circumstances that presented me with serious challenges. Although the university had many non-U.S. graduate students, foreigners were almost completely absent at the undergraduate level. Opting to live in one of the Afrocentric "black dorms" on campus, I found that my background of living in both the Caribbean and Europe made me quite different culturally from the black American students with whom I identified politically, but from whom, I soon discovered, I differed in many significant respects. Most of the latter were living away from home for the first time, for example, whereas I had rented apartments, both on my own and together with other students in London, from as early as age fifteen. It appeared that all of the black undergraduates were from the United States, the majority being scholarship students from California. In contrast, I had grown up on the beautiful, though often conflicted and beleaguered island of Jamaica, which had only gained independence from the United Kingdom and entered the Commonwealth a couple of years before I left the island to attend Charters Towers School in Sussex. I had traveled widely from infancy with both my Jamaican grandmother, a native of the eastern parish of Portland, and my Apache Indian grandfather, who had distinguished himself by being one of the most successful nonwhite businessmen in the United States from as early as the 1940s.

So I was quite pleased when I was soon visited at the Junipero Dorm on the Stanford campus by members of a group who referred to themselves as the Third World Liberation Front. They were a small nucleus of, it was quickly apparent, very brilliant graduate students, who expressed to me the very evening that we met a commitment to radical social change, both in the United States and internationally. Whereas the undergraduates that I had met to date were preoccupied with the issue of race, these young men stressed the salience of class. They hailed from Madagascar, Jamaica, Guyana, and DRC/Belgium and were eager to provide me with the assistance that they sensed I would require to successfully transition from life in the 1960s UK into the radically different social and cultural environment of Stanford University at the beginning of the 1970s. I felt very comfortable in the company of these Third World graduate students, having just spent four years in a high school with students from more than sixty countries—many of them daughters of leaders of anticolonial movements.

It was not long before I found myself drawn to attend several of the classes taught by the recently appointed chair of the Black Studies Department, Prof. St. Clair Drake. A pioneering applied anthropologist who was deeply committed both to African development and to improving the plight of those of African descent in the Americas, his presentations in his very popular classes were riveting. After a couple of months under the tutelage of St. Clair, as well as interacting with members of the Third World Liberation Front, I no longer felt as culturally misplaced, as had been the case upon my arrival at what was affectionately referred to as "The Farm." Like me, St. Clair was both multicultural and multinational. He had spent many years in the newly independent West African nation of Ghana, fulfilling a promise to President Kwame Nkrumah that he would establish and develop the School of Social Studies at Legon University, located just outside of the capital, Accra. The child of a Barbadian father and a black American mother, St. Clair knew what it was like to straddle more than one cultural milieu. He taught me to value my own unique background instead of being embarrassed by it, as I had been during those first few months of struggling to be accepted—despite my marked British accent—by the black American community on campus.

By my sophomore year, I had decided to major in one of St. Clair's disciplines (he was also a brilliant sociologist)—the fascinating field, at least from my point of view, of anthropology. I was privileged to have long conversations with the brilliant scholar and activist that was St. Clair Drake, and he soon became my mentor. I reveled in his never-ending supply of anecdotes, finding them both fascinating and inspiring, as he elaborated on his experiences as both a radical social activist and an anthropologist. He never tired of endeavoring to make his academic skills relevant to his people's struggles for liberation, as well as to further the struggle to end the pernicious racism, prejudice, and discrimination that both limited the horizons and mutilated the souls of victims (Harrison & Harrison 1999). In one of his classes, which focused on the diversity of Caribbean cultures and race relations, I became curious about the experiences of blacks in the Hispanic Caribbean. Growing up in Jamaica, I had always felt close to the Spanish-speaking world. Many of my family friends were from Latin America; a significant number of students attending private Jamaican schools were of Venezuelan and Colombian origin, and the addictive African-based Latin rhythms were very popular during my childhood with Jamaicans of all social strata.

The Cuban Encounter

Upon graduation from Stanford in 1974, I returned home to Jamaica, where I quickly began integrating myself—as a true disciple of St. Clair's—into various projects inspired by the social democratic politics of then prime minister Michael Manley. I managed to secure work as an applied/activist anthropologist on projects ranging from developing a literacy program for a workers-controlled sugar cooperative in the western parish of Westmoreland, to evaluating World Bank-funded housing projects for the homeless in the capital, Kingston, as well as the programs of the Legal Kingston Aid Clinic; I also directed the African-Caribbean component of the Institute of Jamaica. I was also very drawn to the process of intense social transformation and the renaissance of African Jamaican culture that characterized 1970s Jamaican society (McGarrity 2000). I worked closely with the burgeoning reggae music industry and found myself just as inspired by spending long hours watching Bob Marley and the Wailers rehearse until the wee hours of the morning, as I had been by St. Clair's lectures at Stanford.

In 1975, I was invited to join a group of University of the West Indies academics on a trip to explore the legal and judicial systems of "socialist" Cuba. I leaped at the opportunity to see what life in Cuba was really like, particularly for blacks, who I thought, up to that time—as both embassy and other Cuban government officials insisted—constituted only a minority of the total population. The study trip was a real eye-opener for me, and was to be the first of many trips to the island. Several black American revolutionaries, including members of the Black Panther Party—who were exiled in Cuba—sought me out upon hearing of my interest in race relations in what they always considered as their temporary home. They gave me an insight into the true nature of the so-called "revolutionary" process that few foreigners have been able to obtain. They explained to me how they had known from the outset, having lived on the margins of Cuban society for over a decade as they awaited being granted safe passage to any African country, that our group of West Indian scholars would never obtain permission to enter any prisons or jails, despite being assured that we would be able to, when being briefed at the Cuban Embassy in Kingston just prior to our departure. They hinted at the existence of a sinister side of the "Revolution." When I was later, as a graduate student at a Cuban institute of Public Health, without explanation, denied permission to conduct fieldwork on infant and child health and nutrition in the Sierra Maestra—the cradle of the "Revolution"—I became even more determined to learn about the Cuba that existed beyond the carefully guided official tours for foreign visitors.

Life as a Graduate Student on the Island

I returned to the United States in 1976, and soon afterwards entered the doctoral program in anthropology at UC Berkeley. While visiting Cuba for the third time—on this occasion in the company of a group of Native American health workers—we were all given the opportunity to gain an MPH (master's degree in public health) at the Instituto de Desarollo de la Salud (Institute for Health Development) in Arroyo Naranjo, near Parque Lenin, on the outskirts of Havana. Although many in the group were sorely tempted to accept the invitation, I was the only one reckless enough to seize this opportunity to actually live in Cuba. By this time, I had realized that nonwhites, as opposed to being a minority, instead constituted a clear majority on the island, and as a *mulata* or *india* —i.e., mixed African European woman—I was usually identified as a local. I began studies at the Instituto in the fall of 1981, and upon graduation, became the first North American citizen to obtain a graduate degree from a tertiary-level institution in "socialist" Cuba.

As has so often been the case in my life, I was also the first in another important respect. My fellow students at the Instituto were, without exception, all firmly integrated into and products of the Spanish-speaking world—as citizens of Catalonia, Mexico, Panama, Colombia, and, of course, Cuba. Although I understood some Spanish in 1981—thanks to the many years that I had devoted to studying Latin—the first three months as a graduate student were truly challenging. However, as I made a point of not associating more than was absolutely necessary with others in Cuba whose primary language was English, the difficult initiation period soon gave way to my being completely fluent in Spanish. My graduate studies in Cuba were important, not only because of all that I learned about such disciplines as epidemiology, demography, and Marxist-Leninist philosophy. What was to prove equally important to me later as a Latin Americanist scholar was the fact that I learned a great deal about the culture of the Spanish-speaking world of which Cuba, despite being isolated in so many respects during this period, remained and still remains today an integral part.

As a medical anthropologist, I immersed myself in the fascinating materials, courses, and activities that constituted the master's degree in international public health at IDS. I was the only social scientist in a sea of physicians, dentists, and statisticians, and my ethnographic research on Cuban society soon paralleled my official studies. I became close to Dr. Mario Escalona, an esteemed professor at the IDS, a *militante* (trusted member) in the Partido Comunista de Cuba (Cuban Communist Party), and one of Fidel Castro's team of personal doctors. Despite occupying these *oficialista* (related to the Revolutionary apparatus) positions, Mario was critical of many aspects of "socialist" ideology, as he observed it being implemented by Castro's political, social, and economic elite *vanguardia*—members of his inner circle. He confided to me that as a *blanco* (white man) married to a *prieta* (dark-skinned black woman)—who, he emphasized, had always been the love of his life—he had expected to encounter minimal problems living as a married couple within the Cuban "Revolutionary" context. Instead, he had been stunned by the volume of racist insults directed at his wife and him, and the lack of support from his *militante* friends for his decision to "casarse con esa negra"—marry a black woman.

Mario told me, during one of our lengthy conversations, that he had finally concluded that these manifestations of a continued adherence to principles of white superiority (Martinez 2007) could not be dismissed as being simply remnants of a soon to be obsolete socioeconomic order. His considerable analytical skills led him to the firm conviction that deeply entrenched expressions of institutional racism were also being reproduced within the contemporary "Revolutionary" period. I soon came to share Mario's point of view, but struggled for quite some time before fully accepting that all the rhetoric about the "Revolution's" commitment to the destruction of the structural determinants of racism was just that, only rhetoric, easily challenged and dismissed by the glaring realities of inferior treatment meted out to darker-skinned Cuban citizens at every level of society. I saw the racial profiling of young, black males; the easily observable patterns of managers and *jefes* (bosses) being usually *blancos*, while workers were invariably *negros y mulatos/ mestizos* (blacks and those of mixed African European descent); the perpetuation of an antiquated system of education that omitted from the curriculum any mention of the contribution of persons of African descent to the development not only of Cuban society and culture, but also of world civilization; and the creation within the "Revolution" of a repressive state and party apparatus that ensures the continued control of the non-white Cuban majority by a powerful white military, political, economic, and social elite.

The Mini-Sociocultural Laboratory That Was the Instituto de Desarollo de la Salud

My first ethnographic laboratory was naturally, since I was a seasoned anthropologist, the Instituto itself. With the exception of one *mulato* (mixed African European male) and one *prieta* (dark-skinned African female) and myself, all of the students were *blancos*. The comments that the latter made about the neighboring Afro-Cuban community and those who participated in African forms of religion, music, and dance mocked the positions taken by prominent African American supporters of the "Revolution." Given the fact that none of these antiracist activists were fluent in Spanish and that they were all treated as special guests when visiting Cuba, it was unlikely that they would gain any insight, or even catch a glimpse of the living conditions of the nonwhites who were the majority in both the *tugurios* and *solares* (slums) and *barrios marginales* (ghettos/marginal communities), which my Black Panther friends soon introduced me to. As former hijackers, Michael "Maceo" Finney and Jimmy "Ali" Brewton, who were soon to become Revolutionary martyrs, were at pains, when they got to know me, to emphasize what I was, at first, loath to believe—namely, that the reality for people of color in Cuba was little different then, and continues to be little different now, from the plight of working-class African Americans and Afro-Latinos throughout the Western Hemisphere. I often had occasion to wonder about how African American activists, who were unwavering in their uncritical support for the Cuban "Revolution," would react to multiple examples of both insidious racism and deep self-hatred on the part of Afro-Cubans—the self-hatred being a direct result of the racism—that I both observed and experienced while living deeply embedded within the very fabric of Cuban society.

The examples that are engraved in my memory are numerous, but I would like to share only one of them here—an incident that vividly reflects the hierarchical relations that exist in Cuba between the descendants of European immigrants in Cuba, on one hand, and those who arrived on the island as chattel slaves, the majority from West and Central Africa, on the other. As I left the Instituto cafeteria one morning, I heard the *blanca* head of the union that supposedly represented the workers—primarily residents of the surrounding black community. As I passed by, the union representative loudly reprimanded an older black woman, who was clearly both distraught and embarrassed, for making a scene in front of the *medica internacionalista*—roughly translated as the doctor in solidarity with the Cuban Revolution, as she referred to me. I thought to myself: What should be more important to the union representative? Placing emphasis on an adequate and respectful response to the heartfelt grievance of a black female worker, or ensuring that I, as a foreign doctor, was not disturbed by the worker's emotional but justified expression of her concerns? As was clear to me on numerous occasions during the close to a dozen times that I visited Cuba between 1975 and 1979, it is far more important to those who are part of the Cuban "Revolutionary" apparatus of social control to ensure the well-being and comfort of foreigners who bring foreign currency to the island, than it is to satisfy the kinds of pressing workers' problems that lead many to leave the island in desperation—heading for the open sea on virtually anything that will remain afloat.

As a foreigner, who was always careful to carry my U.S. passport whenever I left home, I was usually given the markedly superior treatment accorded foreign visitors and residents. However, because I am *mulata* or *india* in the Hispanic American context that encompasses Cuba, and because I socialized almost exclusively with Cubans, it did not take me long to "buck up" (Jamaican patois for "encounter") the notorious *Ley de la Peligrosidad*—Dangerousness Law. I was the first to write about this discriminatory law that permitted police of all colors to target primarily young black Cuban males and to haul them off to prison, simply on the grounds that they appeared to be "*sospechoso*"—suspicious (McGarrity 1982). Victims of what Bob Marley so aptly designated as "mental slavery," the mostly nonwhite policemen and women racially profile young black men and women, resulting in their constituting more than 80 percent of those in Cuba's penal system. As in so many communities throughout the Americas, walking, driving, or simply existing as a black person in a hostile environment, infused with racism, is sufficient to provoke the wrath of agents of Cuban state repression—the dreaded Seguridad del Estado.

Several of my fellow white students at the Instituto—all of them members of the Partido (a prerequisite for being permitted to study at the university level during the period in which I did the MPH in Cuba)—hastened to advise me, on numerous occasions, to stay out of the sun and to not wear my hair in a very curly style, as I was a *mulata para salir*—a mulata suitable to be seen with in public. The racist connotations of such expressions should be clear to the present audience and do not require much explanation. Suffice it to say that, to me, their disappointing warnings were all too reminiscent of those of my very conservative, upper-class mother, who remained until her death an active member of the right-wing Jamaica Labour Party. Not surprisingly, my relationship with my mother was a very strained one—from as far back in my childhood as I can remember—eventually leading to our being completely estranged for almost a decade prior to her death. Given the fact that I had been an idealistic supporter of the Cuban Revolution from my high school days, I had certainly not expected to hear comments more closely associated with those on the right of the political spectrums that I was familiar with, constantly being expressed by *militantes* (militants) of the Partido Comunista de Cuba (Communist Party of Cuba).

I was subjected to the same kinds of admonitions from my *blanca* female host in Miramar, where I spent my weekends. (During the weekend I, like all other students, was *becada*—a boarder at the Instituto). Also a *militante*, she apparently saw no contradiction between continuously spouting the Revolution's rhetoric about the absence of racism in Revolutionary Cuba—as she claimed was evidenced by the country's military activities in Africa—and her warnings for me not to attend presentations of the internationally acclaimed Conjunto Folklorico Nacional (National Folkloric Group), because "esa gente lleva enfermedades sexuales"—those people carry sexual illnesses (Gutiérrez, personal communication 1981). Of course, I attended them anyway and engaged in several enlightening conversations with then-director Martinez Fure, an eminent musicologist. However, I was quite dismayed at the tiny audience in attendance. The contrast between the amount of people in attendance at events presenting artists committed to both celebrating as well as preserving the rich diversity of Cuban culture, and the huge crowds that flocked to presentations often of markedly inferior artistic quality but more Eurocentric in nature was disconcerting and indicative of the low value attached to Cuban culture in general, and to its more African components in particular.

The decidedly Eurocentric slant of officialdom in Cuba was reinforced for decades by minister of culture Armando Hart. Very European in both appearance and cultural orientation, it was generally accepted that Hart—who, like most who occupied ministerial posts in Cuba, was a member of Castro's inner circle—attached far more importance to the Ballet Nacional de Cuba, directed by Alicia Alonso (another European-Cuban, who was known to have resisted accepting *mulata* and *negra* dancers into her company for years), than he did to Afrocentric expressions of Cuban national culture. The vast majority of Cubans, however, remain strongly influenced by African components of national culture, in everything from food, to gender and sexual relations, to religious beliefs. This was impressed on me on every occasion that I visited one of my favorite night spots in Havana, El Mambi. Never a fan of the cabaret shows at the Tropicana, which was located right next door—with its commodified, oversexualized presentations of *mulata* women, and the offensive portrayal of blackface, long abolished in the U.S. entertainment world—I felt as if I was in Kinshasa or Lagos at the Mambi. Loyal patrons were almost entirely working-class, darker-skinned *negros* and *prietos*, with a sprinkling of *mulatos* and foreigners. When I invited some male, white Cuban colleagues to accompany me there one night, they complained that there were nothing but "negras aquí—ni una mulata, siquiera (only black women present—not even one mulata!)." Obviously feeling very uncomfortable in a social milieu light years away from the one to which they were accustomed in their almost totally white (at that time) Vedado and Miramar neighborhoods, they found an excuse to make a speedy retreat from the very Afro-Cuban atmosphere that they found themselves temporarily immersed in.

For more than thirty years following the triumph of the "Revolution," Comandante en Jefe (Commander-in-Chief and President) Fidel Castro strongly discouraged, and members of the feared "Seguridad del Estado" (the State Security apparatus) even punished young Cubans for listening to U.S. radio stations and for exhibiting symptoms of *divisionismo cultural* (cultural divergence from the "Revolution") by participating in musical forms such as jazz, rhythm and blues, and rock, as well as for sporting North American, particularly Afro, and Rasta dreadlocks hairstyles.

As official statistics according to race were not available during the period that I lived in and frequently visited Cuba—from 1975 to 1997—it was difficult therefore to demonstrate the tangible effects of ideologies emanating from the concept of white superiority on the nonwhite majority of Cubans. Much of the evidence—as can be seen by the approach I have adopted in the present chapter—was anecdotal, based on an analysis of qualitative, as opposed to quantitative data. However, when we students were divided up into field teams—each of which was assigned to a particular Havana *centro de salud* (health center)—the fact that darker-skinned patients had inferior morbidity and mortality patterns compared to lighter-skinned ones was undeniable. As we analyzed epidemiological patterns in communities in which *negros* (blacks) and *prietos* (darker-skinned blacks) constituted the majority, and compared the latter with our experiences in *barrios* (neighborhoods) in which *blancos* (whites) and *mestizos/mulatos claros* (light-complexioned persons of mixed-race background) predominated, it was consistently the case that the health profiles were inferior for those of darker pigmentation. As with marginal communities in other national contexts, the differential morbidity and mortality profiles in Cuba can be blamed only to some extent on historical legacies—like the experience of African slavery. Inferior health status is also linked in the contemporary period to inferior housing, overcrowding, and a plethora of social issues, including domestic violence, lack of meaningful employment opportunities, and alcoholism. The health profiles of working-class and peasant *blancos* are demonstrably not as inferior to those of other whites as are those of *negros* and *mulatos*, across the socioeconomic spectrum.

Interviews conducted with darker-skinned patients revealed that many complained of not being treated as well by medical personnel as their lighter-skinned and white neighbors. The files of darker-skinned residents and interviews with the latter also revealed an increased probability of them suffering from illnesses that are linked by experts on health disparities in other countries (White 2012) to prejudicial and racist treatment on the part of not only medical staff but also members of the larger society. Cuba has one of the highest suicide rates in the Americas (Stusser, personal communication 2010). However, of all citizens, darker-skinned Cuban women are the most prone to attempt to take their own lives. The low self-esteem that continues to characterize most Afro-Cubans in a society in which their sense of inferiority is constantly reinforced also has been connected to higher incidences of high blood pressure and migraines, as well as of various expressions of emotional and mental distress, such as alcoholism, depression, and anxiety. As is eloquently expressed by a young Afro-Cuban woman, interviewed as she sits, perched in a park tree in Havana, the social pyramid that characterizes contemporary Cuban society is as follows: white men at the top, followed by white women; then black men; and then, at the very bottom, black women.

Under a controversial program that places at-risk children (the majority of whom are darker-skinned) in boarding schools in order to mitigate the negative impacts of growing up in impoverished homes—with family members who are ill-equipped to assist with homework, etc.—the educational performance levels of many Afro-Cuban children has improved. However, as several persons whom I maintain contact with on the island assert: What is the point of excelling in school, when even those *negros(as)* and *mulatos(as)* who have taken advantage of opportunities to learn several languages and to obtain postgraduate degrees are systematically excluded from employment in the dollar economies of the mixed-enterprise and tourist sectors, solely on the basis of race? Initially vehemently denying the existence of this form of discrimination, Cuban authorities have more recently justified these exclusionary hiring practices by claiming that Europeans and other foreigners do not like encountering darker-skinned men and women in the hospitality industries, partially foreign-owned businesses, and the like. All whom I have interviewed on this topic have responded that it is not the foreigners—many of whom everyone knows actually visit Cuba repeatedly, specifically in order to socialize with *mulatos(as)* and *negros(as)*—who are racist. Rather, it is the Cuban administrators—members of the privileged class in Cuba—who, being overwhelmingly *blancos* themselves, either seek to place their relatives in sought-after positions in the dollar sectors of the economy, or who are simply acting upon their own racial prejudices when refusing to hire qualified, darker-skinned applicants.

Data collected since 2006 through interviews with Cubans both on the island and throughout the diaspora reveal the manner in which pervasive racial inequality in Cuba is becoming related to increased levels of violence. In the government boarding schools, as well as in penal institutions, darker-skinned individuals are more powerful because of their sheer numbers. There is, therefore, often a tendency for the latter to take advantage of opportunities rarely presented *en la calle* (on the street)—for them to take revenge on *blancos* as well as on *mulatos claros* (mixed- race individuals of lighter pigmentation). The latter are known in Cuba for often being as racist as *blancos* in their attitudes towards and treatment of *negros* and *prietos* (Alarcon 1988, personal communication). The racial tension that permeates these government institutions is considerable and, according to most reports, is increasing as a result of a vicious cycle (McGarrity 1992): darker-skinned Cubans, both male and female, vent their accumulated rage on lighter-skinned individuals, when presented with opportunities to do so in these institutions. Their targets may not even themselves be racist to begin with. However, after being the object of the simmering resentment of *negros y mulatos oscuros* (blacks and dark-skinned mulatos) frustrated by the discrimination to which they are subjected in officially egalitarian "Revolutionary" Cuban society, victimized citizens of lighter complexion in turn develop resentment towards those darker-skinned citizens, some of whom have perpetrated violence against them.

The Relationship between Ethnographic Research on Race Relations in Contemporary Cuban Culture and Society and Applied/Activist, Anti-Racism Anthropology

When I began in 1982 to develop a critique of racist ideology and practices in post- "Revolutionary" Cuba (McGarrity 1982, 1992, 1995), I was still convinced that the latter were the distasteful remnants of a dependent, capitalist social system. I also mistakenly believed that Fidel Castro and his inner circle were well-intentioned, but had not used the correct tools for dismantling the structural foundations of endemic racism in the society, and could be educated on how to do better in this regard. However, as my analysis matured as a result of further research both in Cuba and within the Cuban diaspora, I finally came to terms with the fact that the "Revolution" had actually reproduced certain forms of racism, as well as other forms of social inequality, in addition to introducing new ones (McGarrity 1995). When I complained about this disturbing trend to a socially white but "*sospechoso*" (suspicious—indicating that an individual might be a little too olive-skinned to be included in the privileged *blanco* racial category) Cuban *babalao*-Santeria priest in Miami, he defended the exclusion of nonwhites from employment in the tourist sector by claiming that they lacked a certain "je ne sais quoi"—intangible quality. The "je ne sais quoi" that he was searching for was, quite simply, *blancura* (whiteness), which continues to be a socially valued commodity in contemporary "Revolutionary" Cuba. I was further becoming convinced that the Cuban "revolutionaries" in power were not really so revolutionary after all.

I was recently challenged by a dreadlocked Afro-Panamanian supporter of the Cuban "Revolution" who was a member of the audience during my presentation entitled "Anti-Racist Movements in Contemporary Cuba" at the Conference on Negritude held in San Juan, Puerto Rico, in 2011. He demanded to know why I chose to criticize and attack what he considered to be the most progressive government in Latin American and the Caribbean. I found his numerous interruptions and rather hostile criticisms of my position to be particularly hypocritical because, having been an Afro-Latin antiracist activist since the 1960s, there is no way he can honestly continue to justify his unwavering support for a regime that has finally been forced to come out of the closet—to speak metaphorically—as far as endemic racism is concerned. I have, in the case of African American supporters of the "Revolution," been prone to give them the benefit of the doubt. Perhaps they honestly do not grasp the reality of race relations in contemporary Cuba, as they do not speak Spanish, may not be familiar with the particularly Hispanic variant of anti-black racism, etc. However, my Afro-Panamanian critic has none of these excuses for his ongoing unwavering support of a regime that continues to oppress and to brutalize African-descendants. Perhaps, like many of my activist friends from my days as a graduate student at Berkeley, he has simply adopted the position that the enemy of his enemy is automatically his friend. As a Panamanian leftist, undoubtedly resentful of the U.S. invasion that overthrew General Manuel Noriega and resulted in the destruction of many working-class *barrios* and the death of numerous innocent Panamanians, he will always be loyal to the first nationalist movement to successfully defy U.S. domination, thus becoming an important symbol of regional independence, as well as of anti-U.S. policies.

However, his question about my selection of Cuba for research on race relations is one that I was pleased by and quite prepared to answer. Why should we expect Cuba to be any different than other societies that have experienced the transatlantic slave trade, plantation economies, European and North American colonialism, and neocolonialism? My answer is both clear and unequivocal. When the "socialist" revolution triumphed in Cuba and began its process of consolidation, its leaders declared themselves committed to exalting the culture of the masses, i.e., of the majority of Cubans—who were then, and remain today, workers and peasants—as opposed to emphasizing the culture of the European creole elite, as had been the tradition under previous administrations.

However, although Fidel Castro adopted a rebellious and defiant stance against what he labeled as United States imperialist and neocolonial control over not only his country but also over the rest of the Caribbean/Latin American region, he did not initiate and probably never even envisioned a profound transformation of the status of popular Cuban culture, so that the traditions and customs of the majority, which are largely African in origin, could be gradually elevated to a status equal to that occupied by European-derived cultural practices and beliefs. Those who know or have analyzed him closely (Almeida 2010, personal communication) assert that ex-President Fidel Castro has always had a decidedly Eurocentric view of culture. Hence the kind of statements he has made to the effect that most Cubans had no culture at all prior to the "Revolution." Perhaps he meant to use the noun "*la cultura*" in the sense of formal education, rather than in the anthropological sense as encompassing all expressions of a human group's entire way of life in all of its richness and complexity—that is, a notion of culture that does not involve some cultures being placed higher than others, in a hierarchical fashion.

Cuban culture has always been a potpourri of various European, North American, African, as well as uniquely creolized Caribbean influences. This is evident in musical styles, language, dance, social patterns, religion, language, and food, as well as in many other aspects of Cuban life. The fact that I was repeatedly told by persons who should certainly think about popular culture in a more progressive light by now, from when I was a student on the island in the early 1980s through my last visit to the island in the late 1990s, that African religious forms in Cuba were nothing more than witchcraft and superstition is sufficient evidence of the fact that African culture was, and continues to be, disparaged at both official and popular levels, even though it has historically permeated every stratum of Cuban society. Important scholars had begun to challenge and rewrite colonial versions of African civilization and culture by the time that the "Revolution" took place (Cesaire 2001; Fanon 2008; Nkrumah 2006; Rodney 2011, 2001; Van Sertima 2003, 1985). So, too, had the important Afro-Cuban scholar Walterio Carbonell (1961), the architect of a Cuban policy on Africa that would have had a very different impact on the African Continent, as well as on Cubans of African descent, than the one proposed and eventually partially implemented by Argentine physician and revolutionary commander Ernesto "Che" Guevara. Yet, when blacks of all ages and political tendencies—among them black American exiles on the island—formed study groups to analyze the works of Third World authors and to incorporate these fresh, truly anticolonial and revolutionary ideas into their thinking in the 1970s and 1980s, they were brutally suppressed (McGarrity 2013; Torres 2010, personal communication; Finney 1975, personal communication, 1981; Bryant 1987, personal communication, 1984). This was because Fidel Castro never broke away from his Eurocentric cultural roots to embrace the more popular culture of his mixed-race mother, although he did commit class betrayal of his father, in both political and economic terms. He was so ashamed of his mother, to whom his father was not married at the time of his birth, that he consistently disowned her as he grew up, and did not even attend her funeral.

Since the early 1980s, I have written in both English and Spanish, as well as submitted for publication, both articles and book chapters—mostly on topics related to race and popular culture in Latin America and the Hispanic Caribbean. I continue to give presentations at many different kinds of conferences, held in a myriad of countries, and delivered in French, Spanish, and Portuguese as opposed to exclusively in my first language, English. I do this as a reflection of my commitment to reaching out to and influencing Latin American academics and activists in not only the social sciences, but also in the medical field.

This has not been an easy task. When I first advanced my controversial position—being, at that time, virtually a lone voice in the desert (with the notable exception of my colleague, the Afro-Cuban scholar of the world Dr. Carlos Moore (1988)—to an audience composed mostly of adamant supporters of the Cuban "Revolution," at the Conference Commemorating Thirty Years of the Cuban Revolution, held in Halifax, Nova Scotia, in 1989, the reaction was mixed. Some important intellectuals and politicians, generally considered to be "*oficialista*," actually stood up and applauded my decidedly daring critique of racism in contemporary Cuba. These included Armando Entralgo, director of the Centro de Estudios de Africa y del Medio Oriente (Center for African and Middle Eastern Studies) in Havana, former Cuban ambassador to Ghana in the early years of the "Revolution" and married to a black Angolan wife; and Ricardo Alarcon, president for many years of the Asamblea Nacional de Cuba (Cuban National Assembly). However, white American, leftist supporters of the "Revolution," most notably the director of the influential Center for Cuban Studies in New York, Susan Levinson, actually attacked me in the conference ladies' room, shouting accusations that I was a liar and insisting that she had never encountered any manifestations of racism during the entire period of her relationship with contemporary Cuban society.

On another occasion, this time when representing the University of the West Indies at the Latin American and Caribbean Congress on Social Sciences and Medicine in Caracas, Venezuela, in 1994, I spoke out on what I referred to as "El circulo vicioso: Racismo, violencia y salud en Nuestra América" (The vicious cycle: Racism, violence, and health in Our America) (McGarrity 1995). As is usually the case at the conferences that I attend, the only other person of color was my also mixed-race, female colleague from UWI, Mona campus in Jamaica. Although all of the presenters were informed by the conference chair that they were allotted twenty minutes for their presentation, I was rudely interrupted while in fluent Spanish I was in the course of developing my theoretical argument—one that was so relevant in nature to the central theme of the conference—and instructed to stop my presentation, after only ten minutes.

The chair, an Argentinean academic and prominent Latin Americanist, exploded with a diatribe about me presenting on a problem that only existed in the United States—certainly not in the rest of the Hemisphere. He insisted that my analysis had no relevance to the contemporary Latin American context, despite the fact that, before he had abruptly deprived me of the right to fully advance my argument, I had given several illustrative examples of the impact of institutionalized racism on the self-esteem of nonwhite children—particularly those born out of wedlock to white fathers and their *mulata* and *negra* mistresses—focusing primarily on the Venezuelan and Cuban contexts.

Not one of the delegates present—all of them white and, with the exception of two, all male—came to my defense and objected to the totally disrespectful manner in which a colleague from the English-speaking Caribbean, who was making a statement of solidarity with Spanish-speaking colleagues by presenting in their native language (an unprecedented occurrence at this conference) and thus demonstrating a strong solidarity with the wider Latin American and Hispanic Caribbean scholarly community, was being treated. Furthermore, when we broke for lunch and I sat down at a table in the cafeteria, at which delegates who had just heard my aborted presentation were seated, they all stood up and left. A few minutes later, a female Venezuelan sociologist very surreptitiously approached me in an adjacent hallway and said that she had a colleague, an Afro-Venezuelan woman, who had recently published a book on racism in her country, entitled, revealingly enough, *El Racismo en un País No-Racista* (Montaner, personal communication 1995, 1993). I subsequently met with this brave, pioneering scholar and obtained critical data on the specific nature of race relations within the Venezuelan context.

Apparently blissfully oblivious to my emphasis only a few hours earlier on the manner in which *mulata* and *negra/prieta* women are traditionally viewed solely, and routinely exploited, as sexual objects by *blanco* men—rarely being accepted by the latter socially, neither as wives nor as colleagues—another delegate, a male Costa Rican physician, telephoned me in my hotel room the night following my thwarted presentation, saying that he totally agreed with what I had to say. Before I had a chance to express my appreciation for his words of support, he hastily added that he would like to come up to my room to comfort me! What better proof did I need of exactly the kind of treatment on the part of white men that I had been so severely criticizing, and indeed been sanctioned for daring to describe, only a few hours earlier?

I have learned the hard way that one has to have nerves of steel to discuss the issue of racism in Latin American scholarly and political circles, particularly in my case, as I began doing so when it was a totally taboo subject, in the mid-1970s. Thankfully, it is becoming slightly more acceptable to do so now, given the promising growth of Afro-descendant movements throughout the region; however, there is still a very long way to go. I have neither been silenced nor deterred from my path of applying anthropological methods to the analysis of systematic racial inequality, reinforced by the ideology of white supremacy, within the Hispanic Caribbean and Latin American context.

Although I have never been prone to joining political organizations—sharing Bob Marley's critique of what he labeled "politrix" (which has come to be used as an essentially Rastafarian term for corrupt and tricky politics)—I was recently chosen to be the sole non-Cuban member on the *junta directiva* (directorate) of a civic organization, based in Miami but with a network of members on several continents. The inspiration to establish the organization was derived from a visit made by three prominent Afro-Cuban activists, who finally were able to obtain Cuban visas to leave the island in early 2013. I accepted the position, as I was fully conscious of my ability to help the mostly nonwhite group in their quest to establish links with those of African descent in the United States, as well as throughout the Americas. In the last year, I have provided valuable strategic support, building upon numerous international contacts—some of which I have managed to maintain since my high school days in the UK—to begin educating the many supporters of the Cuban Revolution who continue to be unaware of, or reluctant to believe, the truth about the pernicious and increasingly racist treatment accorded the nonwhite majority population of the island. I contacted a fellow Stanford alumnus—now a very successful African American film producer and director—who is interested in building upon the raw footage provided by young black filmmakers on the island and smuggled out by an important *mulato* dissident, and subsequently made available to me.

My task is often a thankless one. As a seasoned anthropologist, acutely aware of the troubled relationship between the African American and Cuban communities in South Florida, I have nevertheless been dismayed at the level of insensitivity displayed by several Afro-Cuban members of the organization, as regards the racism directed towards their fellow African-descendants resident in the United States. I have often had occasion to ask the worst offenders how they can ever hope to build relationships with not only African Americans but also members of Caribbean communities in this country if their behavior and statements are often indistinguishable from those of white Cubans, who are infamous for their racism. How can they reasonably expect African Americans to take an interest in and join in their struggle to erase racism and construct a more democratic society in their homeland, if they do not at least try, despite considerable cultural and linguistic barriers, to educate themselves on African American history and culture?

Conclusion

I have increasingly come to realize how unique my experience has been—not only as a mixed-race Caribbean/Apache woman educated in Jamaica, the United Kingdom, the United States, and Cuba, but also by being both exposed to, and participating in antiracist movements from the 1960s up until the present. These include, but are by no means limited to, the following:

- My participation in actions designed to force U.S. universities to divest and to sever all ties with the apartheid regime. Focusing on pressuring the United States government, as well as members of the larger international community, to impose sanctions on apartheid South Africa, while a Stanford student in the early 1970s.
- My critical role, while conducting doctoral dissertation research in Nicaragua, in the autonomy process through which indigenous *miskitu*, *sumu*, *rama*, and *garifuna* Nicaraguans, accompanied by sectors of the predominantly African-descendant creole population with whom they share the Atlantic Coast region, continue the struggle to end the marginalization to which they have been subject—due not only to their geographic isolation, but also to their unique history, culture, and particular position within the contemporary Nicaraguan state.

- As a close friend and confidante of Bob Marley (McGarrity 2000), I engaged in many intense and prolonged conversations with this organic intellectual, in the course of which we discussed my experiences on the African Continent, which began at the age of fifteen. We also explored and debated such topics as Pan-Africanism, Rastafarianism, Manley's social-democratic policies in 1970s Jamaica, and the topic so dear to Bob's heart, namely, the critical role of reggae and other forms of popular culture in the liberation of oppressed and exploited people throughout the world. Of particular interest to Bob were the movements for national liberation in Southern Africa. I arranged for a close friend from my London days, Joey Steblecki—a Polish/African "colored"—to visit Jamaica so that he could talk to the Gong (as Bob is affectionately known) about the struggle that was raging during this period of the 1970s to topple Ian Smith's UDI (Unilateral Declaration of Independence) regime in his native Rhodesia. Bob was inspired by his friendship with Joey, who tragically died at a young age of AIDS only a few years after returning to a free Zimbabwe, after opting to marry a local woman and to spend almost a decade in Jamaica. A skilled Southern African entrepreneur, with considerable experience in the music business—in both the European and African contexts—Joey was able to leverage contacts within the liberation movement in the land of his birth to initiate the process that culminated in Bob Marley and the Wailers' historic concert on the eve of Zimbabwe's Independence (McGarrity 2000).

Given this background of international antiracist initiatives and struggle, I have been inspired by my relations with members of the little-known contemporary Black Movement in Cuba (Cuesta Morua, Calvo, Madrazgo, Garro, Antunez, Biscet, Faguas: personal communications), which was brutally repressed by the white-controlled state security apparatus on the island in the 1970s and 1980s. The brilliant Pan-Africanist and Marxist scholar Walter Carbonell's publication of the seminal work on Cuban history and culture (Carbonell 1961) and his participation, along with several Afro-Cubans now resident in the United States (with whom I maintain close contact), along with others committed to improving race relations in Cuba, incurred the wrath of the regime to which he had been loyal since its triumph in 1959. For his convictions, he died a broken man, having endured prolonged periods of imprisonment in the infamous MAPS.[1] I was privileged to meet with Walterio on several occasions, while both living in and visiting Havana. His memory is also a constant source of motivation for my continuing work.

Throughout the years, as mentioned above, I have remained committed to publishing articles in Spanish-language academic journals, as well as in the popular press of Latin American and Caribbean countries, with the aim of contributing to the increasing discourse, and the very limited body of literature in Spanish, on the crucial issues of racism and prejudice. I do so cognizant of the fact that most of the literature, as well as the international discourse on the topic of race, has historically been primarily in English—closely followed by French, particularly as regards the Negritude movement (Césaire 2001). As an applied/activist anthropologist I have, perhaps to a fault, always been more concerned with influencing my Latin American and Hispanic Caribbean colleagues regarding the twin topics of endemic racism and white supremacy—the taboo themes that continue to plague our societies and to thwart the development of our true potential—than with gaining points towards securing academic tenure in the United States. As my commitment from the time of pursuing my undergraduate education has consistently been to applying the methods and principles of several branches of the discipline of anthropology to the resolution of social, cultural, economic, and political problems in the developing world, it was only quite recently that the idea of a secure position within a university setting began to hold some appeal for me.

I take particular delight in observing, as a pioneer in the analysis of race relations in Latin America and specifically in contemporary Cuba, that a growing number of young Cubans are taking increased pride in their *raices* (roots) (Raudell, Cuesta Morua, Calvo, Madrazgo, personal communications; Roland 2011). For decades, mostly—but by no means exclusively—*prieto(a)* darker-skinned black youth, like the most popular hip-hop artist in contemporary Cuba, the Rastafarian Raudel, have been attracted to the international Rastafarian movement. With roots in the ancient northeastern civilization of Ethiopia, as well as in the former British colony of Jamaica, this sect stresses pride in African culture, history, civilization, and aesthetics. It represents a fierce rebuttal of the age-old concept of *blanqueamiento*—whitening—which has held sway throughout Latin America and the Hispanic Caribbean from the time of slavery. Rastafarian ideology appeals especially to African-descendants, as well as to Africans on the Continent (particularly Southern Africans)—many of whom struggle to erase from their consciousness the vestiges of self-loathing and low self-esteem that have kept victims of systematic exploitation and oppression bound in "mental slavery" more than a century following both official emancipation in the New World, and the more recent end of European colonialism and apartheid in Africa. Those whose ancestors were brought to the New World as chattel slaves, and who have been told for centuries that they are descended from ignorant, savage people who inhabit a "dark" continent, find particular solace and inspiration in a religion that stresses the crucial role of Africans not only in the development of Christianity, but also in the development of world civilizations.

The kind of Afrocentric scholarship exemplified by the work of authors like Van Sertima (2003, 1985) and Rodney (2011, 2001)—both natives of Guyana—though not sufficient in itself to liberate the sons and daughters of the enslaved and the colonized, is nevertheless an essential precursor. As Ruben Dario of Nicaragua and Pablo Neruda of Chile—both eminent Latin American poets—have insisted: "Un pueblo que no se conoce, no puede ser libre" (a people who do not know themselves, can never know freedom).

The Cuban educational system, as well as popular Cuban parlance, continues to inculcate in citizens from a tender age—the majority of whom are possessed of varying degrees of African ancestry—the concept of the inferiority of all objects, phenomena, and individuals black. This is both achieved and reinforced by an almost total omission of the role of Africans and African descendants, not only in the development of world civilizations, but more specifically in the development of their own Cuban society. The way that Cubans, both on the island and in the diaspora, seem to always lighten paintings of the brilliant military strategist and political thinker Antonio Maceo, as well as to Europeanize his African features, never ceases to amaze me. Cubans receive clear messages from infancy that Africa and all things African are inferior. Antiracist education (Godreau, personal communication 2011) of the kind advocated by the innovative and creative Puerto Rican applied anthropologist Isar Godreau—which has been introduced into the Puerto Rican school system with encouraging results—should have been introduced into the Cuban system during the early years of the Cuban Revolution, as an effective means of seriously constructing the groundwork for the eradication of manifestations of racist ideologies, manners of speech, and behaviors that have wrought havoc upon Cuban society for centuries. There is evidence to believe that, rather than decreasing as the "Revolution" supposedly matures, the social cancer of racism is instead experiencing a marked rise in twenty-first-century Cuban society. However, antiracist policies such as the ones developed by Godreau and others, throughout the African Diaspora, were not introduced and developed, I would assert, simply because the political will to do so was absent from both the hearts and minds of Eurocentric Cuban *blancos*—who smoothly transitioned into positions of power, replacing the creole elites of pre-revolutionary Cuba as "Revolutionary" rulers of the island in the present era. In this manner, the Cuban tradition of always having whites at the top of, and *negros* and *mulatos* on the lower rungs of, the socioeconomic pyramid is perpetuated.

However, while the Cuban population continues its process of *oscuramiento* (darkening, as opposed to the much yearned for *blanqueamiento*, whitening, idealized by so many) as more and more *blancos* and *mulatos claros* flee their homeland, the *dissidente* (dissident) movement is becoming characterized by an increasing number of *negros(as)* and *mulatos(as)* in leadership positions. The Damas de Blanco (Ladies in White)—an internationally acclaimed pacifist movement for social change, as well as for the protection and liberation of political prisoners—has featured many *negras* and *mulatas* in high positions. Several of the most important figures in the movement to radically reform and refashion Cuban society are also nonwhites. These include such activists as Dr. Oscar Biscet, Guillermo Farinas, Manuel Cuesta Morua, Leonardo Calvo, Juan Antonio Madrazo, Antunez, and the recently unjustly incarcerated heroic prieta activist Sonia Garro—recently imprisoned for her important work caring for, as well as raising the racial and civic consciousness of, Afro-Cuban children. Machismo and sexism continue to be significant features of not only the wider Cuban society, but of the dissident movement as well.

However, the future looks bright, as Cubans are increasingly realizing that in the absence of profound cultural and psychological changes, no amount of purely political transformations will significantly improve the lives of, and empower, the majority. In this regard, the role of members of others in the African Diaspora who know and love Cuba, like myself, is vital. I was fortunate that pride in my own African ancestry was carefully instilled and nurtured from childhood by a very enlightened *mulata* Jamaican grandmother, and was further enhanced by life-changing experiences in the African nations of Ghana, Mali, South Africa, Angola, Zimbabwe, Mozambique, and Madagascar, as well as in Peru, Cuba, Nicaragua, Mexico, Argentina, Colombia, and Puerto Rico on the western side of the Atlantic.

Members of the English- and French-speaking African Diaspora in the New World are uniquely positioned to contribute to the challenge of addressing racism in Hispanic America in the contemporary era. We were more exposed than those in Spanish-speaking America to the philosophies of figures like Marcus Garvey, Malcolm X, Martin Luther King, Kwame Nkrumah (2006), Julius Nyerere, Frantz Fanon (2008), Leopold Senghor, Aimé Césaire (2001), and Nelson Mandela—most of whose writings are more available in English and French than in Spanish and are exceedingly difficult to obtain in countries such as Cuba, in which the proliferation of Afrocentrism, Black Consciousness, and Pan-Africanism threatened the persistence of white dominance in the 1960s and so were, for the most part, banned. I am honored to be part of the multinational and multi-ethnic movement, enhanced by the participation of men and women of varying political positions who are united by their commitment to the construction of a more democratic Cuba, in which whites and nonwhites are treated equally.

NOTES

Dedicated to the memory of Lorenzo Copello, Barbaro Sevillon, and Jorge Martinez, three young black Cuban men executed without the benefit of a fair trial, a week after being charged with attempting to hijack a ferry off the coast of Havana.

1. These were infamous detention centers for homosexuals; young people who were fans of music styles, like jazz and rhythm and blues—deemed to be examples of *diversionismo ideológico* (political incorrectness); and others deemed to be out of step with the "Revolution" by Cuban authorities during several recent periods in "Revolutionary Cuba." Inmates, among them songwriter Silvio Rodrigues, were subjected to an intensive program of *reeducación*, i.e., of "re-education."

REFERENCES

Baber, W. L. (1999). St. Clair Drake: Scholar and activist. In I. Harrison & F. Harrison (Eds.), *African American Pioneers in Anthropology*, 191–211. Champaign: University of Illinois Press.

Bryant, A. (1984). *Hijack*. Raleigh, NC: Freedom Press Public Relations International.

Carbonell, W. (1961). *Como surgio la Cultura Nacional?* Havana: Biblioteca Nacional.

Césaire, A. (2001). *Discourse on colonialism*. New York: Monthly Review Press.

Fanon, F. (2008). *Black skin, White masks*. New York: Grove Press.

Harrison, I. E., & F. V. Harrison (1999). *African-American pioneers in anthropology*. Champaign: University of Illinois Press.

Martinez, I. C. (2007). *The open wound: The scourge of racism in Cuba from colonialism to communism*. Kingston, Jamaica: Arawak Publications.

McGarrity, G. (1982). *Race, revolution and popular culture in contemporary Cuba*. Kingston, Jamaica: ISER-Institute for Social and Economic Research, University of the West Indies, Mona.

McGarrity, G. (1992). Race, culture and social change in contemporary Cuba. In S. Halebsky & J. M. Kirk (Eds.), *Cuba in transition: Crisis and transformation*, 193–205.

McGarrity, G. (1995). El circulo vicioso: Racismo, violencia y salud en Nuestra América. In M. Bronfman & L. Briceno (Eds.), *Proceedings of the International Forum for Social Sciences and Health (IFSSH) annual meetings*, Caracas, Venezuela.

McGarrity, G. (1997). Los determinantes socio-historicos de los diferentes patrones de adaptación de los inmigrantes Cubanos en Jamaica. *Revista de ciencias sociales. Nueva Epoca*, no. 3 (June).

McGarrity, G. (2000). Memories of, and reflections on the Gong: Contribution to Bob Marley—artist of the century. Special anniversary edition. *BEAT* magazine 19 (3).

McGarrity, G., & Cardenas, O. (1995). Cuba. In Minority Rights Group (Eds.), *No longer invisible: Afro-Latin Americans today*, 77–107.

Montaner, L. (1993). *El racismo en un país no racista*. Caracas: n.p.

Moore, C. (1988). *Castro, the blacks, and Africa*. Los Angeles: Center for Afro-American Studies (UCLA).

Nkrumah, K. (2006). *Class struggle in Africa.* Bedford, UK: Panaf Books.

Rodney, W. (2011). *How Europe underdeveloped Africa.* Baltimore, MD: Black Classic Press.

Rodney, W. (2001). *Groundings with my brothers.* Chicago: Front Line Distribution Int'l.

Roland, K. L. (2011). *Cuban color in tourism and* La Lucha: *An ethnography of racial meanings.* Oxford: Oxford University Press.

Van Sertima, I. (2003). *They came before Columbus.* Boston: Random House.

Van Sertima, I. (1985). *African presence in early Asia.* Kingston, RI: Transaction Publishers.

White, A., III. (2012). *Seeing patients: Unconscious bias in healthcare.* Cambridge, MA: Harvard University Press.

Conclusion

Ulrich Oslender and Bernd Reiter

L et's be clear about it. Activist scholarship is not for everyone. As the contributions in this book make clear, there are a great many trials to overcome, difficult situations to navigate in a sea of obstacles placed in one's way as an academic. Institutional structures (university boards, tenure and promotion committees, funding agencies, etc.) typically reward streamlined academic output, thereby discouraging overly activist and time-intensive engagement with research subjects. Activist scholarship also often demands a level of commitment and risk-taking that not everyone is willing, or able, to offer. However, as the accounts assembled here also demonstrate, for many social scientists a basic moral imperative guides their research questions from the outset. Being faced with at times drastic social inequalities in their research settings, the option of activist scholarship becomes more than a simple choice; it is an ethically felt necessity.

Let's also be clear that there are many ways of being an activist scholar. From the organic intellectual who is embedded within a particular social movement, to the efforts of academics who accompany vulnerable communities, at times living among them, at others helping to mobilize from afar, there are innumerable possibilities to bridge activism and scholarship. As Elizabeth Hordge-Freeman (this volume) observes quite accurately in her conclusions, "Activism and research do not always involve elaborately planned protests and institutional transformation. To the contrary, researchers should reframe what activism means for them and their research and work to foster ruptures in the status quo, consciousness-raising, and empowerment that reflect their own capabilities." The writing process in itself can take on an activist shape, for example by providing an outlet for otherwise marginalized voices and imbuing them not only with a space but also status often reserved for the "expert" academic only. Arturo Escobar's (this volume) insistence on the co-production of conceptual language, created *together with* black social-movement leaders of the PCN in Colombia, for example, stresses not merely the epistemological qualities of local knowledge production, but the ontological implications of being-in-the-world.

The chapters in this collection, then, provide a rich kaleidoscope of personal experiences that the individual writers and researchers have gathered in their work with diverse collectivities. In this sense this book wants to be an invitation to others to share their experiences, to collectively enlarge the meaning of "activist scholarship," and to continue to search for ways of making knowledge production meaningful beyond the academy, by speaking truth to power and by supporting marginalized, endangered, or otherwise discriminated-against communities. The authors collectively show how it is possible to successfully negotiate and balance the two roles we choose to play: scholar and activist. As Keisha-Khan Perry has argued, conducting long-term, intensive research in a local community of choice can be a way to belong politically and to be in place emotionally. This is particularly true for those of us conducting ethnographic work, as Perry herself highlights. Anthropologists thus tend to be at the forefront of making sense of their academic work in relation to their role as activists and supporters of local groups. The fact that most contributors to this volume are either anthropologists or borrow anthropological methods of participant observation provides an indicator for this reality. As the general tone of almost all contributions suggests—the "with" is a crucial determinant of a successful marriage between scholarship and social activism. Nothing can be achieved for others without their active involvement.

Seen from this angle, the problem of how to bridge scholarship and activism can only be successfully addressed by those social scientists who have the courage, the means, and the (language) skills to leave the ivory tower and venture into the messy reality of concrete people and their communities. It cannot be done by looking out of the window.

While the predominance of statistical analysis and the search for a harder and more reliable social science is understandable, the social sciences should also look for ways to keep the social in the equation—that is, in their research agendas, ontologies, epistemologies, and methodologies. While survey data is more and more available even for remote areas, nothing substitutes for the direct contact, the interaction, and the learning that researchers undergo when in the field. Respect for local, nonacademic knowledge is but one of the important consequences that often result from extended interactions with local communities. A heightened sense of the limits of academic knowledge, and even a sense of academic humility might also result from such experiences. However, one is not able to detect much of these learnings when attending an American Political Sciences Association annual meeting or another professional association's conference, be it in international studies, sociology, or economics.

For those who have taken the step out of the ivory tower and into local communities, it has become clear that they have to be constantly aware of the different demands and expectations that these two worlds have on them. Whereas local communities are structured by the politics of place, culture, power, violence, and access, universities are structured by specific versions of the same politics. Here, too, insiders struggle over privilege, access, money, and power—but not only are the rules different, so are the power holders and brokers. Anonymous peer reviewers can destroy the careers of young, aspiring, yet still inexperienced and hence idealistic scholars with often devastating reviews, born often out of narrow self-interest or a blind belief in universal standards, which they, the reviewers, think they represent. Job search committees in extremely competitive markets too often fulfill a gatekeeping function whose main guidelines stem from elitist notions of "good" and "bad" universities, where "good" often means private and expensive. Tenure committees, along the same lines, too often pretend to hold up standards for young scholars that do not allow young scholar-activists to conduct meaningful work. Too many times, universities are organized around closed circles of peers, in a club-like fashion, with clear, even if unspoken, historically inherited traditions whose main purpose is to keep certain people and certain research agendas out. The tendency of some American political-science departments to streamline their faculty around rational-choice approaches is but one among many examples. More often than not, social-justice activism is among those characteristics that traditional, conservative faculties seek to keep out or push to the side, into a niche of low-budgeted "ethnic" departments. As a result, most Latin American, Latino, Africana, Asian, and women's studies departments are chronically understaffed and underfunded. For the scholar-activist, awareness of this reality is crucial for their institutional survival, as they have to develop a sort of "double-consciousness" and train their ability to switch codes when addressing different audiences.

As the chapters by those who have successfully navigated this terrain and been able to not only survive but thrive in these two environments demonstrate, the challenges to do a better job never end, as the responsibilities that a serious researcher of a local community faces only seem to grow bigger the better the researcher does his or her job. As the chapter by Rob Benford highlights, successfully negotiating one's roles as activist and scholar can easily lead into a position where the "system" seeks to use and co-opt the activist scholar, expecting him to appease potentially unruly elements. As Ulrich Oslender has highlighted in his contribution, the responsibilities of a responsible activist researcher to local communities are oftentimes difficult to bear and hard to negotiate. However, here as elsewhere, there is no way around transparency and honesty, which must be rooted in a critical self-awareness of the positionality and situatedness of oneself. This not only involves knowing oneself; it also demands knowing how one is perceived by different groups. To know and recognize one's limit is as important as to step up and follow through, as the contributions by Hordge-Freeman, Smith, and Perry clearly show. Much harm can come from overestimating what one can achieve when immersed in local lifeworlds and politics. This does not mean that one is utterly powerless, only because one is in a privileged position. It rather seems that by recognizing the limits of an activist agency, an engaged scholar can direct her efforts towards those things that she can actually do better than the local activists—and offer her contribution as a way to support local efforts. Achieving visibility and a voice is one of the main hurdles that local communities face—particularly poor black communities, and women within these communities. It is precisely here that committed scholars can contribute, as they have more access to different forms of media and outreach. The Zapatistas in southern Mexico provide maybe the best-known example for the potential of this marriage between local communities and international scholars with access to different media outlets. Whenever such a fruitful, and respectful, interchange occurs, it has the potential for mutual learning—the kind of learning where both sides, local communities and scholars, grow. While scholars can offer voice and access to formal structures of power and influence to local activists, local activists can help connect scholars to the stuff that social scientists need as a substratum of their work: the informal world of local community life.

About the Authors

Rob Benford is a scholar/activist who currently serves as a Professor of sociology at the University of South Florida in Tampa. His published works have appeared in a variety of sociological and multidisciplinary journals, books, and encyclopedias. Rob devotes the bulk of his research efforts to identifying, analyzing, and understanding social-movement dynamics. He has been active in the peace, environmental, anti-apartheid, anti–death penalty, gun control, and college-sports reform movements. He previously served as editor of the Journal of Contemporary Ethnography and as the series editor of Twayne Publishers' Social Movements Past and Present Series. He also served as president of the Midwest Sociological Society, and chair of the Peace, War & Social Conflict and the Collective Behavior/Social Movements sections of the American Sociological Association.

Fernando Conceição is a Professor at the Federal University of Bahia, Brazil. He was a postdoctoral fellow at the Freie Universität Berlin's Lateinamerika-Institut and earned both his PhD and MSc. in Science Communication from the University of São Paulo. His work focuses on culture, society, and communication, with an emphasis on policy, antiracism, and ethnicity. He is a founding member of UFBA's Multidisciplinary Graduate Program in Culture and Society. His publications include *Midia e etnicidades no Brasil e nos Estados Unidos* and *Educação comunicação globalitarismo*, among others.

Arturo Escobar is Professor of anthropology at the University of North Carolina, Chapel Hill. His main interests are political ecology, design, and the anthropology of development, social movements, and science and technology. Over the past twenty years, he has worked closely with several Afro-Colombian social movements in the Colombian Pacific, particularly the Process of Black Communities (PCN). His best-known book is *Encountering development: The making and unmaking of the Third World* (1995, 2nd ed. 2011). His most recent book is *Territories of difference: Place, movements, life, redes* (2008).

Cristina Espinosa is an Associate Professor in gender, culture and international development at the Heller School for Social Policy, Brandeis University. Her publications include "Negotiating nature, gender, and modernity in the Peruvian Amazon" (2011); "Globalization and the separation of indigenous genetic resources from indigenous peoples: The alpaca boom in the USA and its impact on Andean alpaqueros" (2010); "Ethnic spirituality, gender and health care in the Peruvian Amazon" (2009); "What has globalization to do with wildlife use in the remote Amazon?" (2009); "Negotiating landscapes, survival and modernity: Goats, migration and gender in arid northern Peru" (2009); "The gender dimensions of inter-ethnic land conflict in Mt. Elgon, Kenya" (Kimkung & Espinosa 2012); "Engendering the global financial crisis: Formal and informal sectors linkages in the mining regions of Zambia and their gender implications" (Namatovu & Espinosa, 2011).

Gustavo Esteva is an independent writer and grassroots activist. He is a practitioner, not an academic. A prolific writer, he is the author of more than forty books, including *Economía y Enajenación* (1980), and he coauthored *Grassroots Post-Modernism* (1998) and *Escaping Education* (1998) with Madhu Suri Prakash. He has also written hundreds of essays, such as "*The Oaxaca Commune and Mexico's Autonomous Movement.*" He is a regular contributor to Mexico's leading daily, *La Jornada*, and occasionally *The Guardian*. Esteva has been a central figure in a wide range of Mexican, Latin American, and international nongovernmental organizations and solidarity networks, including the alternative, community-based organization Universidad de la Tierra en Oaxaca, which he founded and coordinates. In 1996, he was an advisor to the Zapatistas (Ejército Zapatista de Liberación Nacional) in their negotiations with the Mexican government on the San Andrés Accords, and he is a strong advocate of Zapatismo. In 2006, he took part in the Popular Assembly of the Peoples of Oaxaca (APPO). Esteva has received numerous academic honors, including an honorary doctorate (Honoris Causa) in Law from the University of Vermont, the National Award for Political Economy, and the National Award for Journalism. He has served as president of the Mexican Society of Planning and the 5th World Congress on Rural Sociology, and interim president for the United Nations Research Institute for Social Development.

Elizabeth Hordge-Freeman is an Assistant Professor of sociology at the Institute for the Study of Latin America and the Caribbean at the University of South Florida, Tampa. She also serves as the director of the USF in Brazil program. She received her BA in Biological Sciences and Spanish from Cornell University (2001), and completed her MA (2008) and PhD in Sociology from Duke University in 2012. She is one of the coauthors of "Critical race theories, colorism, and the decade's research on families of color," appearing in the *Journal of Marriage and Family* (2010). Her work has been published in other venues and, most recently, she published an article on differential treatment and racial socialization in Afro-Brazilian families, which appears in a special edition on Latin America for the *Journal of Ethnic & Racial Studies* (2013). Elizabeth has received numerous fellowships to support her research, including the Foreign Language and Area Studies Fellowship, the American Sociological Association/National Institute of Mental Health Predoctoral Minority Fellowship, and the Ford Dissertation Fellowship. Her dissertation, "Home is where the hurt is: Racial socialization, stigma, and well-being in Afro-Brazilian families," was selected as Duke

University's nominee for the Council of Graduate Schools/ProQuest Distinguished Dissertation Award in the Social Sciences.

Eshe Lewis is a doctoral student in the anthropology department at the University of Florida. Her general interests include Afro-descendants in the Americas, social activism, gender-based violence, and community development. Over the past five years she has worked with the Afro-Peruvian community, and her dissertation research centers on Afro-Peruvian women and decision making around reporting domestic violence.

Gayle L. McGarrity is an anthropologist who has worked primarily in the Caribbean, South and Central America, and Southern Africa. Her areas of emphasis are race relations and popular culture, as well as health issues in the above regions, mainly malnutrition and HIV/AIDS. Most recently she spent five years as an applied anthropologist, based in Johannesburg but working throughout the Southern African region. Based on this experience, she has written about mixed-race populations in Southern Africa, as well as on her experiences as a Jamaican/Apache woman anthropologist working in the region. Most of her publications, however, reflect her primary research over the last three decades, which is on race relations in contemporary Cuba.

Ulrich Oslender is Assistant Professor of geography in the Department of Global & Sociocultural Studies at Florida International University in Miami, where he is also affiliated faculty at the African and African Diaspora Studies Program. He received his PhD in Geography from the University of Glasgow in Scotland in 2001. He is the author of a Spanish-language monograph on the Afro-Colombian social movement entitled *Comunidades negras y espacio en el Pacífico colombiano* (2008). He has published over thirty articles and book chapters, mostly in relation to social movement theory and political geography. Currently he is finishing an English-language book manuscript on the geographies of social movements, due to be published in 2015. Since 1995 he has worked with the social movement of black communities in Colombia.

Keisha-Khan Y. Perry is Associate Professor of Africana studies at Brown University and specializes in the critical study of race, gender, and politics in the Americas with a particular focus on black women's activism. She recently completed an ethnographic study of black women's participation and leadership in neighborhood associations, entitled *Black Women against the Land Grab: The Fight for Racial Justice in Brazil* (2013).

Bernd Reiter is an Associate Professor of comparative politics at the University of South Florida, where he has a joint appointment with the Institute for the Study of Latin American and the Caribbean and the Department of Government and International Affairs. His recent publications include *The dialectics of citizenship* (2013), *Afrodescendants, identity, and the struggle for development in the Americas* (2012), *Brazil's new racial politics* (2010), and *Negotiating democracy in Brazil* (2009). His research focuses on democracy, participation, and citizenship.

Christen A. Smith is an Assistant Professor of African and African diaspora studies and anthropology at the University of Texas at Austin. Her primary areas of interest are performance, race, gender, violence, and the black body in the Americas, with a particular emphasis on transnational black liberation struggles and state violence in Brazil. She is currently completing her book manuscript on the black body in pain as an ironic transfer point for defining Brazil's Afro-paradise. She has published essays on the performativity of racial formation in Brazil, police violence and the politics of geography in Salvador, and the transnational collective black female body. She continues to work collaboratively with grassroots organizers in Bahia on the politics of race and state violence in Brazil and is currently developing a project on violence and the transnational black female body.